# At the Court
# of the Fish-Eyed Goddess

By the same author

In Xanadu: A Quest
City of Djinns: A Year in Delhi
From the Holy Mountain:
A Journey in the Shadow of Byzantium

# At the Court
# of the Fish-Eyed Goddess

## Travels in the Indian Subcontinent

**WILLIAM DALRYMPLE**

HarperCollins *Publishers* India

HarperCollins *Publishers* India Pvt Ltd
7/16 Ansari Road, Daryaganj, New Delhi 110 002

First published in Great Britain 1998
as 'The Age of Kali: Indian Travels and Encounters'
by HarperCollins *Publishers*, UK

First published in India 1998  by
HarperCollins *Publishers* India

Copyright © William Dalrymple 1998

ISBN BI-7223-332-9

Typeset in Palatino by **FOLIO**
G-68, Connaught Circus, New Delhi 110 001

Printed in India by
Gopsons Papers Ltd
A-14, Sector 60
Noida 201 301

*To*
*Jock*
*who saw the point long before I did*

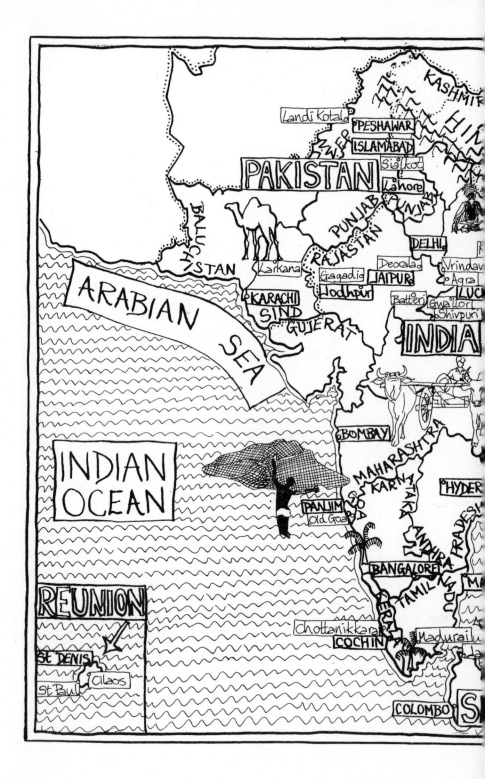

# Contents

# Acknowledgements

'The Age of Kali' was first published in *Granta*; 'The Sad Tale of Bahveri Devi', in the *Observer*; 'Benazir Bhutto', 'Warrior Queen', 'The City of Widows', 'At the Court of the Fish-Eyed Goddess' and 'Shobha Dé' in the *Sunday Times Magazine*; 'Up the Tiger Path' and parts of 'On the Frontier' in *GQ*; 'Parashakti' in the *Independent Magazine*; 'Imran Khan' in the *Tatler*; 'Sati Mata' and parts of 'Imran Khan' in the *Sunday Telegraph Magazine*; 'On the Frontier' and 'In the Kingdom of Avadh' in *Condé Nast Traveler*; 'The Sorcerer's Grave' in *Islands Magazine*; 'At Donna Georgina's' and parts of 'The Age of Kali' in the *Spectator*. In all cases the copyright is retained by the original publishers, and the pieces have been reprinted with permission.

# Introduction

There are very few sensations more annoying than being told what to think about one's own country by some foreigner who rolls in, makes a few perfunctory interviews, then writes some ignorant rubbish in a paper at the other end of the world.

I would hope that I don't fall into that category; but it is nevertheless with some nervousness that I accepted an offer from HarperCollins India to publish *At the Court of the Fish-Eyed Goddess* in South Asia in a separate *desi* edition. For this book is a collection of peripatetic essays about the subcontinent, all of which were specifically written with a *firangi* audience in mind, even though a few are published here for the first time. In some I have explained matters such as caste that would be familiar to any Indian audience since the cradle; in others I have chosen subjects, like the Deorala Sati, which have already been done to death in the Indian media. Yet India is so vast, and so diverse, that I would hope that within these pages there are pieces which may shed new light on some little known corners of the subcontinent. The section on Pakistan, in particular, may hold some surprises for an Indian audience unable easily to travel in a country so close, and yet so very distant, from their own. My book on Delhi, *City of Djinns*, received such a tolerant and generous response from Delhiwallahs—who could easily have decided that no *gora* could tell them anything about their city that they did not already know, that I feel a little less presumptuous at trying everyone's patience a second time.

*At the Court of the Fish-Eyed Goddess* is a distillation of ten year's relentless travelling around the Indian subcontinent, from 1989-1998, six of them based in Delhi while working on *City of Djinns*, the other four on a more nomadic basis since then. It covers a wide geographical range: from the fortresses of the drug barons of the North West Frontier to the jungle lairs of the Tamil Tigers, from the decaying palaces of Lucknow to the great temple of Meenakshi at Madurai, the Court of the Fish-Eyed Goddess of the title. The pieces should be judged by their dates; but every essay is the product of personal experience and direct observation: I have not written about any place which I have not visited in person.

The book covers so many sensitive areas that it is bound to raise a few cries of protest and dissent from patriotic readers understandably touchy about criticism from abroad; but it is a work of love. Its subject is an area of the world I adore like no other, and in which I have chosen to spend most of my time since I was free to make that choice. From my first visit to the region as an eighteen-year-old backpacker, I was completely overwhelmed: India thrilled, surprised, frightened and delighted me. Since then it has never ceased to amaze me; and I hope that that ceaseless power to excite and astonish, if nothing else, is conveyed by this book.

Over the course of the last decade, I have fallen into the debt of many friends across the length and breadth of the subcontinent. There are, after all, few areas where people are so ready to open their house to the weary and confused traveller. I would like to thank the following, all of whom provided invaluable aid, advice and hospitality: Javed Abdulla, Ram Advani, Bilkiz Alladin, S.K. Bedi, Dev Benegal, David and Rachna Davidar, Farid Faridi, Sagarika Ghosh, Salman, Kusum and Navina Haidar, Sultana Hasan, Annie and Martin Howard, Mir Moazam Husain and the Begum Meherunissa, General Wajahat Husain, Dr. S.M. Yunus Jaffery, O.P. Jain, Nussi Jamil, Amrita Jhaveri, Gauri and David Keeling, Sunita Kohli, Momin Latif, Dieter Ludwig, Suleiman Mahmudabad, Sam and Shireen Miller, Sachin and Rosleen Mulji, Mushtaq Naqvi, Saeed Naqvi, Mark Nicholson, Naveen Patnaik, Ahmed and Angie Rashid, Arundhati Roy and Pradip Krishen, Yusouf Salahuddin, Avik Sarkar, Vasu Scindia, Aradhana Seth, Jugnu and Najam Sethi, Mala and Tejbir Singh, Balvinder Singh, Siddarth and Rashmi Singh, Magoo and Jaswant Singh, Khushwant Singh, Mohan Sohai, Tarun and Geetan Tejpal, Jigme Tashi, Tiziano Terzani, Adam and Fariba Thomson, Mark Tully and Gillian Wright, Dr. L.C. Tyagi, Shameem Vardarajan, and Pavan and Renuka Verma.

I would like to give particular thanks to Sanjeev Srivastava who accompanied me on all the Rajasthan stories and provided brilliant insights into the life of the state. Arvind

Das gave me invaluable help with the Bihar story, which was at least partly inspired by his superb study of the state, *The Republic of Bihar*. Rosie Llewellyn-Jones provided me with invaluable contacts and advice for the Lucknow stories. Karan Kapoor and Pablo Bartholomew between them took the pictures which originally accompanied many of the pieces in this book; they also helped set up many of the interviews, and were both wonderful—and patient—travelling companions and friends.

Mehra Dalton of the incomparable Greaves Travel arranged (and on one occasion even sponsored) the travel arrangements.

Nick Coleridge, Lola Bubosh, Jon Connel, Deidre Fernand, David Jenkins, Dominic Lawson, Ian Jack, Sarah Miller, Rebecca Nicolson, Justine Picardie, Joan Tapper, Robert Winder and Gully Wells all commissioned articles from me, and have generously given permission for them to be reproduced although what is published here is in some cases very different from what originally appeared in the articles' first journalistic *avatar*: pieces have been edited, trimmed and rewritten; some have been wedged together; others, where appropriate, have been suffixed with a new postscript to bring them up to date.

Pankaj Mishra, Patrick French, Philip Marsden, Sam Miller, Jenny Fraser and Lucy Warrack all kindly spent hours going over typescripts, while Mike Fishwick and Robert Lacey both performed sterling service with the red pen during the final edit. Mike and Robert, together with Annie Robertson and Helen Ellis, and also Renuka Chatterjee of HarperCollins India, between them provided everything an author could possibly want from a publisher. To all of them many thanks.

Most of all I would like to thank Jonathan Bond who has put me up, for weeks at a time, in his wonderful house in Sundernagar ever since I finally gave up my own Delhi flat. He, Jigme and Tipoo have all put up with invasions of babies, wives, *ayahs*, journalists, friends, colleagues and debt collectors from Airtel, at any hour of the day or night, summer or winter, with almost surreal calm and forbearance particularly on those occasions when the babies decided to rise before dawn and make their presence known.

Finally, as always, I must thank Olivia who accompanied me on almost all the trips, edited and helped rewrite all the articles, and who again provided all the art work. Only she really knows how much she has done and how little I would be able to function without her. To her, Ibby and Sam, yet again: all my love...

*William Dalrymple*
*Pages' Yard, September 1998*

# 1

# Pakistan

# Benazir Bhutto : Mills & Boon in Karachi

KARACHI, 1994

Islamabad—Pakistan's regimented concrete capital, home to Benazir Bhutto and ten thousand of her bureaucrats— is to Pakistan what EuroDisney is to France: it is in the country but not of it.

As you drive in the early morning through its long, deserted avenues, Islamabad still looks strangely like a building site into which no one has yet moved. The bureaucrats' blocks and the Saudi-financed mosques—many still shrouded in scaffolding—rise up on every side. There is little evidence of Pakistan's burgeoning population. Indeed, as you circle the grey, megalomaniac mass of the President's Palace and rise up towards the fortified compound of the Prime Minister's Residence, you realise that since you left your hotel you have seen nobody on the streets at all— except, that is, for the policemen, each clutching his assault rifle as nonchalantly as a banker might hold his brolly.

The summons to interview Benazir Bhutto had come through from the Pakistan High Commission in London two days earlier. After five months of waiting, I had been given forty- eight hours to get tickets and a visa, jump aboard a flight, and present myself in Islamabad. On arrival I had been met by a burly ministry minder who escorted me to my hotel, then reappeared the following morning to conduct me to the Prime Minister's Residence. On the way he had broken his silence to lecture me on protocol: 'You address the Prime Minister as Ms Bhutto, not Mrs Bhutto,' he said. 'And I must warn you that in our society men never shake hands with women.' As the car drew up to the double gates of the compound he held out his identity card to the troop of commandos; the gates swung open.

After the grey architectural brutalism that had gone before, the Prime Minister's Residence crowning the hill was something of a surprise: a giddy pseudo-Mexican ranch house with white walls and a red-tile roof. There was nothing remotely Pakistani or Islamic or Asian about the building, which, my minder said, wobbling his head approvingly, was 'PM's own design'. Inside it was the same story. Crystal chandeliers dangled sometimes two or three to a room; oils of sunflowers and tumbling kittens that would have looked quite at home on the railings around Hyde Park hung below garishly gilded cornices; potted ferns sprouted from kitsch neo-Egyptian bowls. The place felt as though it might be the weekend retreat of a particularly flamboyant Latin American industrialist; but in fact it could have been *anywhere*. Had you seen it on one of those TV game-shows where you are shown a particular house and then have to guess who lives in it, you might have awarded this *hacienda* to virtually anyone; except, perhaps, to the Prime Minister of an impoverished Islamic republic situated next door to Iran.

Which is, of course, exactly why the West has always had a soft spot for Benazir Bhutto. Her neighbouring heads of state may be figures as foreign and frightening as, on the one hand, President Rafsanjani and his cabinet of Teheran mullahs, and on the other a clutch of bearded, fundamentalist Afghan warlords—but Benazir has always seemed reassuringly familiar, has always seemed as if she is *one of us*.

She speaks English fluently because it is her first language. She had an English governess, and her childhood social life revolved around a succession of English colonial clubs with names like the Karachi Gymkhana and the Sindh Club. She went to a convent school run by Irish nuns, and during holidays on the family's country estate she played cricket and badminton with her brothers and friends. She rounded off her education with degrees from Harvard and Oxford. The English media have always loved her, not least because a number of newspaper editors knew her (and in one case even attempted to court her) at Oxford. On top of all these assets she's good-looking, she's photogenic, she's brave, she's a democrat and she's a woman.

For the Americans, what Benazir Bhutto *isn't* is possibly more attractive than what she is: her name isn't unpronounceable, she isn't a religious fundamentalist, she doesn't organise mass rallies where everyone shouts 'Death to America' and burns the stars and stripes, and she doesn't issue fatwas against best-selling authors—even though Salman Rushdie went out of his way to ridicule her as the Virgin Ironpants in *Shame*.

But the very reasons that make the West love Benazir Bhutto are the ones that leave many of her fellow Pakistanis with second thoughts. Her English may be fluent, but you can't say the same about her Urdu, which she speaks like a conscientious foreigner: fluently but ungrammatically, muddling her plurals and singulars, her genders and tenses. Her Sindhi, which for generations has been the mother tongue of her family, is even worse: apart from a few imperatives and a handful of greetings and platitudes, she is completely at sea. Her opponents complain, not unfairly, that she is more British than Pakistani, more Western than Eastern.

More importantly, while she is a star performer at the sort of politics which looks best on Western TV screens— giving fighting speeches, addressing mass rallies through clouds of teargas, touring the deserts of Pakistan by steam train—she is less competent behind closed doors: she has no clear political agenda and champions no obvious political philosophy. Her father was a socialist, but she is not; yet she is no monetarist, Conservative or Republican either. This muddle means that once Benazir actually gets into power she seems to lose momentum and dissipates her energies on petty party politicking rather than getting on with the business of governing the country. Her critics say that she is an intellectual lightweight who doesn't know what she wants to do—they would, of course—but it is certainly true that during her first twenty-month-long premiership, astonishingly, she failed to pass a single piece of legislation.

Even the basis of Benazir's claim to fame in the West— that she fearlessly stood up to the martial law of the sinister military dictator General Zia ul-Haq, then carried on the torch of her father, Zulfiqar Ali Bhutto, after Zia took it upon himself to torture and hang this democratically elected Prime Minister—looks less impressive if you are a Pakistani and remember Bhutto Senior's own antidemocratic tendencies: his propensity for rigging elections, torturing opponents and sacking any provincial assembly that dared to oppose his will. In the most notorious case, after Bhutto unconstitutionally dissolved the elected Baluchistan assembly, the Baluchi tribes rose up against him and several thousand died before the insurgency was finally, brutally, quashed. Moreover, Bhutto's refusal to share power with the victorious Awami League after the 1970 general election led directly to Pakistan's darkest chapter: the civil war between West and East Pakistan, the crushing defeat by India a year later, and the subsequent creation of Bangladesh.

Nor are Pakistanis over-enamoured with Benazir Bhutto's husband, the polo-playing Karachi playboy Asif Ali Zardari, who until his marriage to Benazir was distinguished chiefly for the private discotheque he had built inside his house in an attempt to lure within the leading lights of the Karachi party set. Due to such extravagances, before his marriage in 1988 Zardari was said to be near to bankruptcy. Three years later he was fabulously wealthy—a spectacular financial turnaround that just happened to coincide with his wife's premiership. This led to Zardari being tagged with the label 'Mr 10 Per Cent', and on his wife's fall from power in 1990 he spent two years in jail on corruption and extortion charges. The charges were eventually dropped due to lack of evidence, but rightly or wrongly the mud has stuck, and Pakistanis still perceive Zardari as being massively crooked.

What Bhuttoism represents to Pakistanis, in other words, is not virgin-white democracy fighting the black spectre of General Zia's tyranny and the massed ranks of Pakistan's mad mullahs: there are many shades of grey in between. In 1990, after Benazir's first administration was dismissed by the President for ineptitude and corruption, the people of Pakistan democratically voted in a Muslim League government run by the Zia protégé Nawaz Sharif, a Punjabi industrialist. In the 1993 elections, the Muslim League again won more votes than Benazir's Pakistan People's Party (PPP), but the latter returned to power through a series of strategic alliances with small regional parties.

There is no doubt that Pakistanis are, on the whole, grateful to Benazir Bhutto for bringing back democracy, and that many regard her as a brave and impressive woman. But the fact remains that they have never felt as enthusiastic about her as we in the West would sometimes like to believe.

With a last proud flourish at Benazir's chandeliers, my minder led me out of the Prime Minister's Residence and into the garden, where the interview was to take place. There we sat for ten minutes in mock-Regency chairs beneath the mock-Mexican *hacienda*, before the familiar silhouette appeared at the top of the lawns. On instinct, like schoolboys waiting for the headmistress, we stood up.

If Benazir's campaigning style verges on the frenzied—all hectoring speeches and raucous motorcades—her manner face-to-face is deliberately measured and regal. She took a full three minutes to float down the hundred yards of lawn separating the house from the chairs where we had been sitting. Her eyebrows were heavily darkened, and scarlet lipstick had been generously applied to her lips; her hair was arranged in a sort of baroque beehive topped by a white gauze dupatta. The whole painted vision, wrapped in folds of orange silk, reminded me of one of those haughty Roman princesses in *Caligula* or *I, Claudius*. After such a majestic entrance it seemed only right, when I enquired about her new *hacienda*, that, Thatcher-like, she should answer using the Royal 'we'. 'We didn't want the design to be too palatial,' she said, in a slow, heavily accented purr that managed to make the word *palatial* sound as if it had about five syllables. 'The original [architect's] design was extremely grand—so we modified it, *tremendously*.'

There followed an interlude when Benazir found the sun was not shining in quite the way she wanted it to: 'The sun is in the wrong direction,' she announced. We all rose ancircled one stop around the table, which left her press secretary in the prime ministerial throne, squinting into the sun. Once Benazir had indicated that she was ready, I opened by asking if, after her time at Oxford, she still regarded herself as an Anglophile.

'Oh yes,' she said brightly. 'London is like a second home for me. I know London well. I know where the theatres are, I know where the shops. are, I know where the *hairdressers* are. I love to browse through Harrods and W.H. Smith in Sloane Square. I know all my favourite ice cream parlours: I used to particularly love going to the one at Marble Arch: Baskin Robbins. Sometimes I used to drive all the way down from Oxford just for an ice cream, and then drive back again. That was my idea of sin.'

'So you enjoyed your time at Oxford?'

'I suppose in retrospect it *was* a happy time, because it was free from responsibility and so it had an air of innocence about it...'

'Innoc...?'

'...It was free from all the Machiavellian twists that life can take, free of deception. I think at university one doesn't have the deception or the betrayal which comes about in every career...'

'You think...?'

'...Moreover for me it was a time of security because my father was alive, and he was the anchor in my life. I felt that there was no problem that would be too great for him to solve so I was not worried ever, or too anxious, because I always felt I had my father to fall back on.'

From the beginning of the interview it was clear that trying to halt Benazir in mid-flow was no easier than stopping Lady Thatcher, whom she has frequently cited as her role model (and with whom, incidentally, she had tea and scones at the Dorchester on her last visit to London). She has clearly studied her mentor's interview manner. There was no question of any sort of dialogue: Benazir conducts an interview in much the same manner as she might a public rally, pointedly ignoring all attempts to interrupt her, and treating the interviewer as if he were some persistent heckler.

Her reference to her father also set the tone for the rest of the interview. Benazir tends to mention her father in relation to almost every topic you raise with her. Carrying on her father's flame is still her *raison d'étre*, and she often refers to him with almost mystical reverence as 'the *Shaheed*', or martyr. Recently, in the course of the current Bhutto family feud, Benazir's estranged mother had denied that Benazir was in fact her father's first choice as successor, so I asked if she was actually the closest to him of all her siblings.

'Certainly,' she replied. 'He always had a tremendous sense of pride in me. In terms of politics he would always want to train me. He took me with him to Shimla at the time of the historic meeting after the division of Bangladesh, so that I could see history at first hand. He took me to Moscow, to America, to the funeral of President Pompidou in France. In terms of books, also, both of us would be reading books together...'

'What sort of boo...?'

'...I remember when I came back from university I always used to buy him books as gifts, and he always used to buy me books as gifts. Once I came back for the summer and I gave him a book called *Freedom at Midnight* by Dominique Lapierre. On that same occasion Papa gave me a book, and do you know what it was? *Freedom at Midnight* by Dominique Lapierre!'

Was she being serious? *Freedom at Midnight* is terrible schlock pop-history—the Indian Independence Movement for Imbeciles—hardly the sort of book you would expect to find a senior South Asian statesman admitting to reading. Moreover, its account of the events of 1947 is deeply biased against Pakistan, and presents Jinnah as little more than a crazed megalomaniac. Assuming she was joking and now regarded the purchase as an embarrassing mistake, I laughed—only for it to become immediately clear that she was in fact entirely serious.

'...So it was really rather nice: we were obviously reading the same reviews. We shared a lot in the political, historical, intellectual sense.'

'I never really liked that book,' I ventured. 'I thought...'

'Well, I rather enjoyed it,' she said firmly, before returning to her flow of paternal reminiscences. 'As a child I used to love going through my father's library and sitting and reading the different books. He inculcated in me this tremendous love of reading.'

What about Benazir's siblings, I asked. How did they get on with their father?

'He always spoiled my younger sister, Sanam; he literally didn't have *any* expectations of her,' she said. 'She was born a little prematurely so she was smaller in size than the rest of us. My father was more protective of her, as if she was a little fragile doll who could not weather the storms of life. He thought I had a toughness that would enable me to weather the storms.'

And her brothers?

'They would not be there,' she said, her velvety tone now becoming distinctly chilly. 'They would not be sitting with my father or me discussing these things.'

Throughout our conversation what was very striking was the ease with which Benazir could shift from being Zulfi Bhutto's bubbly, slightly sentimental daughter with a highly developed taste for mint choco chip ice cream, to the tough, sometimes frosty Prime Minister of Pakistan, heavy with the *gravitas* of office. Her 1988 autobiography *Daughter of the East* contains innumerable swings of this sort, most memorably in the chapter in which she describes her father's death. After a brave and genuinely moving passage recording the last meeting of father and daughter, she blows it all by describing how 'my little cat, Chun-Chun, abandoned her kittens' in sympathy. There follows a scene when she suddenly wakes up on the night of her father's hanging. Georgette Heyer or even Barbara Cartland at her most excitable could not have improved on Benazir's rendering of the scene:

> 'No!' the scream burst through the knots in my throat. 'No!' I couldn't breathe, didn't want to breathe. Papa! Papa! I felt cold, so cold. I felt as if my body was literally being torn apart. How could I go on?...The skies rained tears of ice that night...

Those who know her say that there have always been these two quite distinct Benazir Bhuttos. The emotional socialite from the wealthy background is generally the Benazir remembered by her Oxford friends: a glitzy, good-looking

Asian babe who drove to lectures in a yellow MG, wintered in Gstaad, and who to this day still talks of the thrill of walking down the Cannes lido with her hunky younger brother and being 'the centre of envy: wherever Shahnawaz went, women would be bowled over'. This Benazir—known to her friends as 'Bibi' or 'Pinky'—*adores* royal biographies and slushy romances (in her old Karachi bedroom I found stacks of well-thumbed Mills & Boons, including *An Affair to Forget, Stolen Heart, Sweet Impostor, The Winds of Winter* and two copies of *The Butterfly and the Baron*). This Benazir still has a weakness for dodgy Seventies easy listening (*Tie a Yellow Ribbon Round the Old Oak Tree* is apparently at the top of her frequent-play list) and weepy Seventies movies (her favourite, one of her London friends told me, is Barbra Streisand's remake of *A Star is Born*). This is the Benazir who has an enviable line in red-rimmed fashion specs, who still goes weak at the knees at the sight of *marrons glacés* and who deep down, so I was assured by her best friend in Karachi, is still 'as soft as a marshmallow'.

The other Benazir Bhutto is a very different kettle of fish. This is the ambitious Ms Bhutto who stayed on a whole year at Oxford after taking her degree, lobbying relentlessly for months on end to make sure that she would become President of the Union. After martial law was declared in Pakistan in 1979, this Ms Bhutto led marches, fought stave-wielding riot police and sustained long periods of imprisonment in squalid jails in an attempt to save her father from General Zia's noose; then after he was hanged and she was released, she bravely took on Zia and rallied the opposition. This Ms Bhutto did not let herself cry in front of her father's guards after she was led away for the last time from his death cell; nor did she break three years later, when her beloved brother Shahnawaz was poisoned, possibly by Zia's agents. She fought hard for seven long years, until Zia's death and the elections that made her, at the age of thirty-five, the first woman to head a Muslim state since Raziyya Sultana, Queen of Delhi in the early thirteenth century. This Ms Bhutto, Thatcher-like, is today renowned throughout Islamabad for chairing twelve-hour cabinet meetings and for surviving on four hours' sleep. This Benazir Bhutto is, in other words, fearless—sometimes heroically so—and as hard as nails.

In the interview, this side of Benazir emerged most forcefully when we talked about her great *bête noire*—India, and especially India's policy of brutally suppressing the separatist movement in the Kashmir Valley.

'India tries to gloss over its policy of repression in Kashmir, claiming that Pakistan has infiltrated militants,' she said, only minutes after describing the different flavours she used to order at Baskin Robbins. 'India has been quite unable to substantiate these claims.'

'But is it really worth coming into conflict with India over the matter?' I asked. 'India will never let Kashmir go. Isn't it a no-win situation?'

'I don't see it as a no-win situation,' replied Benazir, swinging into Great World Statesman mode, 'because I don't believe that history is the story of Might winning against Right. No matter how great a tyranny is, over time it erodes; and if a struggle is just, and is one in which its people will give sacrifices, then I believe that that struggle will eventually be successful. Might didn't work in Vietnam, it didn't work in Afghanistan. It didn't work in tyrannies all over the world. India does have Might—it has five hundred thousand troops and a hundred thousand armed paramilitary personnel in the Valley—but still it has been unable to crush the people of Kashmir.'

'But by taking on the Kashmiris' cause, aren't you committing both countries to massive defence expenditure that neither can afford?'

'We are prepared to negotiate arms reductions with India, but that doesn't mean that we keep silent, and by our silence collude with the repression which is going on. That would be impossible—particularly for the Pakistan People's Party, which fought so hard for freedom and human rights in Pakistan. It is simply not possible for us to keep silent in the face of Indian atrocities.'

'But isn't the Indian repression in Kashmir not entirely dissimilar to your father's actions in Baluchistan?'

This was a mistake. Benazir glowered—the velvety veneer no longer masking the steely toughness beneath—and set off on a lengthy explanation of why the Pakistan army's murder of around ten thousand separatist Baluchis was in no way comparable to the Indian army's murder of a similar number of separatist Kashmiris.

It was only towards the very end of the interview that I was able to quiz Benazir about her other current bugbears, her brother Murtaza and her mother, Begum Nusrat Bhutto.

The Bhuttos' increasingly acrimonious family squabbles are beginning to resemble one of the bloody succession disputes that plagued the area that is now Pakistan during the time of the Great Mughals. Like many of the Mughals' fratricidal disputes, that of the Bhuttos has long roots. In 1979, on Zulfi Bhutto's death, his children disagreed about the best method with which to carry on his legacy and return Pakistan to democracy. Benazir believed the struggle should be peaceful. Her brothers Shahnawaz and Murtaza disagreed, and turned to terrorism. They flew to Beirut, where they were supported by Yasser Arafat. Under his guidance they received the arms and training necessary to form the Pakistan Liberation Army, later renamed Al-Zulfiqar, 'The Sword'.

In actual fact, for all its PLO training, Al-Zulfiqar achieved little except for a handful of assassinations and murders, and the hijacking of a Pakistan International Airways flight in 1981. This secured the release of some fifty-five political prisoners, but resulted in the death of an innocent passenger. Zia used this as an excuse to crack down on the Pakistan People's Party, and Benazir was forced to distance herself from her brothers, even though they denied sanctioning the hijack. After Shahnawaz was poisoned in July 1985, Murtaza stayed in exile in Damascus as a guest of President Assad, unable to return home due to the multiple charges of murder, sabotage, conspiracy and robbery which had been registered against him.

So things remained until, quite suddenly in October 1993, Murtaza announced his intention of contesting the elections in Pakistan. He remained in Damascus, but registered his name as an independent candidate for nine constituencies, standing for both the provincial Sindh assembly and the national parliament. Begum Nusrat Bhutto, although remaining chairwoman of the PPP, campaigned for her son, often against the official PPP candidate. There were confident predictions that the Bhuttos' followers would defect to Murtaza *en masse*, but in the event Murtaza won only a single provincial assembly seat, while his sister was returned to Islamabad in triumph. Undaunted, Murtaza flew in from Syria on the night of 3 November, only to be arrested at Karachi airport. After his mother protested, she was unceremoniously sacked as chairwoman of the PPP. She hit back by giving a series of interviews in which she denounced her daughter in the most florid Urdu: 'I had no idea I had nourished a viper in my breast,' she told one interviewer. 'If I had known that she would be so poisonous, I would never have given the powers (of the PPP) to her...I will never forgive her.'

I asked Benazir whether she had been upset by her mother's words.

'I am extremely saddened,' she replied in her most dove-like voice. 'But I have been an extremely dutiful daughter, a loving daughter, over many years, and I feel that in due course, given this fact, that she will come back to where the love for her and the respect for her has always been. She says these awful, awful, *awful* things against me and I get mad reading them. But in the end because she is my mother and I know her frailties, in my heart I can't even hold it against her.'

And what about Murtaza, who was threatening to topple her from her position on the Bhutto throne, the brother whom she had left to languish in jail?

'I love my brother and I *always* wanted him to return,' she purred innocently. 'I was the one who gave him his passport: he didn't even have a Pakistani passport until I gave him one. I was bitterly criticised for doing so, but I felt it was his right, and I said I would do justice for him.'

At this point Benazir's smooth press secretary tactfully intervened, saying that in five minutes I would be 'ushered out'. I could, he said, put one last question.

'Don't you feel that political power is increasingly becoming a poisoned chalice for your family?' I asked. 'It has already claimed your father and younger brother, and led to your estrangement from your mother and eldest brother. Do you sometimes feel that the price you are all having to pay personally is just too great?'

Benazir paused for a second before answering.

'Yes. It is extremely difficult. During the election campaign when I found that Murtaza was contesting these seats I thought of my father. I thought how deeply affected he would be to see his children fighting. I was even prepared to step out myself to prevent this ugly family scene. But in the end I had to make a choice: between having this ugly showdown, or being blackmailed by it and submitting. In the end I felt I couldn't do that to my father's political legacy, to his political memory.'

As Benazir rose to go, I asked if there was any hope of continuing the interview for a few more minutes, perhaps the following day.

'Tomorrow the Prime Minister is going to Lahore and Karachi,' said the smooth press secretary.

'But I suppose you could always come too,' said Benazir. 'If you wanted to.'

I was on the tarmac of the military airbase by nine the following morning, being thoroughly frisked by a huge military policeman, when a black Mercedes pulled up beside the Prime Minister's jet. Out of it piled two of Benazir's Filipino nannies, a pile of Louis Vuitton bags, a crate of Evian water and Benazir's youngest child, the beautiful ten-month-old Asifa, decked out in a red OshKosh B'Gosh designer jumpsuit. After the nursery party had been ushered on board, an ADC showed me to my place behind various party functionaries and across the aisle from the Filipino nannies.

Benazir rolled up to the airport a cool twenty minutes behind schedule. She floated up the gangway and appeared, flanked by a pair of liveried ADCs, at the top of the aisle. The entire planeload of passengers rose; a few of the older functionaries actually bowed. The Prime Minister nodded and without a word took her seat. Then she picked up *Vogue* from the pile of glossies which had been left on the seat beside her and gave a signal; the plane taxied along the runway.

When we had reached cruising height I went up and asked Benazir whether we could continue our interview, but was dismissed with a peremptory wave of the hand. 'It's only a thirty-minute flight,' she said. She buried herself in the glossies, and I had to make do with the attentions of her daughter, who sat at my feet making calls with her power-toy, a little red telephone (when you are a part of a political dynasty, you can't start at this sort of thing too early).

Half an hour later we arrived at Lahore. Waiting for us on the runway were a crescent of politicians and dignitaries, flanked by huge Pathan security guards. Behind them stood a phalanx of black Mercedes limousines ready, revved and waiting; at a distance, a little behind the black limousines, stood a single plebeian white Toyota. Benazir waved breezily from the top of the gangway, then descended the steps and passed along the line of waiting dignitaries, nodding and muttering 'Salaam Alekum' to each of them. There was a brief speech of welcome from the Chief Minister of the Punjab, then it was into the limos and off. The Toyota, it became apparent, was for me.

Being Prime Minister of Pakistan has its moments. The whole airport road had been shut off for Benazir's cavalcade. Armed guards lined the pavements; overhead, flags and bunting had been hung across the road, much of it blazoned with welcoming messages to Benazir from admirers as diverse as the Habib Bank and Diet Pepsi. We swept at high speed through the old colonial centre of Lahore—past the Zam-Zammah gun with which Kipling opens *Kim*, and the museum where Kipling's father was curator—the train of Mercedes announced by a posse of open-top police jeeps and flanked by a swarm of motorcycle outriders, all blaring horns and wailing sirens. Another posse of jeeps followed behind. Last of all came me in my dingy white saloon.

Benazir had dropped into Lahore to open an exhibition of Pakistani kilims. Our destination was the Al-Hambra, Pakistan's principal contemporary art gallery. I had been there before on a number of occasions, but had never seen anything like the reception which awaited us now: a Pakistani pipe band, swathed in tartan turbans and merrily wailing *The Gay Gordons*. As Benazir lowered herself out of her limo, the Pipe Major did his stuff with his baton, the drums beat and the bagpipers played the Pakistani national anthem. (According to Benazir's press secretary, whom I later taxed on this subject, Pakistan is now the world's leading manufacturer of bagpipes, and has begun exporting them to Scotland.)

Inside the gallery auditorium, the assembled audience were treated to a half-hour prayer, first in Arabic then in Urdu, by a bearded mullah in a lambskin cap, followed by nearly an hour of speeches on the theme of Pakistan's contribution to the hand-knotted carpet. After this Benazir rose, made another speech, had a four-minute dash round the principal exhibits; then it was back in the limos—a screech of tyres and more wailing sirens—and off to the next city, Karachi, three hours' flight to the south, where the deserts of Sindh meet the Arabian Ocean. Another cavalcade of limousines was waiting on the runway as we stepped out of the plane into the muggy heat of Sindh, and with another blare of sirens we were escorted into the city by yet another swarm of outriders.

Our destination this time was the Presidential Guest House, where Benazir was chairing a meeting of the regional PPP. Inside, the marble passages of the old colonial building were filled with politicians slapping each other on the back or pulling allies aside to whisper political gossip in alcoves. In the main durbar hall, under a huge portrait of Jinnah looking as drawn and emaciated as Christopher Lee in a horror film, thirty-three men sat in a semicircle around one woman.

Without even a minute's break to recover from the journey, Benazir immediately convened a meeting of the party workers from her Larkhana constituency. Most of the men looked about twice her age, but all of them were on their best behaviour—not speaking until they were spoken to, and sitting bolt upright as Benazir lounged on a divan before them. For twenty minutes the Prime Minister grilled the men—'Elaborate, Ali!' 'Thank you, Nadir'—as they stammered to explain themselves: 'Excuse me respected Prime Minister, I'm so sorry, but...' Eventually they were all dismissed with a wave and the command *'Jaldi karo'* ('Do it quick!'). Then the next group was summoned in and another grilling began.

It was ten o'clock at night before Benazir had finished. Throughout the evening, as successive groups of men wilted, she showed not the slightest sign of fatigue.

The following morning I rang up 70 Clifton, for forty years the Bhuttos' Karachi headquarters.

Through the family secretary I managed to arrange an interview with Ghinwa, Murtaza Bhutto's Lebanese wife, but when I asked if I could speak to Begum Nusrat Bhutto I was told that that was impossible: the Begum was out having lunch. Then, after a second's hesitation, the secretary added who she was lunching with: her daughter, the Prime Minister.

Pakistani friends had warned me about these mother-daughter meetings, which were regarded as one of the more eccentric and bewildering features of the current feud. On every trip to Karachi, Benazir would make a point of visiting her mother. Politics would be kept out of the conversation, there would be tears and smiles and all would be well—until two days later, when the mutual recriminations would begin again in the press. For those in political circles this state of affairs was not only confusing, it was potentially perilous, as everyone in the Bhutto camp had been forced to take sides, and no one was quite sure where they would stand if peace was eventually re-established. Ordinary mortals were not encouraged to try to cross the battle lines, and Benazir's press secretary had made it clear to me—in no uncertain terms—that if I attempted to interview the Begum, and focused too closely on the feud, I should not expect to have access to Benazir ever again.

As arranged, at 2.30 p.m. I went over to 70 Clifton to interview Benazir's sister-in-law. The house, located in the centre of Karachi's smartest residential district, had long been chief shrine of the Bhutto cult, but since my last visit a subtle change had come over the shrine's iconography. There were still images of *Shaheed* Bhutto plastering every wall in the vicinity, but those of his daughter, once ubiquitous, had now been removed and replaced by pictures of her brother Murtaza. The largest of these was an enormous hoarding, some thirty feet high, which had been erected on the pavement immediately opposite the main entrance to the house. It was painted in the garish technicolour of Hindi film posters, and showed Murtaza in a Sindhi cap, waving at his supporters. Other posters reproduced press pictures of Murtaza being led away to jail in a Black Maria, handcuffed to a policeman, a new martyr in the making.

I was ushered through the compound by Kalashnikov-carrying family retainers, and left in a reception room just inside the front door. Every surface here—as elsewhere in the shrine—was dedicated to Bhutto imagery: whole tables were covered with signed photographs showing Bhutto Senior with the Shah of Iran, with the Nixons, with Mao. Other frames contained family portraits: Zulfi's father, Sir Shahnawaz Bhutto, various cousins, various children; but again Benazir was notably absent.

After a few minutes Ghinwa appeared. She was younger than I had expected—probably in her mid-twenties—and very beautiful, in the Lebanese fashion. Tea was brought and we chatted for a few minutes about how much she was missing the Middle East, how much her children were missing their father and how hot Pakistani food was. She seemed shy, sweet-natured and naive, genuinely baffled by the chain of events that had led to her husband being escorted straight off to prison within an hour of his return home. 'He only wanted to help Pakistan,' she kept repeating. 'He only wanted to do the best for his country. *C'est un peu bizarre.*'

'Have you talked to Benazir about Murtaza's arrest?' I asked.

'I have never talked to my sister-in-law,' said Ghinwa. 'She has never addressed a single word to me.'

We had been chatting for about half an hour when from outside there came the noise of an arriving car. 'Here's my mother-in-law,' said Ghinwa.

The front door opened and into the room walked Begum Bhutto. Although well into her seventies, the Begum, once a famous Iranian beauty, was still a very striking woman: she had the same remarkable cheekbones as her daughter, and her shapely frame was wrapped in the swathes of a rather dramatic imitation leopard skin *salwar kameez*. I explained that I was writing about Benazir and asked whether it might be possible to talk to her about the difficulties she was having with her daughter.

At that very moment, Benazir herself walked into the room. She must have overheard my last sentence, and she saw me shaking her mother's hand, with Ghinwa standing beside me. I had been caught red-handed talking to her enemies. Benazir narrowed her eyes and looked daggers at me. Then she walked out of the room without a word. Her mother rushed after her.

'*C'est bizarre,*' said Ghinwa, shaking her head. '*Ce pays. C'est trés bizarre.*'

At ten o'clock the following morning, a convoy of jeeps followed by four pick-ups full of police gunmen brought Murtaza Bhutto to the court where his case was being heard. The noise and style was identical to one of Benazir's own processions. The only difference was that Murtaza was unable to wave to passers-by, as his hands were handcuffed to the policeman sitting beside him.

A one-hundred-rupee bribe got me through the police cordon, and I soon found Murtaza with his mother and his lawyer, in an annexe beside the courtroom. Murtaza looked strikingly like his father: he was handsome, very tall—well over six feet—and slightly chubby round the middle; he had a deep voice and like his father exuded an air of self-confidence, *bonhomie* and charisma. He invited me to sit down, and said he was very pleased to talk to the international press. 'Benazir doesn't care what the local press says about her,' he said, 'but she's very sensitive to what her friends in Paris, London and New York get to read about her.'

'Has your sister got in touch with you since you returned to Pakistan?' I asked.

'No. Nothing. Not one note.'

'Not even in her private capacity?'

'Nothing at all.'

'Did you expect her to intervene and get you off the hook?' I asked. 'What kind of reception did you hope she would lay on for you?'

'I didn't want any favours,' replied Murtaza. 'I just wanted her to let justice take its course, and for her not to interfere in the legal process. As it is, she has instructed the prosecution to use delaying tactics to keep me in confinement as long as possible: the prosecution has told several people that these are her instructions. This trial has been going on for three months now and they still haven't finished examining the first witness.'

'But you can understand why she feels threatened by your return,' I said.

'She should regard my return as an aspect of strength (for the family), not a threat. I don't want to lead the PPP. I'm not demanding any party or government post. I just want to be an MNA (Member of the National Assembly, or Pakistani Parliament) and represent the people of my father's constituency. But she's become paranoid and is convinced I'm trying to topple her.'

'Why do you think that is?'

Murtaza then proceeded to allege that his sister's political decisions are sometimes based on superstition: 'Probably been listening to one of her fortune-tellers. She believes in all sorts of voodoo: thinks her first government fell because she sought the advice of one *pir* and another, stronger *pir* got jealous and cursed her. When you base your political decisions on that sort of thing you're in serious trouble.' Murtaza giggled: 'When she came to Damascus in 1990 I had to find an astrologer for her—some Bedouin woman she had heard of, an old hag covered with shells, with tattoos all over her hands, cross-eyed—you know the sort of thing. Benazir spent two hours with the woman. I had to smuggle her into the Presidential Guest House through the servants' entrance. Apparently her ADCs have to do this for her wherever she goes, even in Paris and New York…' Murtaza chuckled happily. 'Anyway, it's easy to realise why she thinks I'm a threat if she's that easily influenced.'

'Do you think she has become harder—more ruthless— over the last few years?' I asked.

This time it was the Begum Bhutto who answered. 'My daughter would not have been capable of her actions today five years ago,' she said, shaking her head. 'The things she is doing now, even General Zia wouldn't have done.'

When I asked what she meant, the Begum went into an emotional description of an incident that had taken place at the Bhutto country estate of Al-Murtaza in Larkhana a month earlier, on 5 January. The fifth was Zulfiqar Bhutto's birthday, and to mark the occasion both the rival claimants to his mantle— mother and daughter—had planned pilgrimages to the *Shaheed's* grave. Fearing trouble if the two groups of supporters clashed, the security forces surrounded the Bhutto compound in Larkhana—the Begum's base—and banned her procession. When the Begum ordered the gates of the compound to be opened and made ready to set off, the police opened fire. One person was killed immediately, and two others died of their injuries after the police refused to let the ambulances through. That night, as the family retainers were bleeding to death, ten miles away in her new farmhouse Benazir celebrated her father's birthday with singing and dancing.

'After three deaths she and her husband danced!' said the Begum, now near to tears. 'They must have known the police were firing at Al-Murtaza. Would all this have happened if she didn't order it? But the worst crime was that they refused to let the ambulances through. If only they had let the ambulances through, those two boys would be alive now. Those two boys who used to love Benazir, who used to run in front of her car.'

The Begum was weeping now. 'I kept ringing Benazir, saying, "For God's sake stop the siege," but her people just repeated: "Madam is not available." She wouldn't even take my call. One call from her walkie-talkie would have got the wounded through. Even General Zia…' The sentence trailed away. 'What's that saying in England? "Power corrupts, more power corrupts even more." Is that it?'

'Don't you talk about this when you meet your daughter for lunch?' I asked.

Tears were running down her face, little rivulets of eye-shadow and smudged mascara.

'No.' The Begum shook her head and broke down. 'I just...just went...off...'

She buried her face in her handkerchief, and Murtaza put his arm around her.

The following morning, my last in Pakistan, I caught the old twin-prop Fokker Friendship which every day makes the passage over the desert wastes of Sindh to Mohenjo Daro, the nearest airstrip to Larkhana.

Nawab Mustafa Lahori, a neighbouring landowner and an old admirer of Begum Bhutto, was there to meet me. As we drove to Al-Murtaza, the Bhutto estate, along the dry salt flats of the Indus plain, the Nawab described to me the events of 5 January, of which he had been a witness. Like all the old Bhutto supporters I met that day, he was mystified by Benazir's behaviour, unable to understand how she had been able to let the police attack her own home, murder three of her most faithful family retainers, then forbid free passage for the wounded. No one believed her claim not to have been informed of the shootings until the following morning; and as for the official police explanation for the siege—that the Begum had been sheltering armed Indian secret agents within Al-Murtaza—there was only contempt.

'Everyone knows this charge is fabrication,' said the Nawab. 'By supporting the action of the police she is only damaging her own reputation in this area.'

That certainly seemed to be true. All over Larkhana, once the heartland of Benazir's most loyal supporters, posters and graffiti on almost every wall proclaimed the town's new allegiance to her brother. In the whole town I saw only one poster of Benazir, and that looked old and faded.

Al-Murtaza was a large walled compound in the centre of the town. Inside the walls, the dust of the desert gave way to a lovely irrigated Persian garden, the lawns broken by lines of palms and flowering bougainvillaea. Two old gardeners took us around, pointing out where police bullets had left holes in the gates and buildings or had knocked the bark off the trees; a clutch of teargas cylinders that had been fired during the siege were produced with a great flourish.

'We are very proud of our Bibi Sahiba (Benazir),' said one of the gardeners. 'But this time...it was very bad. It was not reasonable to stop the Begum Sahiba going to the grave of her husband. What happened on the fifth was done on Bibi's orders.'

'Bibi Sahiba is the Prime Minister,' agreed the other gardener. 'She gets to know what happens everywhere in Pakistan. She knew what the police were doing. No person should behave like this to her mother, or to her home.'

'Will people here vote again for her?' I asked.

'It's not certain,' said the first gardener. 'After the fifth our minds have been changed. We want Murtaza, not Bibi. All Sindh is unhappy with her. Everyone is angry.'

As they guided us around the flowerbeds the gardeners changed tack to the happier subject of Benazir's father, whom they clearly adored.

'The *Shaheed* was a wonderful man,' said the first gardener. 'Other politicians forget your name once they have your vote, but *Shaheed* Bhutto, he always remembered.'

'When the *Shaheed* was martyred,' said the second man, 'we all wept.'

I asked about the rumours I had heard that the villagers of Larkhana had begun seeing miracles at his grave.

'It is true,' said Mohammed Ibrahim, the Bhuttos' *chowkidar* (guard), who had joined us. 'Women who want babies go to his grave and soon the *Shaheed* fulfils their wishes.'

'Others who want work get employment,' said the first gardener.

'Many people have seen him in dreams,' said the second. 'They call him "*Shaheed* Baba". For all us people of Larkhana the *Shaheed* is the same as the great saints of Islam.'

'I myself have seen him in a dream,' said Mohammed Ibrahim. 'I was asleep in this garden when I had the dream. *Shaheed* Bhutto was sitting in a big chair in the company of the Prophet.'

'God is specially with this family,' said the second gardener. 'That we can say with certainty.'

'So do you believe that in due course Benazir may also become a saint?' I asked.

The three retainers looked at each other uncertainly.

'There are not so many female saints in our Islam,' said one gardener.

'Well, what about Murtaza then?'

'I believe he too will reach this peak,' said Mohammed Ibrahim. 'He is the true heir of *Shaheed* Bhutto. We all pray that he too will be a great saint one day.'

*Postscript*: Two and a half years later, in September 1996, Murtaza Bhutto and six of his supporters were shot dead in a hail of police bullets, a few yards from the front door of 70 Clifton. The police claimed it was an accident, but when the officer in charge of the shooting was found hanged a few days later, officially having taken his own life, the circumstances began to look more and more suspicious. Benazir denied any complicity in the killing and made an operatic display of public mourning, but when her government was dissolved by the President on 5 November 1996 for gross corruption, her husband was immediately charged in connection with the murder and is currently imprisoned in Karachi, awaiting trial. There seems, however, to be little hard evidence against him, and there is a strong possibility that he will again succeed in avoiding conviction.

After her husband's death, Ghinwa Bhutto and her stepdaughter Fatima took over Murtaza's PPP—*Shaheed* Bhutto faction, using it to launch a vigorous campaign against Benazir. Partly as a result of their efforts, and partly due to increasing evidence of the massive scale of Benazir and Zardari's corruption, with more and more details emerging of a succession of lavish foreign properties and Swiss bank accounts containing hundreds of millions of dollars, in the general election which followed in February 1997, Nawaz

Sharif's Muslim League won by a record margin. At the time of writing Sharif remains in the saddle, though Pakistan is being consumed by ever-worsening sectarian violence and is undergoing a major economic crisis, made much worse by the sanctions imposed after the country detonated its nuclear bomb in May 1998.

Discredited as she is, Benazir remains leader of the opposition. Her children have been sent to Dubai 'for their own safety'. It seems highly unlikely that Benazir can mount a credible comeback—although stranger things have happened in Pakistan—and it is now said to be open to question whether she even wants to do so: some of her friends believe that all she desires is to get Zardari out of jail, and then to leave the country. In this case, the move of her children to Dubai may be the precursor to her own departure. On the other hand, Benazir's almost messianic sense of her own destiny may preclude her from ever totally giving up politics, however strong the evidence of corruption against her.

One last serendipity: in 1997, as chance would have it, Christopher Lee was cast to play Jinnah in a forthcoming biopic of the Quaid-e-Azam's life. I was clearly not alone in noticing the uncanny resemblance between Dracula's most memorable incarnation and the man who must take much of the blame for the bloodbath of Partition.

# On the Frontier

PESHAWAR, 1989

Violence is to the North-West Frontier what religion is to the Vatican. It is a *raison d'être*, a way of life, an obsession, a philosophy. Bandoliers hang over the people's shoulders, grenades are tucked into their pockets. Status symbols here are not Mercedes or Savile Row suits; in Peshawar you know you've arrived when you can drive to work in a captured Russian T-72 tank.

The pathological frame of mind of the frontier people is partly derived from the harshness of the landscape. It is hard, barren, dry country, drained of colour, warmth and softness. The mountainsides are grey and sheer, covered with sharp mica schist, the tedium relieved only at the valley bottoms with windbreaks of poplar and Ashoka. There is no snow here—it is too dry—but the winds from the snow peaks sweep down the slopes and the scarred valley sides and brush the streets clear of people. The sky is grey and the air is grey and the greyness seeps into the ground and the stones and the buildings. The only colours are the red and yellow silk flags flying over the new graves in the graveyards. As you wander past, you can feel winter lying like a curled dragon across the land.

The people here are as cold and hard as the schist. Blank, stony faces with long, drawn features look out from blank forests of facial hair. The subzero temperature makes them withdraw into themselves, both mentally and physically. They lift up their knees to their chins and wrap their heavy Kashmiri shawls around both. On top, their heads are covered with woollen rollmop caps. You see only the dark eyes peering out into the cold. Eighty per cent are illiterate. Yet they are proud. They sneer through their moustaches, eyes levelled straight, in contempt as much as in curiosity.

These people—the Pathans—have never been conquered, at least not since the time of Alexander the Great. They have seen off centuries of invaders—Persians, Arabs, Turks, Mughals, Sikhs, British, Russians—and they retain the mixture of arrogance and suspicion that this history has produced in their character. History has also left them with a curious political status. Although most Pathans are technically within Pakistan, the writ of Pakistan law does not carry into the heartland of their territories.

These segregated areas are in effect private tribal states, out of the control of the Pakistan government. They are an inheritance from the days of the Raj: the British were quite happy to let the Pathans act as a buffer zone on the edge of the Empire, and they did not try to extend their authority into the hills. Where the British led, the modern Pakistani authorities have followed. Beyond the check points on the edge of Peshawar, tribal law—based on the institutions of the tribal council and the blood feud—rules unchallenged and unchanged since its origins long before the birth of Christ.

The tribal areas are officially closed to all foreigners, as their safety cannot be guaranteed by the Pakistan government: kidnapping and murder are so frequent here that they are virtually cottage industries. To visit you have to smuggle yourself quietly across the tribal border, ideally in the company of some tribal elder. It is not difficult to do this, but it does require a little care and preparation.

In the shops in the bazaar in Darra Adam Khel, just over the border in the tribal territories, lines of high-explosive warheads sit in glass cupboards facing on to the street as innocently as jars of humbugs in an English village store. The stacked mortar shells and the anti-tank ammunition are available over the counter, for cash, as if they were tins of Heinz baked beans. Nearby the belts of machine-gun bullets are hung up like strings of onions. Outside, left lying around in the streets like so much discarded gardening equipment, can be found heavy machine-guns, rocket-launchers and field-guns. There is a fantastic, almost surreal feel to the place: here we go round the arms bazaar, half a pound of tuppenny shells, five green gasmasks sitting on a wall.

Mohammed Rafiq, prop., Khyber Military Supplies, (Pvt) Ltd, is a serious man with thick black glasses, a pinstripe waistcoat and a tall Astrakhan hat. He serves cardamom tea in delicate porcelain bowls and moans about the end of the Afghan war.

'Sahib, I am telling you the truth,' he said, sipping at his bowl. 'Five year ago we were selling forty or fifty Kalashnikovs a day, no problem. Now business is not good. Occasionally we are selling some anti-aircraft missiles, now and then an RPG (rocket-propelled grenade). But the Afghan war is over. Now it is only our tribesmen who are buying.'

This thought appeared to depress Mohammed Rafiq. But his assistant Abdul Qadir was more optimistic.

'Our tribesmen are still good customers,' he said, wobbling his head from side to side in the Indian manner. 'Everyone is still wanting many guns.'

Mohammed Rafiq nodded in agreement. 'Our people are liking too much these arms. In the tribal areas you do not need permit, not even for tank.'

'Take middle-rank man,' said Abdul Qadir philosophically. 'He does not have the comforts of life. But he has gun and pistol and rifle, maybe two: one Lee Enfield for tradition-sake, one Kalashnikov for killing people.'

'If he is big man—a *malik*—he may have rocket-launcher and anti-aircraft gun. Too many gun. Is good business.'

'And they actually use these guns?' I asked.

'Often they are using.'

'On who?'

'On each other.'

'Oh yes,' said the assistant proudly. 'Our tribal people are having these enemies and they are having to kill them. All the people of the North-West Frontier are gunfighters.'

As we spoke, the wail of a muezzin pierced the air from a loudspeaker outside.

'Excuse me,' said Mohammed Rafiq. 'This is the time of our prayer.'

The two partners got out strips of carpet from under a heavy machine-gun and laid them down behind the desk. Intoning their prayers, they began rising and falling so that all you could see was two Astrakhan hats bobbing up and down between the telephone and the stapler on the desk.

On the way back to Peshawar I called on Khan Abdul Wali Khan, once one of the great landlords and politicians of the area, now a frail and half-blind old man. We sat in his summer house in the middle of his irrigated garden, beneath great jungles of climbing bougainvillea, looking out on his flowerbeds full of yellow narcissi, roses and chrysanthemums. There was a sound of birdsong and running water. The Khan poured jasmine tea and gestured at the bowls of walnuts, dates and raisins on the table. I told him what I had seen at the Darra arms bazaar.

'Yes,' he said. 'There are now more than one million Kalashnikovs in this province alone. It has got completely out of control.'

He shook his head sadly.

'I feel,' he said, 'as if I'm living on an ammunition dump.'

The bazaar in Peshawar is the great meeting place of the tribes. It is here that the region's produce is brought to be sold, here that goods smuggled over the Afghan border pass into Pakistan, here that news and gossip is passed on and exchanged. Appropriately enough, the main street of the bazaar is known as the Qissa Khawani, the Street of the Storytellers.

It is only here, as you wander through the bazaar, that you realise the great diversity of racial types that the different invasions have left behind them. The genes of a hundred different races meet here and intermingle. The passage of Genghis Khan and his Mongol hordes has elongated many eyes and turned to silky down the normally thick beard of a Pathan chin. Bright Aryan-blue eyes flash beneath mountainous turbans, calling to mind the old tales of Alexander's lost legions left stranded in these mountains—and also the taste for British memsahibs that the Pathans developed over the century following 1840. Curly hair and Semitic noses remind one of the (admittedly slightly far-fetched) legends which maintain that the Pathans are a lost tribe of Israel—those who got separated from Moses during the forty years wandering in the desert and mistakenly stumbled into the Hindu Kush while looking for the way back to Egypt.

The contents of the bazaar are as diverse as the people within it. Along with the rugs and sheepskin coats, the *karakul* caps and the Chitrali cloaks, the pavements of Peshawar appear to be the end of the line for many of the knitted woollies and discarded trousers proudly donated by tens of thousands of Home Counties grannies to Save the Children or Oxfam. Ten yards further down the street plastic mirrors, broken toy tanks and red waterpistols all appear to have fallen off the back of a lorry *en route* from Taiwan. The fraudulent Rolexes, brass idols, cassettes of wailing music and garish calendars have been smuggled across the border from India.

But alongside this small-scale junk business is hidden another much more lucrative trade. In the last few years many of the mud-brick houses in Peshawar have been faced with marble. Goatherds have become millionaires and bazaars boulevards. The same transformation has left the lobby of the Hotel Pearl Continental in Peshawar one of the strangest sights in Pakistan. The Pearl Continental is one of the most lavish establishments of its kind in South Asia, but unlike its rivals it is not full of Western tourists and businessmen. The people who dine in its five restaurants and spend in its lavish shopping arcade are wild-looking tribesmen, hung with ammunition belts and weapons, eating with their hands, looking to the casual observer too poor to be eating anywhere more luxurious than the kebabji of the bazaars. Yet these men have money, and in no small quantity. They pay for their meals in cash, handing out bundles of notes from the sports bags they keep tucked by their sides.

The source of this money is no mystery to the inhabitants of Peshawar, although it is a matter for some indignation. 'I am number two in this hotel,' I was told by Mohammed Riaz, the assistant manager of the Pearl Continental. 'I work thirteen hours a day and have been working like this for eight years. But in that time how much do I manage to save? Perhaps one hundred thousand rupees (£2,000) in two years. With that I can afford a small motorbike. But I see my classmates: they have beautiful Suzuki jeeps, some even have Mercedes. I ask, "How much do these cost?" They reply, "Seven hundred thousand." I ask, "Where did you get that money?" They reply, "We have shops." Shops! Shops do not make this sort of money. Of course it is drugs money. Go to the tribal areas—you will see there bad land and no industry. Everyone there is uneducated and illiterate. But many of the tribesmen are driving around in big BMWs. They are all in it up to their necks.'

According to US drug enforcement officials, about thirty per cent of all American and perhaps eighty per cent of all British heroin passes through Peshawar. The poppies are grown in the tribal areas and in Mujahedin-held areas of Afghanistan. From there the poppy heads are brought to one of sixty illicit processing laboratories dotted around the Khyber Pass. The processed heroin then passes to Peshawar, where it is loaded on to lorries—or occasionally on to military transports—and taken to Karachi. Then it is shipped to the West. Pakistani customs officers actively encourage the trade. Their monthly salary is equivalent to about £40, but payoffs from the drug mafias are so lucrative that highly skilled graduates compete to bribe their way into the customs service. A recent survey at Karachi University found the customs service to be the single most popular career.

Most of the rich men in Peshawar are involved in the drug trade in some way, as is much of the Pakistani civil and military establishment: known heroin smugglers sit in parliament. In Pakistan they can buy themselves out of trouble. Only when they venture abroad are they in danger of being arrested: the brother of the Chief Minister of the North-West Frontier and the son of the province's Governor are currently both in jail near New York on narcotics charges.

Yet even the Americans have to tread carefully here. Pakistan is a valuable and fragile ally, which cannot be bullied and invaded like Colombia or Panama. Pakistan is a base near the Gulf, a base for the operations in Afghanistan, and a base on the Iranian border. For this reason the Americans put up with the martial law of General Zia, and now they put up with the new and ever-expanding drug culture for the same reason.

Landi Khotal, at the top of the Khyber, is the nerve centre of the opium trade and home to many of Pakistan's biggest drug barons. Hiring a guard armed with an American-made automatic rifle, I managed to wangle a pass from the tribal authorities and set off soon after dawn in an old Morris Traveller, still in service as a taxi after thirty-five years.

We passed a clutch of mud-walled Afghan refugee camps and then were out of the town and on to the plain of Peshawar. As we came to the border of the tribal area two ominous signs reared out of the scrub:

SEEK HELP FROM ALMIGHTY GOD

and beyond it:

BETTER ALONE THAN IN BAD COMPANY.

I looked nervously at the guard. He smiled blankly back.

We snaked into the narrow mouth of the Khyber Pass, and rose, past a series of castellated farmsteads, higher and higher into the barren hills. On one bend we passed a huge marble-faced enclosure surrounded by high-tension electrified wire. Guards holding Kalashnikovs flanked the marble gateway.

'Zakir Afridi—big drugs man,' explained the guard.

Every so often we would pass a fort—a succession of bleak, mud-walled fortifications—at least one of which, Kafar

Kot, the Fort of the Unbelievers, dates back to the time of Alexander the Great. Few places in the world have seen such a succession of armies pass through them. When Alexander's generals, Hephaestion and Perdiccas, led their Macedonian legions down the caravan road which threads through this narrow defile, they were already following in the footsteps of Darius and no doubt countless other earlier prehistoric armies. Since then the same snaking road has seen Seljuk, Mughal, Khajar, Afghan and British armies come and go. All have left their mark, but none has managed to hold the Pass for more than a century or two.

On the outskirts of Landi Khotal we passed the station. When it was built in 1925, in the aftermath of the third Afghan war, it was the last railhead in British India and the terminus of the Khyber Railway, one of the most remarkable—and expensive—engineering projects ever undertaken by the British in India. Costing more than £2 million to complete, it wound its way up fifteen miles of impossible gradients through thirty-four tunnels and over ninety-two bridges and culverts. But since 1985 the railway has been closed. 'The tribesmen were firing Stinger missiles at it,' I was told by a friend in Peshawar. 'It was the drugs barons that were behind it: it was crossing their territory so they closed it down.'

Certainly, Landi Khotal station looked as if it had been built to expect the worst. It seemed more like a castle than a railhead, with solid stone walls pierced by tiny arrow-slits. Projecting turrets on its four corners covered every angle. All around the houses had been cleared to leave a free field of fire. Afghanistan is less than half a mile away: this was once the British Empire's first line of defence.

The windows were covered with thick metal grilles, and the doors were of reinforced steel. One, however, had been smashed off its hinges, and I climbed inside to explore. The interior—a quadrangle of rooms giving off an overgrown cloister-garth—had something of the air of Custer's last stand. You felt instinctively as if something terrible had happened here: that the tribesmen had crucified the stationmaster perhaps, or garrotted the ticket collector. This was the sort of place where Kipling's short stories came to an end, the true-blue Victorian hero lying disembowelled on a frontier pass, and the vultures hovering nearby:

> When you're wounded and left on Afghanistan's plains,
> An' the women come out to cut up what remains,
> Jest roll on your rifle an' blow out your brains,
> An' go to your Gawd like a soldier.

Inside the stationmaster's office, everything was as it had been when the last train pulled up the Pass. The *Pakistan Railways Almanac 1962* lay open on a desk and old ledgers gathered dust on a shelf. It was an eerie place and I had no wish to linger.

It was now mid-morning and the market in the centre of Landi Khotal was in full swing. Old men were gathered around a fire drinking Pathan *kahwa*. *Kebab-wallahs* fanned little charcoal grills while butchers disembowelled chickens and tanners skinned dead goats, leaving little rivulets of blood running into the open sewer. Nearby a scrap merchant was weighing a crate full of spent shell-cases. I explained to the guard what I was looking for, and he nodded and led me further into the labyrinth.

Along an alley, down a dark, slimy staircase we arrived at a gateway. The guard knocked three times, and the door swung open. Inside eight bearded tribesmen were sitting in the half-lit gloom under some trellising. For a moment I looked at my companion, wondering why he had brought me here. Then one of the tribesmen took from his pocket a paper envelope. He tipped the contents—some browny-white powder—out on to a piece of silver foil, then held it up to his face. He lit a match and warmed the foil until the powder liquefied. Then he took a small white tube and inhaled the vapours. The sweet, sickly stench of heroin filled the air.

Landi Khotal was awash with narcotics. Heroin itself was generally kept out of sight under the counter, but hashish and opium were freely available, and as casually displayed as cigarettes and betel nut. Some of the hash was set in great toffee-like blocks; other pieces were folded into hash chapattis or tortured into spaghetti strands. One roadside stall moulded its hash into curvilinear arrangements that looked like liquorice allsorts.

'The US tried to bribe us to stop growing the poppy,' one vendor told me. He tore a little lump of opium off a block, nonchalantly rolled it into a ball and popped it in his mouth. 'They promised us irrigation and improved roads if we destroyed our crops. We let them spend their money, then used the wells to grow better poppy.'

Drugs were not the only illegal trade flourishing in Landi Khotal. The town also has one of the largest smuggling bazaars in Asia. Electrical equipment from Hong Kong and Japan and cheap Russian household goods (huge washing machines; vast, outdated air conditioners) are brought by rail or air from the former Soviet Union to Kabul. They are transferred to lorries and driven towards the Pakistani border, then loaded on to pack-mule or camel and wind their way by night across the border and into the tribal territories. There they are either sold direct or passed on to middlemen who smuggle them into Pakistan proper. No duty is paid at any stage. The profits are colossal.

The question that currently exercises the intelligence agencies is how long will it be before nuclear warheads from the former Soviet Union join the hardware passing on donkey-back into the Frontier—and thence on to the international market.

It is not the first time that these barren and remote hills on the edge of the Hindu Kush have been both prosperous and strategic. For centuries the area has been a natural border zone between the rival cultures of India, China, Persia and Central Asia, the place where the goods of the different civilisations have been exchanged and where all the porous cultures, religions and languages of the area have mixed and intermingled—not for nothing does 'pesh awar' mean 'frontier town'. But however large the profits of the opium trade in

Peshawar today, they are nothing compared to the riches brought to the area by the silk route, especially during the first five centuries A.D. It was at this time that the area around Peshawar gave birth to the civilisation of Gandhara, one of the most remarkable composite cultures in South Asian history.

I first stumbled across Gandhara when, a couple of days after hitching a lift out of Peshawar, I found myself climbing up a goat path in Swat, one of the most beautiful valleys on earth. Here the snow peaks of the Karakorums widen and thaw into a landslide of cultivation terraces. Below, the Swat river—in autumn the colour of lapis-lazuli—meanders lazily around a green plain of orchards and wheatfields. As you wander past, scenes from a Mughal miniature take shape in the fields around you: men are bent double beneath stooks of corn, reaping with sickles; others carry bundles of juniper branches for feeding to their goats.

The tarmac road had given up far below, and a shepherd boy had offered to lead me to my destination. Although he must have been barely twelve years old, he strode on ahead, scrambling up the track at a pace that only one born among mountains could set. I followed in fits and bursts, stopping every few minutes to wheeze and catch my breath. In this fashion we climbed up past mud-brick farms and through unharvested fields, the track getting ever smaller and steeper. Behind us the dying sun was sketching deep-cut shadows in the hills. We passed a group of hayricks, and above them a herd of cows chewing their evening cud. In the distance I could hear the ringing of bells as the shepherds led their fat-tailed sheep home for the night. We climbed on; and eventually, doubling back up the side of the hill and turning a corner, we arrived.

It was an extraordinary sight. Perfectly preserved in the middle of nowhere, miles from the nearest main road, lay the ruins of a sophisticated and beautifully constructed monastic complex. It was built in a style that would not be out of place in Athens, Rome or Constantinople: the porticoed and pedimented façades were supported by carved Corinthian pillars. Halls, chapels, *stupas* (burial mounds)—all were built in a style immediately recognisable as classical Greek. Yet these were Buddhist buildings, a few miles from the Afghan border, and they dated from the early centuries of the Christian era, long after the demise of classical civilisation in Europe.

I stood on top of the highest *stupa*. A crescent moon had just risen, though it was not yet dark, and the cicadas were singing. Pillars of dung-smoke rose from the valley villages. I looked out over the landscape, astonished by what I was seeing; it was only later, in the libraries back home, that I was able to make sense of it.

It seems that the origins of these extraordinary buildings date back to the summer of 327 B.C., when Alexander the Great swept into the highlands of Swat at the head of his victorious Macedonian army. Intending to conquer even the most distant provinces of the ancient Persian empire, Alexander had crossed into the Hindu Kush; and there, high on the Afghan plateau, he had first heard stories of the legendary riches of the Indian subcontinent—of its gold, said to be dug by gigantic ants and guarded by griffins; of its men who lived for two hundred years and its women who made love in public; of the Sciapods, who liked to recline in the shade cast by their one enormous foot; of the perfumes and silks which, the Afghans told the Greeks, grew on the trees and even in the cabbage patches of India; of the unicorns and the pygmies; of the elephants and falcons; of the precious jewels which lay scattered on the ground like dust; and the unique variety of steel which could avert a storm.

It was the end of the hot season, the beginning of the rains, and Alexander had arrived at the edge of the known world. Now he made up his mind to conquer the unknown world beyond. Easily defeating the Hindu Rajahs of Swat on the banks of the river Jhelum, he prepared to cross the last rivers of the Punjab and to conquer the Indian plains. But on the swollen banks of the Beas he was brought to a halt. His homesick soldiers refused to go on; the torrential monsoon rain had destroyed their spirits where everything else—heat, starvation and disease—had failed. Alexander was forced to turn back, leaving a series of Greek garrisons behind to guard his conquests. On the return journey Alexander died— perhaps poisoned—in Nebuchadnezzar's empty palace in Babylon; and his empire split into a million pieces.

In the ensuing anarchy the Greek garrisons of India and Afghanistan were cut off from their homeland. They had no choice but to stay on in Asia, intermingling with the local peoples and leavening Indian learning with Greek philosophy and classical ideas. Over the following thousand years, further cross-fertilised by Central Asian influences brought by the conquering Kushans, an astounding civilisation grew up in the fastness of the Karakorums, deep within the isolated and mountainous kingdom known as Gandhara. Hellenic in spirit, Buddhist in religion, worshipping an encyclopedic pantheon of Greek, Roman, Iranian, Hindu and Buddhist deities, Gandhara's principal icon was a meditating Buddha dressed in a Greek toga.

Gandhara survived for a thousand years, long after Greek civilisation had disappeared in Europe; and when it was extinguished by a further wave of Central Asian invaders in the seventh century it left behind a legacy of finely constructed monasteries—in the plains around Peshawar Fa-Hien, a fifth-century Chinese traveller, counted no fewer than twenty-four hundred such shrines—and a scattering of well-planned classical cities, *acropoli*, *stupas* and superb sculptures. Most of these illustrate the Buddhist scriptures, but to do so use the motifs and techniques of classical Greek and Roman art, with its vine scrolls and cherubs, Tritons and centaurs. The slowly decaying remains of the civilisation which emerged from this extraordinary clash of cultures still litters much of northern Pakistan.

I had left Peshawar early in the morning the day before, and hitched out of town on a succession of brightly painted trucks.

It was both harvest and election time in Pakistan, and the little roadside villages were suffering from the head-on collision of agriculture and politics. As I approached a village bazaar I would come across a traffic jam made up of bumbling herds of fat-tailed sheep, strings of bad-tempered camels and heavily-laden tractors bringing in farm-folk with their crops. I would not have to wait long to find the cause of the obstruction: from the opposite direction a float bearing a parliamentary candidate and his supporters would be making slow progress through the village lanes, waving banners, pasting posters and shouting slogans.

For all their dour machismo, the Pathans have a great love of festivities and bright colours, and to their minds elections seem to come under the same sort of heading as New Year celebrations, pilgrimages and religious festivals. They much enjoy festooning their mud-brick houses with the colourful flags of the different political parties, even if it sometimes means that one house carries the flapping colours of three rival parties. Processions and meetings are well attended, and even the most hopeless candidate can gather a cheerful crowd of tribesmen.

This is all very well for the candidate, but is less of a boon to a traveller trying to get anywhere at election time. In one village where the streets were clogged solid, my truck driver was forced to give up and retire to a tea shop until the procession had passed. Pin-ups dotted the walls: Benazir Bhutto, a selection of election candidates, Sylvester Stallone, Madonna and the Ayatollah Khomeini.

'Which of these is the best candidate?' I asked the *chai-wallah*, gesturing at the posters.

The man shrugged his shoulders: 'Who knows?' he replied, glancing up at them undecidedly. 'All are good Muslims.'

Because of such delays, it was well past noon by the time we arrived at the ruins of Pushkalavati, the City of the Lotus. Once upon a time, Pushkalavati was a rival of the great Babylon, but its conquest by Alexander began a decline from which it never recovered. Today it is a strange and romantic ruin, more like a ziggurat in desert Mesopotamia than the remains of the one-time capital of the fertile Punjab. The barren grey clay walls rise eighty feet out of the cane-breaks, huge and sheer and craggy. Their original shape has been washed away by two and half thousand years of rain, and all that remains now is a Herculean block of mud and a series of local legends of a city made of gold.

I climbed to the top of the vallum, unrolled a rug and sat munching away at my packed lunch; while I ate I listened to a shepherd boy playing a reed flute in the cane-breaks below. Afterwards I picked around the ramparts, trawling through the mass of pottery, bones and arrowheads which lay scattered across the hillocks of the ruin. Handles of ancient amphorae, painted shards and fragments of geometric decoration lay strewn around like autumn leaves—tens of thousands of broken shards poking out of the mud as if some ancient sledgehammer-maniac had run amok in a pottery kiln. At its height, traders came to Pushkalavati from all over the world: archaeologists have found alabaster from Rome, painted glass from Antioch and Alexandria, porphyry from Upper Egypt, ivories from south India and lacquers from the China coast. But now it was just the shepherd boy, the shards and the mud and the ruins and me. I pocketed a couple of glazed pot-handles and returned to the road.

Beyond the ruins of Pushkalavati the first lavender-coloured peaks of the Himalayas rose into the sky. I flagged down a passing Morris Traveller driven by an unusually small and round Pathan named Murtazar, and together we set off towards the Malakand Pass, the gateway to Swat.

In the nineteenth century the valley's ruler was the Akond of Swat, who inspired the Edward Lear comic poem:

Who or why, or which, or what,
Is the Akond of Swat?
Is he tall or short, or dark or fair?
Does he sit on a stool or a sofa or chair,
Or squat,
The Akond of Swat?

But there was nothing in the least comical or whimsical about the Malakand Pass. Here the road rises some five thousand feet in a near-vertical ascent of only a few miles. It is a most dramatic drive up a virtual cliff-face, unspoilt by such tiresome impediments as crash-barriers or fences to break your fall. It is emphatically not a road to be travelled by anyone suffering from vertigo; nor is it recommended for anyone driving an ancient Morris Traveller—as we soon discovered.

We had only turned the first of the great U-bends when the car began to shake and rattle like a boiling kettle. 'Car going ruk-ruk,' observed Murtazar. 'This ruk-ruk not good noise.' It certainly wasn't. But the car jolted grudgingly on. Below, the fields of the plain of Peshawar receded into a quilt of patchwork squares, broken by seams of poplar avenue. We crawled on, up and up, and suddenly we were there. The Traveller gave a last metallic groan and turned its nose triumphantly down into the valley on the far side. 'Olden car is golden car,' said Murtazar in a tone as much of surprise as of pleasure, and as if to reward the car for its good behaviour, he turned the ignition off and let the Traveller freewheel down the slope to the banks of the Swat river.

So relieved was I to have achieved the top of the pass that it was several minutes before I began to take in the astonishing beauty of the valley into which we were rapidly plunging. It was like entering a lost world, a forgotten Eden isolated on its high Himalayan plateau.

We were passing rapidly through the vortex of an Ashoka avenue, flanked on one side by the blue Swat river and on the other by green orchards watered by bubbling irrigation runnels. There were mangoes and cherries, quinces and apples, apricots and almonds, and beyond the orchards there were thickets of tamarisk and casuarina as well as groves of mulberry trees belonging to silk farmers. There were children paddling in the streams, and girls carrying brushwood bundles on their heads, and old men sitting in the shade, sucking at their silver hookahs. Everywhere you looked were the undecayed remains of the Gandharan golden age: colossal Buddhas and reliefs of the Kushan King Kanishka cut into the rockface; huge stupas rising from hexagonal drums; and a series of fortresses sitting on vast bluffs of rock overlooking the old silk road.

Though many of the most remarkable surviving Gandharan remains lie around the top of the Malakand Pass, Gandhara's ancient capital is sixty miles to the south, at Taxila. When Alexander appeared at the mouth of the Khyber, the King of Taxila wisely decided against challenging the Greeks. Instead he met Alexander in Swat and guided him through the forests of rhododendron and alpine clematis to the walls of the city. Here, for the first time, Alexander's troops were able to rest and take in the Indian scene.

To the Greeks, familiar with the glories of Athens, Babylon, Susa and Egyptian Memphis, the buildings of Taxila were unremarkable: the houses were made of mud and uncut stone, and were laid out without any central order or plan. But what did amaze them were the Pathans who lived there. 'Physically, the Indians are slim,' wrote Alexander's Admiral Nearchus. 'They are tall and much lighter in weight than other men...they wear earrings of ivory (at least the rich do), and they dye their beards, some the very whitest of white, others dark blue, red or purple or even green...they wear a tunic and throw an outer mantle around their shoulders: another is wound round their head. All except the very humblest carry parasols in summer.'

Others wore no clothes at all. Two miles outside Taxila, the Greeks came across fifteen naked wise men who laughed at their cloaks and knee-high boots. They demanded that the foreigners should undress if they wanted to hear some words of the ancient wisdom of India. 'But the heat of the sun,' wrote one of Alexander's men, 'was so scorching that nobody could have borne to walk barefoot, especially at midday.' So the Greeks kept their clothes on, and the senior guru questioned them about Socrates, Pythagoras and Diogenes. Later, the gurus, still naked, dined at Alexander's table: '(They) ate their food while standing,' wrote one witness, 'balanced on one leg.'

Although Alexander stayed at Taxila only for a matter of weeks, his visit changed the course of the city's history.

Visiting the museum at the entrance to the archaeological site, I wandered through the rooms looking at the Gandharan sculptures, some of which dated from nearly a thousand years after Alexander's death. Even the Buddha, that symbol of Eastern philosophy, had undergone a process of Hellenisation: his grace and easy sensuality was thoroughly Indian, yet the images in the Taxila museum were all defined by Western ideas of proportion and realism; moreover the Buddha was wearing a toga, European dress.

Most remarkable of all was the coin room. Over an entire wall were scattered the gold and silver coins of a millennium of Taxila's rulers. It wasn't just that the coins were all modelled on Greek originals. What was amazing were the names of the rulers: Pantaleon, King of North India; Diomedes, King of the Punjab; Menander of Kabul; Heliochles, King of Balkh. They hinted at the strange, hybrid world these kings inhabited. They brought East and West together at a time when the British, the only other Europeans who ever succeeded in ruling the area, were still running through prehistoric fogs dressed in bearskins. The coins of Heliochles of Balkh were typical: they showed a Roman profile on one side—large nose, imperial arrogance in the eyes—but on the reverse Heliochles chose as his symbol a humped Indian Brahmini bull.

Outside, among the ruins—which are spread out over a distance of some fifteen square miles, and overgrown with hollyhocks and wild foxgloves—it is this strange mix of Europe and Asia that continues to grip the imagination. At Sirkap on the edge of Taxila, the Bactrian Greeks founded a classical Greek quarter in 190 B.C. It was to be the New Taxila, a great advance on the old city, and they carefully laid out the streets in a grid of straight lines, like a chessboard. As at Athens, a magnificent boundary wall loops around the residential areas and rises up to the fortified citadel, Sirkap's answer to the Parthenon.

From there you can stand on the citadel walls and see the expanse of houses unfold beneath you. It is a scene of striking, almost suburban, regularity: it could be any modern New Town, except that each street is punctuated with Buddhist shrines, not supermarkets, and that the whole city was built nearly two hundred years before the birth of Christ. Most intriguing of all, one of the shrines bears the insignia of the double-headed eagle. Centuries later the same symbol was to become the crest first of Byzantium, then of the Habsburgs, and finally of Imperial Russia. Its first appearance, here in a lost city on the edge of the Karakorums, is one of Gandhara's great unsolved mysteries.

My favourite of the Taxila ruins, I decided, was that of the monastery of Julian, named after its founder, an Imperial Roman envoy who converted to Buddhism. The monastery was always a place of retreat, and even today, a ruin, it still retains its original calm. I arrived there late in the evening, just as the smoke from the village fires was forming a perfect horizontal line above the fields. At the foot of the hill, below the olive groves, leathery black water-buffaloes sat with their legs folded beneath them. Above, there were parakeets among the olives, and as I walked up the hill flights of grasshoppers exploded from beneath my feet.

I was shown around by the elderly *chowkidar* who as young a man had participated in Sir Mortimer Wheeler's excavation of the site. He was a fascinating old man, and as he explained the function of the different ruins the monastery came to life. Soon I could see the orange-robed monks tramping clockwise around the stupas, queuing for their food in the refectory, or snuffing out their oil lamps in their austere stone cells.

Best of all, I could visualise the builders. They were men with a sense of humour, for they had included in the design a hundred little conceits, all lovingly pointed out by the *chowkidar*. Here were a series of grotesque Atlantes—they had narrow Mongol features, handlebar moustaches and giant earrings—groaning as they sank under the weight of the *stupa* which was resting on their shoulders. Here—and this was obviously the chowkidar's favourite—was a scene from the temptation of the Buddha: as he sat meditating under an arch, two girls appeared around the corner flashing their breasts at him, trying to distract him from his spiritual quest. Round the base of the stupa the *chowkidar* pointed out more temptresses—some extending their legs, others baring their bottoms, others proffering amphorae of wine: 'Girls, dancing,

drinking—all no-problem to Mr Buddha. He liking only
prayer, preaching and hymn-singing,' said the *chowkidar*
approvingly. 'Buddha-sahib is very good gentleman.'

Remarkable as these remains are, it is difficult at first to
understand how the warlike Pathans could be descended
from the gentle Hellenistic philosophers who created the
civilisation of Buddhist Gandhara. Yet they are, and if you
visit the museum in Peshawar you can slowly begin to
understand the connection which links the warlike tribesmen
in the bazaar to the philosopher-soldiers of Alexander's army.

The most obvious link is material. In the wonderful
friezes of sculpture which illustrate the ancient Buddhist
scriptures, the Gandharan sculptors included details from the
everyday life they saw around them, details which one can
still see repeated in the lives of the people of the Frontier
today. The writing tablet and reed pen which the Buddha
used as a child are still used in the more remote Frontier
primary schools. The turbans which the Gandharan chieftains
sported in the sixth century A.D. have yet to disappear, and
many of the tribesmen still dye their beards, just
as they did when Nearchus wandered through the streets of
Taxila in the third century B.C. The sandals of the Bodhisattvas
are still worn; their musical instruments still played; their
jewellery still manufactured in the silver bazaar today. Even
the design of the houses remains more or less unchanged by
the passage of time.

But the link with the world of Gandhara runs even
deeper than this. The Peshawar museum is home to one of
the most magnificent collections of Buddhist images in
existence. Room after room is filled with spectacular black-
schist figures, standing, meditating, preaching or fasting. The
images follow a prescribed formula. The physique is
magnificent: muscles ripple beneath the diaphanous folds of
the toga. The saviour sits with half-closed eyes and legs

folded in a position of languid relaxation. His hair is oiled and groomed into a beehive topknot; his high, unfurrowed forehead is punctuated with a round caste-mark. His face is full and round, the nose small and straight, the lips firm and proud.

It is only when you have stared at the figures for several hours that you realise what is so surprising about the Gandharan version of the Buddha: it is its arrogance. There is a hint of rankling self-satisfaction in the achievement of *nirvana*; a sneer on the threshold of enlightenment. This is the Buddha as he was in life—a prince. And soon you realise where you have seen that haughty expression before—outside in the bazaar. Unlike the tendency to grovelling subservience which you find in some of the other peoples of the subcontinent, the Pathans meet your gaze. Hawk-eyed and eagle-beaked, they are a proud people; and as the Buddhas demonstrate, their poise and self-confidence directly reflect that of the Gandharan Bactrian Greeks who sculpted these images in the plains of Peshawar nearly two millennia ago.

The institution that perhaps most directly links the modern Frontier with the area's primeval past is the blood feud. These small but incessant inter-family battles cause literally thousands of deaths every year, the ancient penalties of the system magnified a hundred times by the killing power of modern weaponry.

What most surprised me was the level of culture of some of the families caught up in the cycle of violence. Blood feuds sound the preserve of mafiosi, but in the North-West Frontier the most gentle and civilised families are involved in tit-for-tat killings of appalling brutality.

Hajji Feroz din-Khel is a charming old man who lives in a tumbledown stronghouse near the tribal village of Barra. He has twice visited Mecca, has eighteen grandsons and is held in great respect by everyone in Barra, where he is the main landlord and the honorary muezzin in the mosque. He has a long white beard and on a dark night could easily be mistaken for Father Christmas. Yet with his own hands he has murdered three men and a number of children. This is what he told me:

'Feuds usually start over a dispute about land or money. In this family we have feuds with two other families, both of which started simultaneously about forty years ago. Those two families have formed an alliance against us although they are not related. I have lost a father, two sons and one nephew aged about seven. The other two families have lost nine people altogether, so at the moment we are winning.

'The feuds started over a completely petty matter. There was a stream which flowed between our lands. It was divided by a line of stones, and on our side of the stream the water was diverted to a water mill. One day I was removing some of these stones to build a wall. My neighbour saw me and said, "Stop, these are my stones." We had a quarrel and I insulted him. The next day he killed my father, Faizal Akbar.

'After thirty years of killing we arranged a truce. But that truce was broken last year. My youngest brother Said Lal was walking along the road towards Barra when a car stopped and five men jumped out. They tried to kidnap his son who was walking with him. Said Lal shot at them and chased them away, but as they went one of them sprayed his machine-gun behind him. They killed my nephew. He was only seven.

'Despite this killing I want to make a settlement. But the other side have had more people killed, so they have to get their own back.'

I visited the Hajji several times during the autumn I was staying in Peshawar, and on my last trip I saw the effects of the blood feud for myself. Up to then, all the talk of guns and violence had been just that—talk. Now I saw what it actually entailed, the stark reality.

It was late afternoon and I was chatting to the Hajji in the shade of his verandah. We drank tea and the Hajji told me about his most recent visit to Mecca. Suddenly four men came rushing in, screaming in Pushtu. The Hajji rose to his feet, apologised to me and made straight for his jeep. 'There has been some trouble in the bazaar. My brother tried to kidnap a man who owed him money. The man resisted. Now Said Lal's been shot.'

I sat in the Hajji's house for an hour before the messenger came. Said Lal was dead. His body had been brought back to a house further down the road.

By the time I got there about a hundred people had gathered in and around the compound. The Hajji greeted me, his face distorted with sadness, but his eyes dry. He whispered a prayer and went back into the house. I could hear muffled wailing from the women within the harem, but the men outside were completely silent. They sat on *charpais*, heads lowered, hands cupped around their faces. Others pulled their beards. The dry, silent male mourning seemed much worse than the noisy grief of the women. Despite the frequency of violence in the tribal territories, the shock of loss was no less tangible here than it would have been anywhere else.

I was still holding my notebook, and my cameras were slung over my shoulders; I was a journalist intruding on a moment of private tragedy. It would have been quite wrong to stay. At the gate, I passed a friend of the din-Khels whom I had met with the Hajji earlier in the month.

'What will happen now?' I asked.

'There will be a truce for the funeral,' said the man, 'and then the Hajji will be required to recover his honour.'

'What does that mean?' I asked.

'It means,' said the man, 'that he must seek revenge.'

# Blood on the Tracks

It is barely dawn, and the sky is as pink as Turkish delight. Yet already, at 5.45 a.m., Lahore Central Station is buzzing like a kicked hive.

Bleary-eyed, you look around in bewilderment. At home the milkmen are abroad at this time, but no one else. Here the shops are already open, the fruit and vegetables on display, and the shopkeepers on the prowl for attention.

'Hello, my dear,' says a man holding up a cauliflower.

'Sahib—what is your good name?'

'*Subzi! Subzi! Subzi!*'

'Your mother country?'

A Punjabi runs up behind the rickshaw, waving something horrible: a wig perhaps, or some monstrous vegetable. 'Sahib, come looking! Special OK shop! Buying no problem!'

Lahore station rears out of the surrounding anarchy like a liner out of the ocean. It is a strange, hybrid building: the Victorian red-brick is imitation St Pancras, the loopholes, battlements and machicolations are stolen from some Renaissance palazzo—Milan perhaps, or Pavia—while the towers are vaguely German, and resemble a particularly extravagant Wagnerian stage set. Only the chaos is authentically Pakistani.

As a tape of the Carpenters' greatest hits plays incessantly on a Tannoy, you fight your way through the surge of jammed rickshaws and tottering red-jacketed coolies, through the sleeping villagers splayed out on the concrete, past the tap with the men doing their ablutions, over the bridge, down the stairs and on to the platform. In the early-morning glimmer, Platform 7 seethes with life like a hundred Piccadilly Circuses at rush hour. Porters stagger towards the first-class carriages under a mountain of smart packing cases and trunks. Further down the platform, near third class, solitary peasant women sit stranded amid seas of more ungainly luggage: cages and boxes, ambiguous parcels done up with rope, sacks with lumpy projections—bits of porcelain, the arm of a chair, the leg of a chicken. Vendors trawl the platform selling trays of brightly coloured sweetmeats, hot tea in red clay cups, or the latest film magazine. Soldiers wander past, handlebar moustaches wobbling in the slipstream.

The railways are now so much part of the everyday life of the subcontinent that it is difficult today to take in the revolution they brought about, or the degree to which they both created and destroyed the India of the Raj. Before the arrival of the railways in 1850, travel in India meant months of struggle over primitive dirt roads. Just fifty years later, tracks had been laid from the beaches south of Madras to the Afghan border, more than twenty-three thousand miles of railway in all. It was the biggest, and most costly, construction project undertaken by any colonial power in any colony anywhere in the world. It was also the largest single investment of British capital in the whole of the nineteenth century.

By 1863 some three million tons of rails, sleepers and locomotives had been shipped to India from Britain, in around 3,500 ships. Engineers had looped tracks over the steepest mountains in the world, sunk foundations hundreds of feet in to the billowing deserts, bridged rivers as wide and as turbulent as the Ganges and the Indus. It was an epic undertaking, even by the standards of an age inured to industrial heroics.

The railways also brought about a social revolution. There could be no caste barriers in a railway carriage: you bought your ticket and you took your place. For the first time in Indian history a Maulvi who spent his days contemplating the glorious Koran might find himself sitting next to an Untouchable who skinned dead cows. Moreover, as journey times shrank, India became aware of itself for the first time as a single unified nation. As the bullock cart gave way to the locomotive, a subcontinent disjointed by vast distances and primeval communications suddenly, for the first time, became aware of itself as a single geographical unit. It was the railways that made India a nation.

Ironically, a century later, the same railways also made possible the irreparable division of the subcontinent. The partition of India and Pakistan on 15 August 1947 led to what was probably the greatest migration in human history. More than twelve million people packed up and left their homes and their countries. Muslims in India headed *en masse* for Pakistan, while Hindus and Sikhs made their way in the opposite direction. In the course of the mass migration, suppressed religious hatreds were viciously unleashed: over a million people lost their lives in the riots and massacres that ensued. Yet Partition would have been impossible without the railways; and it was on the railways that much of the worst violence took place. Lahore station was the eye of that whirlwind

The fate of Lahore remained uncertain until the final maps of the boundaries between the two nations were released on 14 August. In the event the city went to Pakistan, just fifteen miles from the Indian border, and Lahore and its people were torn apart. Thousands of Hindus and Sikhs fought their way to the station to flee to India. At the same time train after train began arriving from south of the border carrying hundreds of thousands of Muslims to their new homeland. The station became a battleground.

On the night of Independence the last British officials in Lahore arrived at the station. They had picked their way through gutted streets, many of which were littered with dead. On the platforms they found the railway staff grimly hosing down pools of blood and carrying away piles of corpses on luggage trolleys for mass burial. Minutes earlier a last group of desperate Hindus had been massacred by a Muslim mob while they sat waiting quietly for the Bombay Express. As the train finally pulled out of Lahore, the officials could see that the entire Punjab was ablaze, with flames rising from every village. Their lives' work was being destroyed in front of their eyes.

The massacres of Partition brought the Raj to a cataclysmic close. Now, only half a century later, that period can seem as distant as that of the Romans. But the buildings—like Lahore station—still survive. They are the keys which can unlock the history of a period, a history which, though it may seem impossibly foreign, is as much part of the British heritage as that of the Indian subcontinent.

With its great round bastions and tall machicolated towers, Lahore station may look like the product of some short-lived collaboration between the Raj and the Disney Corporation, but it was in fact built in deadly earnest. According to its architect, William Brunton, the whole station had a 'defensive character', so that 'a small garrison could secure it against enemy attack'. The twin towers may look as innocent as Swiss cuckoo clocks, but they were designed to be bomb-proof, while the loopholes across the façade are not the mock arrow-slits they appear to be, but placements for Maxim guns, drawn down carefully designed lines of fire. Even the cavernous train sheds could, in an emergency, be sealed with huge sliding metal doors, turning the whole complex in to a colossal fortified bunker.

Straddling the Grand Trunk Road leading south to Delhi and Calcutta, Lahore is marching-distance from the North-West Frontier. At the time of the Great Game the Victorians saw it as an important defensive post against a potential Russian invasion through the Khyber Pass. Moreover, the station was built in the immediate aftermath of the Indian Mutiny of 1857, and for that reason it was designed to function both as a station and as a fort. Brunton was particularly pleased with the masonry, which he called 'the best in the world' and which he felt confident could survive even full-scale howitzer fire.

In the event, however, Brunton's extraordinary architecture was never put to the test. Instead, in the course of the late nineteenth century the station became a symbol of the surprisingly profitable partnership Britain developed with its greatest colony. For India took to the railways in a way that could not have been imagined by the British engineers who first drew lines across the plains of the subcontinent. Just as

India has always seduced and transformed its conquerors, so in the same way it slowly took over and indigenised the railways. Soon the stations were inhabited by whole villages of people washing, sleeping and cooking in the ticket halls, arriving days early for a train and building encampments on the platforms. Within a few years something quintessentially English had been forever transformed into something quintessentially Indian.

Then there was the bureaucracy. Somehow the idea of multiple forms, triplicate permissions and strict codes of practice—ideas that originated in Crewe perhaps, or maybe Swindon—took on a new lease of Indian life in the plains of the Punjab, in the hands of Hindu bureaucrats brought up from birth with gods who had multiple incarnations, three faces and the strictest of codes of practice regarding their representation and worship. The hierarchy of the railways seemed directly to echo the Hindu caste system, with a pyramid that rose, rank after rank, from the lowly armies of sweepers through the parcel clerks, goods clerks, booking clerks and special ticket examiners to the twice-born apex of stationmaster and general manager. For the Muslims too, there may have been something appealing in submission to a railway timetable at once as merciful, omnipotent and loftily inflexible as the great Koran itself.

The railways were the ultimate symbol of all the Raj prided itself on being: pioneering and up-to-date, intrepid and impartial; on the cutting edge of the Industrial Revolution. Even today harrumphing Home Counties colonels will point first and foremost to the railways as a symbol of everything they like to think the British 'gave' to India. Yet the railways were not works of charity. They were sound commercial enterprises, and the private investors who put up the initial capital saw their money returned many times over. Nonetheless, the railways did inspire a real feeling of *esprit de corps* among those who worked for them, a spirit which survived until very recently.

Walking around the station one day this summer, I met Abdul Majeed. He was an old man with hennaed hair and heavy plastic spectacles. He wore a sparkling clean *salwar kameez*, and sat on a magnificent throne raised on a mahogany dais above Platform 1, underneath a plaque with the message: 'Our objective—Speed Cum Safety.'

Abdul Majeed told me that he had retired from the Pakistani railways ten years earlier, but he still chose to come to the station and sit in the information booth: 'I spent forty years in the railway department,' he said, lowering his face shyly. 'I come back to this station because I am loving these railways of Pakistan—to them I have dedicated my life—and because my colleagues are my best friends.'

I remarked to Mr Majeed how many of the older men in the Pakistani railways seemed to regard its running almost as a sacred duty.

'I think we should,' replied Mr Majeed. 'I always took my duty as a sacred duty, just like my religious function. I never came to the station without washing myself, just as I prepare for my prayers in the mosque.'

I asked him how the railways had changed in the forty years he had been part of them.

'Sahib,' said Mr Majeed, 'it's not only the railways. The change is in the general sphere of life.'

'In what way?'

'In the shape of corruption, in the shape of requirements, in the shape of evils, in the shape of thinkings, in the shape of harassment, in the shape of sabotages. Now the young men are not so dutiful, I think. There has been big change.'

'You think corruption has eaten into the railway system?'

'Sahib, you can imagine. When I was working as a stationmaster, people used to adjust their watches by the passage of trains. Now we adjust our watches from the public. Today there is no punctuality. Yesterday's train arrives today and today's train arrives tomorrow. No one thinks to mention it when a train comes in ten or twelve hours late. Things are very bad.'

Abdul Majeed, it emerged, was born in the half of the Punjab which is now part of India. Expelled from his ancestral village at Partition, he and his family were made to walk to a refugee camp in the monsoon rains. There was no drinking water or facilities for even the most basic sanitation. Soon cholera broke out.

'In the camp my mother died at about two a.m. due to cholera,' said Abdul Majeed, eyes still lowered. 'The same day my father died at fourteen hours.'

'You lost both your parents on the same day?'

'Yes. We buried our mother that evening, then buried our father on the morning of 9 October.'

'You had to bury them yourselves?'

'Yes; we buried them ourselves near a mosque, offering our religious prayers. I was just fifteen years old. The following day we were made to walk to the new place from where we had to catch a train. In the crowd, my younger brother was separated from the rest of us. I never saw him again. In the morning, when the train passed the Beas river I looked down and saw hundreds of corpses scattered in the riverbed from point to point, being eaten by crows, dogs and kites, giving bad smell. After many hours we eventually crossed the Pakistan border from Atari at about fifteen hours. We were stunned when people said "Pakistan zindabad!" Long live Pakistan! They welcomed us and gave us food and water. We had not eaten for four or five days. Then we thought, we are still alive.'

Pakistan's birth-pangs had also been India's holocaust. Everyone you met had their story, but the most horrific were told to me by Mr Majeed's elderly friend Khawajah Bilal, who had had the unenviable job of being the stationmaster of Lahore in 1947.

'I have been coming to Lahore station since I was a student,' Khawajah Bilal told me as we sat on a bench outside what had once been his stationmaster's office. 'Before Partition took place the station was a landmark of beauty. The platforms were clean and the carriages were spotless. The people were calm and quiet. The staff were well dressed. The uniforms they wore were immaculate. The buttons were polished, the braid was golden and shone under the lights. All that ended with Partition.'

'What happened?' I asked.

'On 14 August I was on duty. We heard an announcement that Partition had taken place. Soon after that the killing started, the slaughter began. Everywhere we looked we saw carnage and destruction of human life. There was no law and order, even when the soldiers came and made a barricade with barbed wire outside the station. Despite their presence, many were being killed—on the platforms, on the bridges, in the ticket halls. There were stabbings, rapes, attempts at arson. I had my charpoy in the stationmaster's office: I didn't dare go back to my house. But at night I could not sleep because of the screams and moans of the dying coming from the platform. In the morning, when the light came, bodies would be lying everywhere.

'One morning, I think it was 30 August, the Bombay Express came in from Delhi via Bhatinda. We found dead bodies in the lavatories, on the seats, under the seats. There had been around two thousand people on this train. We checked the whole train, but nobody was alive except one person. There had been a massacre when the train stopped at Bhatinda. The sole survivor told us he had approached the train driver, an Englishman, who gave him refuge. He hid the man in the watertank by the engine. When the Sikhs arrived they could not see him so they went away and he survived. Only one man out of two thousand. After that every train that came from India was attacked. We used to receive one hundred trains a day. Every one was full of corpses.'

Listening to these horror stories, it was clear that for the people of India and Pakistan the horrors of Partition were not just the stuff of history, consigned to the memories of a few old men: for most people they were still livid scars, unhealed wounds which were still poisoning relations between Hindu and Muslim, India and Pakistan, half a century later.

Today the old main line from Lahore to Delhi, once the busiest in India, is hardly used. These days only one train a week passes from Lahore station down the line to India—and that is largely empty.

# Imran Khan: Out for a Duck

*I interviewed Imran Khan twice: once in 1989, when he was still a bachelor-playboy and captain of the Pakistan cricket team; then again seven years later, after his marriage, when he had entered politics to campaign against corruption in Pakistani public life.*

LAHORE, 1989

If you brought together Kylie Minogue, George Michael, Princess Diana, Ian Botham, Prince Charles and Joanna Lumley, bred them, and created some monstrous celebrity super-creature, that being might possibly figure in British gossip columns as prominently as Imran Khan does in the press of Pakistan.

The man is a national obsession. He combines the status of royalty, the prestige of a cabinet minister and the gossip value of a pop star in a country which doesn't have any royals, whose cabinet ministers are hopelessly corrupt and whose pop stars are mostly Indian, and therefore national enemies. Every *chai-wallah* in the country can—and will—give you a breakdown of Imran's batting and bowling statistics, the details of his horoscope and a list of his girlfriends in pidgin English or Urdu, whether or not you ask him. His sex life is a matter of national speculation.

'Imran Khan has too many girlfriends,' my rickshaw driver announced on the journey from the border.

'I've heard he has a soft spot for English girls,' I said.

'English girl, yes,' replied the rickshaw driver. 'Also Pakistani girl, Indian girl, German girl, Bangladeshi girl. Also they are saying Sri Lankan girl and American girl, French girl, Italian girl, Spanish girl, African girl and Chinese girl. All girl. Lots of too many girl.'

Those not busy worrying about his sex life spend their time trying to marry him off. 'You see, he is intelligent, educated, and comes from a good family,' explained the tweed-jacketed schoolteacher in the bus. 'He's a very eligible young man.'

More to the point, he is the captain of the Pakistan cricket team. He is the man who turned Pakistan from a very mediocre side into what is now the world's second-best team (after the West Indies), and he is also, in many people's opinion, the best all-rounder currently playing. And he is all this in a country which is utterly fixated on cricket, a game everyone plays and which no one can ignore. Pakistani television is dismal even by subcontinental standards: so as far as entertainment goes there is pretty well only cricket and cricket and more cricket; it has a captive audience of hundreds of millions. The collective gasp as a Pak player is dismissed can be heard several miles into Afghanistan.

When Pakistan beat India in the 1986–87 Test series, 150,000 people turned up to welcome the team at Lahore's airport, lining the road into the city for ten miles. Less than a year later, when India narrowly beat Pakistan in the World Cup, the newspapers reported twenty-seven coronaries and brain haemorrhages up and down the country, and Pakistan went into national mourning for a week. No wonder then that General Zia personally intervened to beg Imran to come out of retirement, and that he later offered him a prominent ministry in his cabinet.

Following Imran around Pakistan, I soon discovered the extent to which his aura rubs off on those even distantly associated with him. Just having a copy of his autobiography in my hand got me through customs unchecked, and allowed me to change my traveller's cheques at a special rate. Judicious dropping of his name provided free taxi rides, free meals, discounted hotel bills and enough cups of tea to rupture my bladder. In Sialkot, where every hotel for thirty miles was booked up for the Test match, mentioning the magic word 'Imran' got me the manager's own room. It was handed over to me with the solemnity of a Papal Indulgence. 'Do not thank me, Sahib,' said the manager. 'It is not choice, it is duty.'

Imran Khan is, indisputably, a very good-looking man. I first saw him on the balcony of the players' pavilion during the Pakistan v. India Test at Sialkot. He was leaning forward on to the balustrade, his familiar dark features and mane of coal-black hair offset by the white of his cricket jersey.

When, a little later, it was his turn to come out to bat, the already volatile crowd exploded into an orgasm of cheering, horn-tooting, banner-waving and general unabashed idolatry. The people on the terraces leapt to their feet and began dancing and screaming and waving Imran's picture, until they were commanded to sit by a nonchalant hand signal from their hero. But one section of the crowd refused to obey him. Pakistani cricket is strictly segregated by gender. The men may have got the hint, but no one was going to stop the normally silent Pakistani sisterhood from having their fling. From behind the canvas shelter of the women's enclosure came a deafening racket of adoring screams and a slow, high-pitched chant in Punjabi.

'What are they saying?' I asked the man sitting next to me.

'These ladies are saying that they want to marry Imran Khan,' he replied, blushing slightly. 'And they are saying that their love is like an ache in their belly.'

Yet Imran is in many ways an unlikely sex-symbol. When I arrived for supper at the house where he was staying, I had to sit waiting for five minutes while he finished his prayers. The names of the internationally glamorous may trip off his lips in his conversation ('Sting and I never really hit it off...' 'Ian Botham's just a common bully...' 'When Mick Jagger was here...') but Imran is nevertheless a practising Muslim who prays to Mecca five times a day and goes to the mosque on Fridays. When he came to greet me, I expressed surprise at the intensity of his devotions.

'I am a humble sinner like anyone else,' he said. 'But I have a very strong faith in God and try to live by the rules of the Koran.'

It was not the reply the gossip had led me to expect. But then again, it was not totally impossible to believe. Imran was sitting cross-legged on a divan, swathed in a voluminous white woollen *salwar kameez* and a matching Kashmiri shawl. His friends were sitting around a pile of rice and spicy chicken, eating with their hands. There was no alcohol: Imran is a strict teetotaller. Like everything in Pakistan, the meal was segregated. The men ate in the living room amid the Afghan carpets, the tribal pillows and the portrait of Mr Bhutto. The women prepared our food in the kitchen. Whatever he gets up to in England, Imran Khan is a Pakistani Muslim at home. I mentioned, as delicately as I could, that I had heard he was not always exactly puritan in his lifestyle.

'Well, I am someone who likes to enjoy himself,' he admitted. 'But I'm not extravagant. I have simple tastes. I love the wilderness. I like shooting, I like walking. I don't like spending my time in the South of France or Monte Carlo hanging out in nightclubs.'

He picked a lump of chicken from the pilaff and munched it thoughtfully. 'I suppose I like a bit of both lifestyles. I spend summer in England seeing my friends—ten appointments a day—then come home to Pakistan in winter. Time slows down. I get mobbed if I go into the streets, so my life here is very private. I have a close circle of friends who I see a lot of, but I hardly ever go out. I'm very shy. I get awkward if I'm recognised.'

Imran is an intriguing compendium of contradictions: extrovert and cripplingly shy, openly arrogant yet disarmingly modest, austere and sensual, jet-set yet oddly primitive. He can switch from one persona to another with remarkable ease. The cricketer and the gossip-column playboy are the familiar façades, the pious Muslim is another face. There is also Imran the Oxford graduate who has strong and fairly coherent political views, has written a very readable autobiography and is working on a travel book on the Indus.

Yet perhaps the most surprising aspect of his character is his tribal sympathies. Imran is a Pathan of Afghan origins, and is highly conscious of it (even if his critics like to point out that he doesn't actually have more than a bare smattering of Pushtu, the Pathans' tribal language). The friends with whom he was staying were Pathans, as was Zakir Khan, the only other member of the Pakistan team invited to supper. Imran's cricket bat and sportswear are made by a company owned by a Pathan of his own tribe. If he eventually submits to an arranged marriage—which he thinks a possibility—it will only be to a Pathan girl: 'All my sisters have married Pathan husbands. If I let my father choose my wife, he would almost certainly choose a Pathan. My family came to the subcontinent from Afghanistan about five hundred years ago but we kept our identity by refusing to marry outside the tribe. That pride of race is deeply ingrained in every Pathan child.'

I asked him if he was therefore irritated by the entire country acting as his personal marriage broker.

'I just can't understand this massive concern for my marriage,' he replied, throwing his shawl around his shoulders. 'Whenever I'm doing badly in a match the crowds always start screaming, "You're getting old, you should get married." I've never yet understood why they think marriage would improve either my batting or my bowling. Then there's the press. I seem to get engaged about three times a year. My father used to get upset when he woke up and read the news—thought I hadn't bothered to tell him—but even he's stopped believing it all by now.'

'Is it just the Pakistani press?'

'No. It's worse in India. As a result I get about eighty per cent of my mail from India: these strange letters saying, "You appear arrogant and ambitious, your hair's thinning and you're not half as good-looking as you used to be. I just can't work out why I'm in love with you."'

The next morning, a rest day in the Test match, Imran went duck-shooting.

It had dawned foggy and we drove fast through the early-morning mist, narrowly missing bullock carts, pack-donkeys and old men wobbling along on ancient bicycles. After a few miles we came to a border post. The border rangers stood to attention and saluted Imran. We left the car and transferred to an open-topped Suzuki jeep belonging to the rangers. We drove along a straight poplar avenue, once the main road to Delhi, but closed since the Indian border was sealed at Partition. After a few miles we left the avenue, swerved off over stubble fields and arrived at the edge of the marsh.

The fat District Commissioner was waiting for us. He bowed to Imran, crossed over to our vehicle and signalled to the beaters sitting in another jeep. In convoy, we sped off along the causeways. In the near distance, over the marsh, you could see the line of conning towers that marked the Indian frontier. The District Commissioner pointed them out. 'Better keep down. There was a border skirmish there last week. Three killed.'

Then one of the beaters blew his whistle. The front jeep skidded to a halt and the beaters leapt out and disappeared into the marsh. Ignoring the Commissioner's words of warning, Imran jumped on to the bonnet of the jeep. In the distance a small covey of black partridges broke cover. Imran fired twice. He missed with the first barrel, but brought down a male bird with the second, almost at the limit of the gun's range.

'It's the hunter's instinct,' he said, beaming boyishly from the jeep's bonnet. 'I can never hit duck, because I hate the taste. But a black partridge in a spicy tomato sauce—it would be a sin to miss it.'

After a few minutes a beater appeared from the reeds holding the dead bird above his head. Its markings were stunning: black and red, with the white wingtips offset by the duff khaki of the chest. Imran took the bird and held it aloft. 'The male is prettier in every species,' he said, 'except the human race.'

The Pakistanis are as superstitious as the Irish. The two nations share a phobia of spirits and witches as well as a love and reverence of hermits and healers and holy men.

Imran is no exception. He is the patron of a Sufi *pir* who, he believes, has the second sight. The *pir* spent five years naked above the snowline in the Hindu Kush with a wizened guru who taught him to control and discipline his gift. One day the *pir* returned unannounced to his village in the Punjab. Since then he has never left it except for a single pilgrimage to Mecca, at Imran's expense. At the Ka'ba in the Great Mosque the *pir* saw the doors of heaven open and angels stream down to earth and back again.

Imran has complete faith in his *pir*, and has consulted him on all the important decisions of his life. It was the *pir* rather than General Zia who brought him out of retirement, and he never embarks on a team reshuffle or a romance without the man's consent. 'I have been consulting him for three years and he has never yet been wrong,' Imran told me. 'He has extraordinary powers. Everything he has said has come true.'

We drove to the holy man's village through the evening Punjab. Smoke from dung fires rose from the villages, and the bullock drivers pulled their blankets around them as the sun ebbed and the shadows grew.

We were expected. Urchins clustered around the holy man's door waiting for a glimpse of Imran as he hopped out of the jeep and into the darkness of the *pir's* hut. Like a rabbit into a burrow, I followed.

What surprised me was the normality of the man. I had expected an elderly, bearded hermit in flowing Old Testament robes. Instead, he was middle-aged, balding and a little plump. His face was honest, almost credulous, and he lived alone in a one-room dive, decorated with pictures of Imran, General Zia and the Great Mosque at Mecca. On one wall he had hung a Cindy doll still wrapped in its cellophane box and surrounded by tinsel. We exchanged pleasantries, accepted cups of tea, fended off the growing crowd outside, then got down to business.

Perhaps sensing an air of scepticism from my corner, the *pir* turned first to me. Without any prompting or introduction he told me, correctly, that there were six in my family—myself, my two parents and three brothers—then he advised me to stop wasting my time travelling and to get on with writing my book on Delhi. With his silent critic dumbfounded, he turned to Imran.

His visitor drew up his legs and sat cross-legged on the sofa. He had two questions for him, he said. Firstly he wished to know who had stolen a golden chain from his house six months before. He suspected one of his servants. The *pir* asked him a few questions about the date, the servant's horoscope and the circumstances of the chain's disappearance. He scribbled a calculation on a piece of paper, then announced that the chain had been stolen by a female visitor who had been staying that night. Imran nodded. There had indeed been a female visitor that night. The *pir* checked his calculations and got the same result. Finally, just to make sure, he asked Imran to write down the names of ten people who could conceivably have stolen the chain. Imran complied. The *pir* ripped the page up and folded the names into ten identical squares. He got Imran to pick out one at a time, dropping each in turn into the wastepaper bin. Sure enough, with the inevitability of a card trick, the name left at the end was Imran's female guest. She, it seemed, was the thief.

Then Imran asked about the next day's cricket. The Indians' lead was less than two hundred, and Pakistan looked like snatching an easy victory. Did the holy man foresee any problems? The *pir* did a calculation, then checked it. His face fell. Imran, watching him closely, began to look worried. The *pir* did a last calculation, then turned to face his friend.

'Imran,' he said. 'I've never lied to you. You must fight hard tomorrow. All is not lost. But the odds are against you. Very heavily against you. I cannot pretend to you that it is otherwise.'

The next day, as a vortex of vultures wheeled overhead, the game started sharp at 11 a.m. Imran scored three runs, and was then bowled a bouncer. As he ducked to avoid it, the ball caught the edge of his bat and went through to the wicketkeeper. There was silence over the entire ground. The umpire raised his finger, and Imran was out. After that the Pakistan batting collapsed. They were all out, for 170, a few minutes before lunch.

Five days later, the corridors of the Hotel Pearl Continental, Peshawar, were seething with cricket fans. They searched out the rooms of the Pakistani players with the instincts of bloodhounds, armed to the teeth with Instamatics and autograph books. Imran, staying under a false name at the very top of the hotel, using the back entrance and the service staircase, managed to elude them. But as an additional precaution he refused to answer the telephone, and had arranged to have his corridor blocked off by paramilitary police. Getting through to have a drink with him after the end of the one-day international was like a military operation.

Before long we were joined by our host for that evening, an elder of the Afridi tribe. Mohammed ud-Din Afridi—not his real name—was not at all my idea of a tribal elder. He was tall, sleek, good-looking, wore a crisp Savile Row suit and drove a white Mercedes. Heroin arrived in Peshawar about twenty years ago, and since then it has changed everything. According to Mohammed ud-Din, his money comes from 'a family business' and 'electricals'. According to Peshawar gossip, Mohammed's family business amounted to the two hundred goats his father used to herd, and everything Mohammed owns he has earned himself in seventeen years— he is still only thirty-seven. His money, so the gossip goes, actually comes from the opium-processing laboratories he owns in Landi Khotal at the top of the Khyber Pass. Whatever the truth, he is also a fanatical cricket fan, and he laid on a party for the captain of the Pakistan team like few that I have ever seen.

We crossed the checkpoint into the tribal areas, and our Mercedes was joined by an escort of two jeeps filled with armed men and a swarm of motorcycle outriders. We drove for half an hour through the no man's land of the tribal reserve until we came to Mohammed ud-Din's palace. Thirty-foot-high walls reared out of the scrub, studded double gates opened before us, and we were presented with a view of a pleasure complex that could have been a James Bond set. Spotlit fountains rained down water in glistening waterfalls. A white neo-classical *porte-cochére* gave on to a Georgian mansion; it was whitewashed but otherwise looked as if it had been magically transported from Oxfordshire. On one side was a miniature marble mosque, on the other, partially lit by eddies of reflected light, the ha-ha of a deer park, filled with gazelles and peacocks. Round everything was wrapped the great crenellated walls, loaded with climbing roses, honeysuckle and jasmine.

Inside, two hundred of Mohammed ud-Din's cousins, retainers and tribesmen were waiting. Huge baroque mirrors reflected glistening chandeliers; stags' heads studded the walls between fans of nineteenth-century muskets and flintlocks; guards armed with Kalashnikovs flanked the doorways. Imran led the way, and after drinks had been served, we filed past the tribesmen into the dining room. There, a forest of kebabs, skewered lambs and charcoal-roasted pullets had been laid on long trestles, amid great tent-flaps of *naan*.

Pathans are good eaters, but less talented conversationalists. After supper was finished we returned to the sitting room to grunt and burp and meditate. Dialogue was intermittent. Soon however the conversation turned to armaments, a subject dear to the heart of every Pathan.

'What defences do you have here?' asked Imran.

Mohammed ud-Din considered.

'Well,' he said, adding up slowly, 'I have about fifty gunmen, ten anti-aircraft guns, and...ooh...about four hundred batteries of missiles. They're only small missiles—you know, four kilometres range.'

Imran looked nonplussed. 'A show of strength is very important in the tribal areas,' he explained to me in a matter-of-fact tone.

'I'm one of the largest landowners in my tribe,' added Mohammed, 'so it's my duty to support my poorer relatives. Most of my guards I employ for this reason.'

'It surely can't be healthy having this amount of weapons in private hands,' I said lamely.

'You Westerners are always telling us this,' he replied. 'But for poor people the tribal system is very good. In the settled areas in Pakistan there is much violence. But here no one can rape any girl. No one can steal. They know the tribe will rally round and there will be a blood feud if they do. In Pakistan you can kill a man in broad daylight and if you have the money you can buy justice. But with tribal law rich men and poor men are equal. You cannot buy the tribal council—you pay with your neck.'

Several large joints passed around the room before someone suggested it was time to go outside and play with the Kalashnikovs. We piled out on to the *porte-cochére*, and Imran was handed a rifle and a magazine of tracer. He pointed the gun in the air and fired off the whole clip. Scarlet shooting stars streaked up in a glowing arc and fell outside the walls, beyond the deer park.

'At my friend's wedding, I alone fired eight hundred rounds,' said someone behind me. Other tribesmen were muttering in Pushtu, out of which emerged, as solitary comprehensible islands, the names of weapons: 'Rumble, rumble, rumble, anti-tank gun. Rumble, rumble, Stinger! Stinger rumble? Kalashnikov rumble, SCUD rumble, T-72 rumble. RPG. Acha.'

On the way back in the Mercedes, Imran was in high spirits.

'What did you think?' he asked.

'Terrifying.'

'Yes,' he said, proudly. 'These are my people.'

*Two years later, Imran retired from cricket but remained in the news: first by raising funds to build a cancer hospital in Lahore following his mother's death from the disease; then by announcing he had 'reawakened' to his Muslim faith; then by marrying Jemima, daughter of the Europhobic tycoon Sir James Goldsmith. Following Jemima's conversion to Islam a ludicrous—and sadly characteristic— wave of anti-Islamic hysteria swept the British press. The* Sun, *anxious that the glamorous Jemima would not be able to wear figure-hugging clothes in Lahore, filled its front page with the query 'HOW KHAN JEMIMA COPE WITH ALLAH THIS?' Andrew Neil in the* Sunday Times *described Jemima as 'sleepwalking into slavery', while the* Evening Standard's *front page showed her*

*leaving San Lorenzo 'after throwing off the shackles of her Muslim religion to enjoy a traditional hen night with her friends'.*

*The following year Imran founded his own political party, the Tehrik-e-Insaaf, or Justice Movement. Following the dismissal of Benazir Bhutto's venal government on 5 November 1996, he mobilised his new party to fight the election, amid high hopes that he would change the face of Pakistani politics by riding the wave of public disgust with corrupt politicians. Shortly afterwards I returned to Pakistan to cover his election campaign. It quickly became clear that, despite the enthusiasm of both the crowds and the British media (who sometimes made it seem as if the election was already in Imran's pocket), it was by no means going to be an easy ride for the former cricketer.*

LAHORE, 1996

'I will vote for Imran Khan,' said the man on the motorbike, 'because he is a very good cricketer and because he has very nice inner beauty.'

Imran's convoy had been ambushed by cheering fans as it drew to a halt at the toll gate on the Lahore-Islamabad highway. Amid a pall of smoke, an arsenal of Chinese firecrackers exploded by the side of the road, while nearby a Punjabi wedding band in mock-regimental finery struck up 'For He's a Jolly Good Fellow'. From every side a thousand overexcited supporters closed in on the candidate, bawling out the chant '*Imran zindabad!*' (Long live Imran!) '*Imran Khan Vazir-e-Azam!*' (Prime Minister Imran Khan!)

After baskets of rose petals had been showered and speeches made, the convoy began to move off again, now led by a squad of fifty boys on Vespa scooters, all flying the red and green flag of Imran's new party, the Tehrik-e-Insaaf. Bringing up the rear was Imran's battered Mercedes, which following the floral welcoming ceremony looked as if it had crashed into a stand at the Chelsea Flower Show, its bonnet thickly carpeted with rose petals while several strings of marigold garlands dangled from its wing mirrors.

The Mercedes looked nearly old enough to have been a Nazi staff car, but it was painted bright yellow and plastered with lurid posters of the aspiring politician. They all carried a photograph of Imran which must have been shot in the late 1970s, when he had sported a bouffant hairdo that made him look more like John Travolta in *Saturday Night Fever* than the cropped, chiselled, more austere figure he cuts today.

Inside the car, Imran looked profoundly tired and slightly haggard. He had been on the road, holding three or four rallies a day for two weeks now, and every day the campaigning had been followed by late nights in an endless chain of committee meetings. These days, he said, he considered himself lucky to catch even four hours' sleep a night. This latest rally had been organised only two days before, and as it was being held on the land of a feudal landowner hostile to Imran everyone had been worried that nobody would turn up. Certainly no one had expected a reception like this.

As we approached the venue, a one-horse *mofussil* nowhere-town called Lala Mousa, the crowds lining the pavements began to spill out on to the motorway itself, reducing our speed to a crawl. Over the motorway signs, banners had been hung: 'Victory to Imran Khan!' 'Imran Khan the Conqueror!' Every roof was lined with cheering fans and supporters; out of every window fluttered Justice Movement flags.

'You're seeing the beginning of a revolution,' Imran shouted to me, struggling to be heard above the noise. 'When our supporters started work six months ago people dismissed them as lunatics; they said we had no chance. Now those same people are queuing up to join us. The people are sick of the old politicians. Just look around you: something very, very big is brewing up.'

As our pace slowed, in our wake there built up a tailback of some two hundred vehicles. Immediately behind us was a brightly painted coach (or rather, as the inscription on its side put it, a MERCEDES RAJAH SUPER AIRBUS) whose passengers, caught up in the excitement, had begun to dance on the roof, and who only narrowly avoided being decapitated when the bus passed underneath a low-slung power cable. All the while Imran waved regally from the open window, shaking some of the outstretched hands thrust towards him, while his driver endeavoured somehow to plough slowly through the milling multitudes without killing anyone. When he finally pushed through to the base of the platform, Imran leapt out and sprang up to the dais. His baggy khaki *salwar kameez* billowing in the breeze, he began to thunder out his pitch:

'For fifty years the politicians have been exploiting the people of Pakistan,' he declaimed, punching the air like a demagogue. 'They've been looting and plundering the country! The thief protects the thief! We want to bring the plunderers to justice! We will hang the corrupt! The people of Pakistan should unite to achieve their cause!'

At the side of the platform, the District Superintendent of Police and the local magistrate gazed down at the ecstatic crowds which now stretched for at least two miles down the road, totally blocking both lanes of Pakistan's principal motorway.

'I have been here for ten years,' said the DSP, 'and I've never seen anything like this. In fact I've never seen a crowd even one tenth this size. How many are here? Thirty thousand? Thirty-five thousand? Benazir's people had to throw money around to get even two thousand when she came here.'

The District Magistrate, a portly, moustachioed gent in a tweed jacket, nodded his head in agreement. 'Actually,' he said, 'this is something quite new.'

Imran Khan might have been pulling in record crowds out in the provinces, but in the political lobbies of Islamabad and the establishment drawing rooms of Lahore, it was extremely difficult to find anyone who really rated his chances at the election.

In many ways this was hardly surprising. Imran had launched his Tehrik-e-Insaaf only six months earlier. At the time he believed he would have two years to prepare the new party for a general election, to form a set of coherent policies, set up offices across Pakistan and find clean, capable candidates to run them. In the event, less than a month after he had formally announced that he was entering politics, Benazir Bhutto's government was prematurely dissolved for gross corruption by the President, Farooq Leghari. Suddenly Imran found he had only three months in which to mobilise his embryonic political movement.

The result was that, for all his undoubted popularity, few commentators in Pakistan took his challenge seriously. As the election drew near, they began to point out that he still had no credible grassroots organisation, no big-name candidates and no clear policies. Moreover, his enemies questioned whether he had the intellectual capacity to form them.

'Not for nothing is he known here as Im the Dim,' said Abida Hussein, a former Pakistani Ambassador to the United States and a candidate for Nawaz Sharif's Muslim League, which most people expected to win the election. 'It's a classic case of overdeveloped pectorals and underdeveloped brain cells. If you put any of our big movie stars up on a podium they'd probably pull the crowds, but it doesn't mean anyone with any sense will vote for them. Would you vote for Ian Botham?'

Others dismissed Imran as a hypocrite. What can you make of a man, they asked, who castigates what he calls the 'VIP culture', then sends his wife to have her baby in the most expensive suite at the Portland Hospital? The Oxford-educated and thoroughly Anglicised Pakistani who attacks the 'brown Sahibs' and their Westernised ways? The ladies' man, once the darling of a hundred Fulham bedrooms, who now thunders from his podium about rooting out the Western disease of promiscuity?

Even his friends had reservations. 'I love Imran as a person,' said one Lahore socialite. 'He's honest, he's sincere, he's got great integrity and he's totally incorruptible. But I still have the nagging worry that if he got into power he might have me stoned to death for adultery or cut my head off for drinking. He's got some pretty strange ideas. Have you heard how he's been promising to string up all corrupt politicians? And he means it, you know.'

Many of Imran's 'strange ideas' are linked to his recent religious reawakening, the product of a midlife crisis following his mother's slow and painful death from cancer. This has brought about a profound change not only in his outlook but in his manner. The old *joie de vivre* of the cricket pitches has given way to a new seriousness. Imran subscribes to the tolerant Sufi tradition of Islam, and is no bearded fundamentalist, but he takes his religion very seriously, and his conversation is now peppered with Sufi anecdotes and even the occasional quotation from the Koran.

More alarmingly, he believes that the Islamic Sharia law has much to recommend it, comparing the almost complete absence of petty crime in the tribal areas of Pakistan, where Sharia is in force, with the anarchy of New York at night. 'In the tribal areas there has never been one single case of rape,' he said at one point. 'To me that is a million times more civilised than America, where there are one million rape cases every year.' He has also expressed a rather unnerving admiration for some aspects of the Iranian Islamic Revolution, pointing out, for example, that the Iranian literacy rate has risen from sixty to ninety per cent since the fall of the Shah, a stark contrast to the situation in Pakistan, where literacy is actually falling year by year. When, as a joke, I asked him whether he saw himself as Pakistan's answer to the Ayatollah, he thought for a second before replying, 'Not exactly.'

While this sort of thing probably plays well with the Pakistani electorate, who are no doubt as keen on hanging and flogging as their British counterparts, the pundits point out that there is one major obstacle to Imran's party translating its undoubted popularity into votes: the Justice Movement had no money, and therefore no muscle, in a country where politics depends on little else.

In Pakistan, as in India, elections are not really about ideology: they are about outbidding rivals by making a string of extravagant local promises. Typically, a parliamentary candidate will go to a village and give a sum of money to one of the village elders, who will then distribute the money among his *biradhari*, or clan. The *biradhari* will then vote for the candidate *en bloc*. To win an election, the most important thing is for the candidate to win over the elder of the most powerful clan in each village. As well as money, the elder might also ask for various favours: a new tarmac road to the village, or gas connections for his cousins. All this costs a considerable sum of money, which the candidate must then recoup through corruption when he gets into office.

According to the conventional wisdom in Pakistan, the only thing that can overrule loyalty to a clan is loyalty to a *zamindar*, or feudal landowner. In many of the more backward parts of the country the local *zamindar* can automatically expect his people to vote either for himself, if he is standing, or for the candidate he appoints; as one commentator put it, 'In some constituencies, if the feudals put up their dog as a candidate, that dog would get elected with ninety-nine per cent of the vote.'

Such loyalty can be enforced. Many of the biggest *zamindars* are said to have private prisons, and most have private armies, or at the very least access to gangs of local *goondas*, or hired thugs. In the crowd at Lala Mousa, several of Imran's supporters said that they would like to work for the Justice Movement, but did not dare: 'I would like to help Imran,' said one boy, 'but I'm afraid I'll get my legs sawn off. It happens. The candidates of the other parties here are very strong and have many gunmen. When the election comes they will threaten anyone who works for the Tehrik-e-Insaaf.' In the more remote and lawless areas there is also the possibility that the *zamindars* and their thugs will bribe or threaten the polling agents, then simply stuff the ballot boxes with thousands of votes for themselves.

As part of his drive to clean up Pakistani politics Imran made it quite clear that he intended to do no deals with landowners or clan chiefs. If individuals wish to support him, he said, well and good. But only by breaking the system of patronage did he believe that corruption could be brought under control. This was clearly true, but in the eyes of most of the Pakistani journalists I talked to, it relegated Imran to the position of a hopelessly naive idealist who had spent too long on the cricket pitches of the Home Counties, and who had no grasp of the brutal realities of political power in Pakistan. He may pull the crowds, they said, but that was a very different thing to winning a Pakistani election.

Later that week in Lahore, I began to grasp what *biradhari* politics actually involved.

It was a warm Punjab night, and Imran's best friend, but political rival, Yusouf Salahuddin was dressed in a thick white *salwar kameez*. He lay curled up on a long divan, his arm resting on a bolster of Kashmiri cloth of gold. From beyond the cusped Mughal arches of the wooden canopy came the patter of a small fountain; beneath the trellis the air was heavy with the scent of frangipani and tuberoses.

'Baby, I've told you,' repeated Yusouf into his portable phone, 'I'm not going to stand this time. It's going to be a dirty election; it's going to be rough, really rough. No, no, I'm not ducking out. Honey, listen a second. I'm in control, OK? I'm running the politics of this city from my *bedroom*. Right, OK, baby. See you.'

Yusouf clicked the machine off, retracted the aerial and snapped his fingers in the air. Two liveried bearers came running.

'Sorry about that,' he said to me. 'You want a drink?'

'Sure. What have you got?'

'Everything.'

I ordered a glass of malt, my first real drink since I had arrived in dry Pakistan. As the bearers scurried off, I asked him whether he was telling the truth. Was it going to be a dirty election?

'Yup,' he said. 'The worst. All kinds of goons are standing: underground figures, drug smugglers, real crazies...'

'But if—as you say—you are still pulling the strings in Lahore, won't it be dangerous for you?' I asked. 'Shouldn't you be armed?'

'I don't think I need to be,' replied Yusouf. 'I haven't got any enemies...'

He paused, and made a slight sweeping gesture with his hands. 'But still, you know, these days you can't be too careful. I keep five bodyguards, ex-commandos, just in case. They are all armed.'

'Pistols?'

'Oh, no big deal,' said Yusouf. 'This isn't the Frontier. They've only got five Kalashnikovs, MP-5 sub-machine guns, Chinese-made Mausers and some Italian pump-action ten-shot repeater shotguns. No heavy artillery.'

I had met the bodyguards. They had smiled sweetly as I passed by them, under the stuffed animal heads in the great gateway of Yusouf's *haveli*; I had thought them loiterers, friends of the *chowkidar*. I hadn't seen their hardware. I asked, 'You really need all that?'

'You need it at election time,' said Yusouf. 'Pakistani elections are...rather different from British ones.'

'What do you mean?'

'Let me tell you a story,' Yusouf said. He lay back on the divan and sipped his drink. 'Last time around, on polling day, late in the evening, I was checking out some booth— there had been talk of violence. Just as I arrived there the Jamaat-i-Islami candidate appeared. He had about a hundred men, all armed. They closed in, and fired five shots, wounding one of my guards. My boys had just got their new Italian guns, and one of them fired ten shots in the air, rapid fire. No one had ever seen anything like those guns in Lahore, so while the Jamaat goons hesitated, we managed to get into the car and get the hell out.'

'I see what you mean.'

'I'm not finished yet. The Jamaat then made their mistake. They gave chase, and came into my territory, into the diamond bazaar, shooting. The police fled, but my *biradhari* were outraged. They could not bear to see me attacked. They thought my family had always protected them, so they considered it their duty to protect us.'

'They had guns too?'

'While I was a member of the Provincial Assembly I'd given out a lot of licences, so there was quite a bit of hardware about. The whole population went up on to their roofs and began shooting down at the Jamaat boys with whatever they'd got. It was a bloody great gun battle—uncontrollable. We thrashed them. After half an hour they fled, taking their dead and wounded with them.'

I was quickly becoming familiar with the talk of guns and shooting and street fights. It is very much par for the course in Pakistan these days, and has been so ever since the Afghan war turned the country into one of the world's biggest ammunition dumps. What interested me was Yusouf's support from his *biradhari*. I asked him who his supporters were, and why they followed him.

Yusouf's family, it appeared, were Kashmiri landowners who had come to Lahore at the beginning of the nineteenth century after some unpleasantness—a property dispute, a death, an execution order. They brought with them their gold, and invested it in property. By the time Yusouf's great-great-grandfather died, the family owned about a third of Lahore. They had been good landlords and pious Muslims, giving away much of their fortune as alms, and they were always popular as well as powerful.

After Partition, Yusouf's family, co-founders of the Muslim League and connected through marriage to the national poet Iqbal, easily managed to transform themselves from the city's most powerful feudal landowners into its leading politicians. At every election they could count on the support of a great chunk of the population of the old city—partly Kashmiri relations, partly tenants and ex-tenants, partly neighbours and admirers. It did not matter which party the family chose to support, the *biradhari* votes would come with them. And even if one of the family did not stand, they could transfer their support to the candidate of their choice, just as Yusouf was doing now.

'It's not just a tribal thing—we are more like honorary clan leaders. So when the Jamaat invaded our territory, the people took it as a personal insult. Their love for us flared up, and they...well, they just massacred our rivals,' said Yusouf.

As he talked, the bearers reappeared carrying our supper: kebabs and rice on silver trays. Yusouf shrugged his shoulders:

'Privately, of course, I wish Imran the best of luck. But as you can see, the Pakistanis are very loyal to their traditional leaders. With the best will in the world, I doubt whether his party will win a single seat in this election. In fact, he'll be lucky to get in himself.'

What happened in Lahore—the most powerful feudal family transforming itself into the most powerful political family—was repeated over much of Pakistan when democracy came to the new country in 1947. Since then, despite three periods of martial law, the system has not changed. Landowning—feudalism—is still almost the only social base from which Pakistani politicians can emerge: the Bhutto family are big landowners in Sindh, and most of what they do not own in that province is controlled by Ghulam Mustafa Jatoi, one of Benazir's main rivals. The traditional wrangling of rival feudal landowners that is the very essence of north Indian medieval history (just open a page of the *Baburnama* or any other Mughal chronicle) has continued into the present in the guise of political vendettas. The huge and highly educated middle class—the class which seized control in India in 1947, castrating the might of the maharajahs and feudal landowners almost immediately—is still to a remarkable extent excluded from the political process in Pakistan.

If clan and tribal allegiances can survive in a modern cosmopolitan city like Lahore, these links are still more potent in rural districts. The difficulties this presents for Imran were graphically brought home the next afternoon when we drove to Wando, a remote constituency famous for its shoot-outs and blood feuds. This notoriety is partly the result of the penchant of the local heavies for attacking police stations and thus initiating a series of spectacular gun battles, remarkable even by Pakistani standards of carnage. But Wando's reputation for epic violence has recently been enormously enhanced by a film called *Maula Jat*. The movie tells the true story of its eponymous hero's blood feud with a local *goonda* who rejoiced in the name of Nouri Nutt; in terms of blood spilt, *Maula Jat* succeeds in making *Rambo* look like *Bambi*. It has now become the most popular Punjabi movie ever made in Pakistan, and takes the form of a kind of long, ritualised slaughter interspersed with occasional dance sequences. It ends with a pile of corpses of which even Genghis Khan might have been proud.

'We've got a bit of a problem in this constituency,' admitted Imran as we drove into the badlands of Wando. The nub of the problem, he explained, was that the last time someone had stood against the local *zamindar* that man had been shot dead, then his entire family had been tracked down and wiped out, one by one. This had led to an understandable reluctance among supporters of the Justice Movement to step forward and contest the election. But in due course a candidate had been found. This man, said Imran, feared no *goondas* and bowed his head to no *zamindar*.

'Why is that?' I asked.

'He's Nouri Nutt's nephew.'

We picked up Ansar Nutt a few minutes later. He was a huge, burly figure with curling moustaches and the physique of a wrestler. He sat beside me in the back, and as we drove I asked him about his uncle Nouri.

'He was a good-looking man,' said Ansar, shrugging his shoulders. 'He killed a few people and went to lots of jails.'

'So the film was accurate?'

'My family objected to him being shown as the villain. We went and saw the director.' Ansar smiled. 'When he saw us he soon apologised.'

'Has anyone threatened you now you're standing for Imran?'

'They sent some people. But Nutts are the majority in this area. The last time we had a blood feud over a hundred died. So they quickly went away again. It was not a big problem. My *biradhari* is behind me.'

'Did you have to kill anyone?' I asked. Alarmed by my question, Imran looked around anxiously from the front seat to hear the answer.

'I don't like violence,' said Ansar, sidestepping the question. 'Except when it comes to my self-respect. Only then am I like my uncle.'

'So you are not worried?' I asked.

'I'm not scared of anyone. With my family I need no bodyguards. Also I've done a commando course. When the appointed time comes I'll go to my grave,' said Ansar Nutt. 'But not before.'

Political violence may leave Ansar Nutt unruffled, but not all the Tehrik-e Insaaf workers are equally fearless. After Imran had spoken at a dusty village rally—more ecstatic crowds, more garlands, more promises to hang corrupt politicians—the convoy retired to the house of a local worthy for *chai*. There a succession of anxious villagers pleaded with Imran for protection if they did take their life into their hands and stand up and support him.

'Khan sahib,' said one gnarled old farmer with henna-dyed hair. 'Promise us that if you lose you will not go off to England with your wife and leave us alone.'

'We are poor people,' said another. 'If you are not there the *goondas* will kill us.'

'These looters will go to the police. Then the police will arrest us and create many problems for our families.'

Imran raised his hands, calling for silence.

'If you have trouble,' he said, 'my workers and I will come to this constituency and fight for you. We have many educated people with us, many lawyers. We will provide justice through the courts.'

The farmers looked at each other uncertainly. Lawyers were clearly not the kind of defence they had had in mind.

'This election is just a battle in a long war,' continued Imran. 'If we win, then the real struggle will begin. If we lose, we will become more organised. Either way, do not fear. I will look after you.'

By the time the meeting finished, darkness had fallen. Imran's convoy passed slowly along the rutted village roads. The driver was clearly a little uneasy, and cast nervous glances into the shadows around him.

'These *zamindars* can be very rough,' said Imran. 'One area we went to, a landowner's wife entertained us. She was trying to impress us, and over tea she remarked, "My husband is a very powerful man around here. Do you know he had eight hundred people killed last year?" '

Suddenly a figure emerged from the gloom at the edge of the road  and pulled a gun from under his shawl. It was a Kalashnikov. He began firing into the air; in the dark you could see the sparks shooting from the end of the barrel. I jumped, but Imran merely smiled. 'In this part of the world that is the way you welcome your guests.' He got out, shook the man's hands, patted him on the shoulder and then got back in the car.

'What was I saying?'

'You were talking about a man who had killed eight hundred people in one year.'

'Wherever we go, my supporters' main concern is whether I can give them protection.'

'And can you?'

'In one sense I can't, because I haven't got any gunmen. All I can promise is lawyers. Already we've had three or four of my party workers beaten up. In Sindh in particular—the area where Bhutto comes from—the people are terrified. The *zamindars* are always sawing the legs off anyone who stands up to them.'

'Literally?'

'Literally. Under Benazir there's been a total breakdown of law and order. It's like the last days of the Mughal Empire...Uh oh. Here is a *real* hold-up.'

I looked up from my notebook to see a tractor and trailer totally blocking the road ahead of us. All around were men swathed in shawls, carrying pistols and assault rifles. Only when we drew closer could we see that some of them were wearing police uniforms under their shawls. One portly man with a walrus moustache walked up to us, pistol cocked and levelled. Imran turned on the light inside the car and slowly wound down his window. I locked the rear door. Still pointing his gun at us, the policeman bent down and looked inside the car.

'Oh. Good evening, Khan sahib,' he said, recognising Imran. 'Please go through.'

We swerved around the tractor and quickly headed on.

'They were certainly up to something,' said Imran. 'Did you see how startled he was when he saw me?'

'What were they doing?' I asked.

'In this part of the world the police are part of the organised crime network,' replied Imran. 'They are supposed to protect the people from *dacoits*, but they are the real outlaws. They are on less than two thousand rupees (£35) a month, so they're all forced into crime to survive. Only when their salaries are raised will anything change. Until then the best police stations go to the highest bidder. Around here they're involved in smuggling across the (Indian) border— narcotics, mainly. The rest of the time they just stop people and demand money.'

'What happens if you refuse?' I asked.

'If you create trouble they usually plant a gun on you,' said Imran. 'Then they shoot you dead.'

The situation at Wando dramatically illustrated Imran's principal charge: that under Benazir Bhutto corruption and lawlessness has now reached such endemic proportions in Pakistan that only a complete clean-out of the entire political system can solve the problem.

In 1995 Transparency International, a Berlin-based corruption-monitoring organisation, named Pakistan as the most corrupt country in Asia and the second most corrupt in the world, pipped at the post only by Nigeria. Partly as a result of this, the International Monetary Fund suspended a $1.5 billion loan to Pakistan. At the same time Amnesty International accused Benazir's government of massive human rights abuse. According to their report, Pakistan had one of the worst records of custodial deaths, extra-judicial killings and torture anywhere in the world, despite which not one policeman had ever been charged with or convicted for abusing his authority.

In such a situation, with Pakistan hurtling towards its worst crisis since the crushing military defeat by India in 1971, it was difficult to see how Imran, despite his political inexperience, could act as anything except a positive force. The Tehrik-e-Insaaf had resolutely refused to take on as a candidate any existing Pakistani politician, while a scrutiny committee grilled all potential candidates on their tax returns and sources of income.

Indeed, even if the Justice Movement failed to perform well in the elections, most observers agreed that it had already been an important catalyst in putting corruption at the top of the agenda. It was research by Imran's workers that had led to the revelation of Benazir Bhutto owning a £2.5 million manor house in Surrey, a £3.5 million Chelsea townhouse, two luxury apartments in Belgravia and a Normandy chateau. Benazir naturally denied all knowledge of the properties, but the charges, which are well documented, certainly contributed to the President's decision to dismiss her government. Now the caretaker government had begun taking steps to ban convicted criminals from standing for political office, and to force all candidates to declare their assets. The following day, Benazir's famously corrupt husband Asif Ali Zardari—recently upgraded from 'Mr 10 Per Cent' to 'Mr 30 Per Cent'—announced that he would not contest the forthcoming elections. Many more of the most notorious politicians in Pakistan may follow his lead and think twice about facing the caretaker government's scrutiny of their accounts.

'We want to make a completely fresh start,' said Imran the next day, when I went to his house for lunch. It was a Friday, the Islamic Sabbath, and Imran was taking the day off. He had just returned from visits to the gym and the local mosque, and for once was wearing a tracksuit rather than his trademark *salwar kameez*. 'The politicians are now the most hated people in this country. Do you know that sixty-five per cent of them have jumped parties at one stage or another in their career? They are totally unprincipled.'

While Imran tucked into his meal, I asked him if he was worried by his lack of experience.

'On the contrary,' he replied, scooping up a mouthful of *dal* and rice with his right hand. 'I think my lack of experience is an asset. It means I know my limitations. And as for the lack of experience among my workers, I regard it as our single biggest achievement that we haven't let in a single professional politician. We've started again completely from scratch.'

'But do your people have the qualifications to solve Pakistan's problems?' I asked.

'Pakistan's problems are not complicated,' replied Imran. 'They stem from straightforward corruption. At root it's a very simple problem. The level of corruption is so great it has put off all foreign investors; even overseas Pakistanis don't send their money here any more. In the 1960s Pakistan's exports were neck and neck with those of Hong Kong. Now our exports are worth barely a tenth of theirs. The government is now so poor, its resources so badly looted, that it cannot afford to spend anything on health. We have one of the worst infant mortality rates in the world. The education system has almost completely broken down.'

He paused to lever another handful of rice into his mouth: 'It is straightforward embezzlement and corruption that has brought us to this position,' he said. 'The nationalised banks are looted. Half the funds apportioned for development simply disappear. I didn't have to know anything about surgery to run my cancer hospital. It's no different with politics. As long as you can put the right people into the right jobs everything else will follow.'

That afternoon Imran was to have his portrait taken by the French photographer Alexandra Boulat. So after lunch he disappeared to shower and groom himself for his modelling session, leaving me in his flat on the first floor of the large house he shares with his father, his sisters and their families. Despite Jemima's year in Lahore, she did not appear to have made much impact on Imran's former bachelor pad: one half of the drawing room was dominated by a low teak table on which lay Imran's large collection of tribal stabbing daggers, the other half by his outsized running machine. Only two large black and white pictures of Jemima's parents and an unread copy of her father's anti-European tract *The Trap* indicated that she had ever been there.

Imran's bedside reading was almost endearingly austere: *Towards Understanding the Koran, The Road to Mecca* and *The Sayings of Nizam ud-Din Auliya* rubbed spines with *The Emergence of Islam* and *The Meaning of the Glorious Koran*. The only remotely racy title I could find was the *Encyclopédie de l'Amour en Islam*. All this formed a somewhat striking contrast to the stacks of Mills & Boons I had found a year or two earlier in Benazir's Karachi bedroom.

On the coffee table, however, by Imran's precious daggers, was one of my favourite biographies, Fawn Brodie's wonderful life of Sir Richard Burton, *The Devil Drives*. Relieved to find something more exciting than *The Meaning of the Glorious Koran* to occupy me while I waited for Imran to finish his epic shower, I opened the book, to discover that it belonged to Jemima. On the title page had been written a 'To Do' list in large, round, girly script. It read:

David Frost
Bikini Line
Chemist
Gym
Ring Parmesh—dress for Vogue

Such are the concerns of the rich and famous.

At that moment Imran finally emerged from the bathroom, wearing his best *salwar*. While the photographer rearranged him in a chair, trying to persuade him to prop his head on his knuckles in the manner of Rodin's *Thinker*, I asked him what Jemima thought of his entry into politics.

'She understood the dilemma I was facing,' said Imran. 'I never particularly wanted to go into politics. But the country was quite literally on the verge of collapse. Every day, people would come to me and say, "You've got to do something." Now I'm going to try to get Pakistan out of this mess. If I fail, at least I'll know I've given it my best shot.'

But was Jemima not horrified by the dangers, I asked. I hardly needed to remind him that the life expectancy of senior politicians in South Asia was not very high. On the day he had announced that he was planning to stand for election, a bomb had exploded in his cancer hospital, timed to coincide with his arrival at the building. Had he not been detained and arrived late, he would now be dead.

'Of course there is a danger,' he replied. 'Everyone in my party is worried I will be assassinated. If you take on the political mafia, this is something you must expect.'

Later I discovered from his friend Yusouf Salahuddin that many years before, when he was still a young cricketer, Imran had visited a renowned fortune-teller in Spain. She had told him that he would live to a happy old age. Only one thing troubled her. 'Do not ever go into politics,' she said, 'for if you do, you will be killed.' Imran at this stage had never for one minute considered entering politics. But according to Yusouf he had never forgotten the prophecy, and in due course it had made him hesitate for several years before he finally decided to go ahead and take the risk .

'Then again, I could die this evening in a car crash,' continued Imran. 'Or tomorrow, from cancer. Anything can happen. It's not really worth worrying about. Fear is the biggest barrier in anyone's life. Fear makes you a small person. Faith gives you courage. In the end, you die when you die,' he said, nonchalantly shrugging his shoulders. 'There's nothing to be done about it. Such things are in the hands of the Almighty.'

*Postscript*: In the event, Imran was not assassinated, but nor did he or any of his nominees win a single seat in the election. Indeed, the Tehrik-e-Insaaf was so disorganised that Imran discovered he was not even eligible to vote, as no one had bothered to register him. As the Pakistani pundits had predicted, the crowds at the rallies did not translate into votes, and the better-organised political parties made electoral mincemeat of the Justice Movement.

When the votes had all been counted, Nawaz Sharif's Muslim League stormed home to a stunning victory, with one of the largest majorities in Pakistan's history—much to the bemusement of the British press, which by and large had presented the election as a two-horse contest between Imran and Benazir, and which had almost totally ignored Nawaz. A few months later, in the British general election, Imran's failure was closely reproduced by his father-in-law Sir James Goldsmith, whose Referendum Party gained almost as much publicity as Imran's Justice Movement, and to equally little effect.

The Tehrik-e-Insaaf remains in existence, albeit on the very margins of Pakistani politics. Despite the virtual meltdown of Benazir's PPP, the prospects for Imran's political future remain fairly modest. His party has, however, succeeded in putting the issue of corruption into the centre of Pakistani political debate, no small achievement in a country which has become so inured to the dishonesty and venality of its politicians that before Imran's intervention, corruption was considered par for the course—as much a part of everyday political life as addressing rallies or attending parliament.

# 2

# In Rajasthan

# The Sad Tale of Bahveri Devi

Of course, she said, after the politician had sworn to take revenge, had sworn that the vendetta between the two families would last for seven generations, they had expected some sort of trouble.

Already, when they returned from their fields at the end of the afternoon they had become used to finding that someone had broken down the door of their hut and ransacked their possessions. Perhaps their pots had been broken as they sat drying by the kiln; or maybe their trees had been uprooted and their wattle fences damaged or destroyed. That sort of trouble, that sort of petty harassment, they had learned to cope with. After all, they were poor, and he was a politician, and there was nothing they could do. But, she said, they had not thought that he would dare to risk open violence, not when everyone in the village knew about his vow of revenge and of his intention to destroy the family.

So, on that evening, they had taken no precautions. One of their buffaloes happened to have died the night before, and as was the custom they had spent the whole day giving the animal the last rites. For that reason the sun was already setting when both of them went out to fetch the fodder from the fields. When they arrived at their land, Bahveri had gone off a short distance to cut grass, while Mohan, her husband, had begun gathering in the animals. It was only on her return that she had heard his cries, and she had run over to find out what was the matter.

What she saw was this: in the shadows, five men had surrounded her husband, had got him on the ground and were kicking him and viciously beating him with lathis. She recognised them immediately. Facing her was the politician, Badri Gujjar himself. Three of the other men were members

of his family—Badri's son, nephew and brother-in-law. The
fifth man was the Brahmin from the village temple.

'I asked them: "Why are you beating up my husband? It
was I who caused the problem for you. He has done nothing."
So Badri came over, grabbed me by the shoulders and shook
me and began abusing me. I said: "Don't shout. I was forced
to give your name to the authorities, but I did not send for
the police. It was the District Collector; he sent them. Why
don't you go and abuse him instead of us?" But the men did
not listen. They repeated over and over again: "It was your
fault. It was all your fault. We have been dishonoured and
we must have our revenge." And Badri said: "I will have my
revenge now—if I am man enough to take it." '

Two of the men held Mohan down while Badri raped
Bahveri Devi. Then two other men—Badri's son and nephew—
raped her too, one after the other. They were all sober at the
time, but when they left her lying there in the dust, she
remembers that they went away laughing like drunkards. As
they disappeared into the dusk they shouted behind them
that what they had just done should teach her a lesson,
should teach her that a woman of her caste—a potter, an
Untouchable—did not interfere with men of their caste,
Gujjars—proud yeoman farmers, cowherds and landowners.
What they had done would teach her her place in the village.
If she forgot it again, she knew what she could expect.

That, at any rate, is her version of events.

Village Batteri is an hour and a half's drive from Jaipur. You
leave the bazaars of the Old City by the Agra Gate, and head
off, past the domes and *chattries* of the Maharajahs' cremation
ground, out into the plains beyond.

For a while the country is green and fertile. Sometimes
you turn a corner and the fields ahead blaze bright yellow
with a ripening crop of spring mustard. But the further you
drive, the drier and hotter it becomes. Winter wheat gives

way to drooping sunflowers; dust-devils circle; melon beds tangle amid the sand-flats of the scrub. Turning right off the tarmac road and across a level crossing, you pass for miles and miles along narrowing dirt tracks. The settlements grow poorer; the camel thorn closes in. The colour drains away, but for the odd flash of red sari as a woman winds her way to a well.

Batteri clings to the edge of the cultivation, a border fort on the edge of the desert. It is an old village with a scattering of small eighteenth-century *havelis*, a silent, half-deserted and strangely sinister place. As you drive down the main street, wild-looking men glance up from the *hookahs* they are smoking on the verandahs of their houses, then spit on the ground in front of them. There are no children playing in the lanes; only the wind rakes down the main street.

We stopped and asked a cowherd for directions to Bahveri Devi's hut.

'Tchh! That slut!' said the man, speaking in a coarse Marwari dialect. 'What do you want with her?'

'We want to interview her,' said Sanjeev, a journalist friend from Jaipur who had agreed to come and help translate some of the thicker accents.

'Hasn't that bitch already brought enough shame to this village?' replied the man.

'She's a liar,' said another man, coming up to the car with his big, leathery water-buffalo. 'Nobody believes her and her stories. Everyone hates her.'

'Badri Gujjar is a good man,' said the first cowherd. 'Everything she says about him is untrue.'

The men pointed us down a side road and, again warning us not to believe a word that Bahveri Devi said, went on their way.

We found Bahveri Devi sitting on her verandah, chopping up chillies and onion on a stone. She was small, fragile and grey-haired. Although she was well into her middle years, she was still beautiful, with fine, well-pronounced cheekbones. She wore an old sari over a torn red *choli* ; she was barefoot, but around her left ankle was wrapped a single silver torc. Bahveri put down her knife and indicated that we should sit on the *charpai*, while calling into the hut to her daughter to bring us water from the well. Drawing up her feet underneath her, she asked in a soft, surprisingly high-pitched voice, how she could help us.

'Why are the villagers so hostile to you?' I asked.

'They say I have brought shame to the village,' said Bahveri. 'They say that such incidents should be dealt with by the village *panchayat* , not by the police or by any outsiders. They say that by bringing in the authorities I have sullied the name of the village for one thousand years.'

'Do none of your neighbours support you?'

'We have been boycotted,' said Bahveri. 'Now no one talks to us or buys our pots or milk or helps us with our animals.'

'Even other *kumars* (members of Bhaveri's own potter caste)?' asked Sanjeev.

'Even other *kumars*,' replied Bahveri. 'Our caste *panchayat* has declared us outcastes. No one, not even our families, will acknowledge our existence now.' She sighed. 'It has become very difficult for us to make ends meet.' She looked down and continued chopping the onions. In the silence you could hear the cooing of the rock doves on the byre at the back of the hut.

'Can't you leave this village?' I asked. 'If it is so bad here, couldn't you make a fresh start somewhere else?'

'It is not practical,' replied Bahveri Devi. 'But more importantly, I don't want to give the impression that I am afraid, that I'm giving in and running away.'

Bahveri's daughter, a slim girl of thirteen, came back from the well with two steel cups full of water. Sanjeev and I drank. When we had finished, I asked Bahveri to tell me her story, right from the beginning. Pushing her chopping stone away from her, she cleared her throat, rearranged her sari, and began.

It was five years, she said, since she took on the job as Village Batteri's *sathin*. *Sathin* means friend, and a *sathin's* job is to act as an informal social worker among the women of the village in which she lives. In most parts of India, *sathins* teach the other village women about health, hygiene, the mysteries of family planning and the benefits of sending their children to school. But in conservative and backward Rajasthan, where the literacy rate is one of the lowest in Asia (thirty-eight per cent, although among rural women the rate is as low as eleven per cent), *sathins* have had to concentrate on even more basic matters: discouraging female infanticide and child-marriages, both of which are alarmingly common in the more remote areas of the state. By covertly murdering baby girls at birth, or by marrying all of their young daughters off together in a single ceremony, villagers can drastically cut the prohibitive cost of dowries and marriage ceremonies, either of which can eat up whole decades of earnings for a poor family.

In rural India, women have little say in the running of village affairs, and lower-caste women have virtually none. But over time the *sathins* have proved that by working quietly among a village's women, and by rallying them together in a cause, it is possible to encourage slow social change. Thanks to the patient work of the *sathins*, fewer and fewer female babies have been drowned, while the financial benefits of sending children to school, rather than marrying them off in a job-lot, have been slowly but successfully demonstrated.

In 1992, however, official figures published in Delhi showed that child-marriage was still more prevalent in Rajasthan than anywhere else in India. Embarrassed by these statistics, the Rajasthan government ruined years of gradual progress by overreacting and ordering *sathins* to act as informers on any family planning a child-marriage. The police would then be sent in and the marriage stopped by force. In several cases the parents were arrested and sent to jail. Overnight, the *sathins* changed from respected figures in the villages to being perceived as interfering spies capable of bringing great shame and humiliation to a family at their most important and public ceremony.

Bahveri Devi was caught in this dilemma in the summer of 1992. She protested to the authorities, warning that only quiet persuasion would eradicate child-marriages in the long term; but as a poor woman reliant on the government for her salary, she eventually had no choice but to cooperate. In the end she provided the District Collector with a list of the names of seventeen families planning such ceremonies. Four of the families went ahead with the weddings despite warnings, and these ceremonies were all forcibly stopped by the police.

One of them was the marriage of the two young granddaughters of Badri Gujjar, the local *sarpanch* and the political leader of the district's dominant caste, the Gujjars.

'Twice I went to Badri's house and pleaded with him,' Bahveri Devi told me. 'I said: "Go ahead and marry your fourteen-year-old granddaughter, but why marry your one-year-old too? With the money you save on her dowry you could send her to school; in due course she will get a good job in Jaipur and earn much money herself." Badri would nod, but said nothing and kept going on with the arrangements. So a third time I went and talked to him. I got the one-year-old from out of the house and held her in my arms, showing her to Badri, saying: "Look! See how young she is!" But he just replied: "Everything is fixed. It will not be stopped now: it is too late. Now it is a matter of my family's prestige." Finally my Project Director came from Jaipur to talk to him, but when he persisted we had no option but to tell the Collector. On the day, two old policemen did turn up, but they were Gujjars, Badri's caste-men, so all they did was join in the wedding celebrations and eat their fill of the wedding sweets.'

The wedding went ahead, but the damage had been done. Badri had been humiliated at his granddaughters' wedding, and he publicly vowed to avenge himself for this dent to his prestige in the village. According to Bahveri Devi, Badri and his friends came for her on 22 September 1992. The day after the rape, she rose at dawn and took the early-morning bus to Jaipur to tell her Project Director. By the time she arrived, the Project Director was out, and he did not return until late that night. It was thus not until the morning of the twenty-fourth that Bahveri was persuaded to go to a police station and actually report the rape.

Bahveri felt that reporting the incident would help no one and only cause further trouble; she also correctly suspected that the police would be completely unsympathetic to a lower-caste woman lodging a complaint against a prominent local figure. Yet even she was surprised at the degree of hostility she encountered. The Jaipur police said that the matter was of no concern to them, and that she should report it to the police headquarters in Bassi, the district in which the rape actually took place. Once she had got to Bassi, four hours' bus ride away, the police there made it clear from the start that they disbelieved her story, treating her, she says, 'as if I were a prostitute' and keeping her waiting in the station for three days before getting around to giving her even the most basic medical examination.

Bahveri Devi now believes that the delay was deliberate, as according to many authorities, sperm tests are no longer valid or accurate three days after intercourse. Moreover, despite a 1982 amendment to the Indian penal code which provides that the police should take it as a premise that a rape victim is telling the truth, and take the suspect into custody as soon as the crime is reported, no attempt was made to arrest Badri Gujjar. Indeed, ten days passed before he was even questioned.

Badri Gujjar's family have a very different version of the events of 22 September. According to the Gujjars an incident did take place on that day, but it was only a fight between the priest from the village temple and Bahveri Devi's husband Mohan, over a cow which both claimed as their own. Mohan was getting the better of the priest when Badri's nephew and brother-in-law passed by and intervened 'because we could not bear to see a Brahmin being beaten up by Mohan, a *kumar*'. By the time they had finished with him, Mohan had been badly mauled.

I had gone over to Badri Gujjar's house as soon as we left Bahveri Devi. It was a much bigger affair than Bahveri's hut, made of cut stone rather than mud, with a shady verandah decorated with carved stone pillars. Outside, some twenty water-buffaloes were lined up by a byre; one of them was being milked by a servant girl. Most of the Gujjar menfolk were away, but Ram Sukhar, Badri's nephew, was there, a lean, muscular farmer with a thick moustache, smoking his hookah on the verandah.

'Badri wasn't even here that day,' said Ram Sukhar. 'Nor was his son. They had both gone to Dosa on their tractor. Yes, I certainly helped protect our Pundit from Mohan, but Bahveri, she was nowhere to be seen. The first we heard about any rape was when the police came around and questioned us.'

'But it is true that you were angry with her for interfering in your marriage ceremony?'

'Certainly,' he replied. 'We all agree that a child-marriage is not proper, not ideal, but it saves us so much money if we marry all the girls at the same time. If not, we have to bear the expense of four separate marriage parties, and we cannot afford that—we are only a poor family. Bahveri Devi should have understood that. But these *sathins* are very bad women. They are very bossy. Everything they say is wrong. Bahveri Devi had no business to send the police around at such a time. We had a reputation in this village. She has ruined that now.'

'So did you try to seek revenge?'

'No. But we did stop talking to her family. So did the other villagers. They said: "You have sullied the reputation of a good family." It was because of that boycott that she made this accusation. She wanted to punish us for isolating her.'

'But why would she make up a rape? It is the most humiliating thing a woman can admit to.'

'What is Bahveri Devi's reputation? What is her prestige? She is a *kumar*. And a whore. No one respects her. She has nothing to lose.'

'And the village still supports you?'

'Of course,' said Ram Sukhar. 'No one in the village believes Bahveri Devi's lies. Not one person. When the police saw this, they agreed with us that she had made up the whole incident.'

The following day in Jaipur I talked to Pratab Singh Rathore, the Inspector General of Crime in the Jaipur police. He confirmed what Ram Sukhar had said.

'Frankly we are 99.999 per cent certain that Bahveri Devi was not raped by these persons,' he said, twirling a pencil in his fingers. 'We have questioned everybody and made sperm tests, and on the basis of that evidence have dropped the case. There were traces of several different semen types in her sample, but none of these belonged to the accused. Nor, incidentally, did the sperm match with that of her husband.'

'What are you saying?'

'I don't think I have to spell it out,' replied the Inspector General. 'Ask anyone in the village about that woman's reputation.'

'So are you trying to imply that Bahveri Devi is not only a liar, she is also a slut?'

'Those are your words,' said the Inspector General. 'Not mine.'

I had planned to write about Bahveri Devi in January 1993, when I first heard about the case and went over to Jaipur to investigate. But faced with the Inspector General's claim to have scientific evidence that Badri Gujjar could not possibly have raped her, I dropped the story and put my notebooks in a bottom drawer. Initially there had been a wave of support for Bahveri Devi among women's groups, but following the publication of the Jaipur police report, the marches, the lobbying of MPs and the campaign all dried up.

So the case rested until May 1993, when Kavitha Srivastava returned from a year's sabbatical in England. Kavitha was a social worker with the Jaipur Institute of Development Studies, and had known Bahveri Devi well since she first came to Jaipur to be trained as a *sathin* five years previously. She was in no doubt that a woman of Bahveri's honesty and integrity would be quite incapable of making up a false rape allegation. As far as she was concerned, the whole case stank of caste and gender prejudice.

'You see, rape is actually very common in Indian villages,' she explained, 'particularly the rape of lower-caste women. But because of the shame and stigma it goes largely unreported: in all of India, astonishingly, only four or five cases are reported each year. The victim knows she will be labelled for life; moreover, everyone around will encourage her to hush it up, as the stigma will be attached not only to her, but also to her family and to her village. So in most cases women just hide such things, and if necessary go off and have an abortion.

'This is why the village would not support Bahveri. They are angry that she has gone public and so brought disrepute to Batteri. Moreover, they are all terrified of the Gujjars. Badri is a powerful local politician, while his son Gyarsa is the *panch* of his *jati*, the head of all the Gujjars in the neighbouring eighty villages. With him rests the final decision on marriage, society and death for all the local Gujjars. If you fall out with him he can ostracise you. You won't be allowed to smoke or eat or drink with anyone from the Gujjar community, and your children may not get the chance to get married.'

The more Kavitha investigated the case, the more she became convinced that the police had acted suspiciously, even improperly.

'In a rape case, the penal code makes it clear that the accused should be arrested and the evidence examined by a court. It is not up to the police to start making moral judgements and announce that the victim is an immoral character who might or might not be telling lies. And why didn't they arrest Badri Gujjar? The answer can only be that Badri was a prominent local politician, and that in Bassi

District the Gujjars are incredibly powerful: the local MP is Rajesh Pilot, who is not only a Gujjar but also a cabinet minister in the Central Government. In 1993 a state election was due, and no party could win seats in the area if they alienated the Gujjar vote. I have absolutely no doubt that political pressure was put on the police both to delay the medical and to clear Badri.'

Kavitha believed that if Bahveri was not cleared, no *sathin* would ever be able to work in Rajasthan again, nor would any Rajasthani rape victim ever again dare to come out in the open and seek justice. It was no longer just a matter of clearing the name of one woman: the stakes were now far higher.

'Four of us got together and made a solemn commitment to see the case through,' said Kavitha. 'We were aware that it might take as long as seven years to settle, as the appeals would take it from the Sessions Court to the High Court, and from there to the Supreme Court. But we knew that if we didn't see this one through we all might as well go home and pack our bags.'

After discussion, Kavitha and her supporters decided that their only hope was to create a political lobby to rival the influence of the Gujjars. They rallied the women's groups of India, and organised a new wave of marches and petitions and a series of articles in the press. On 27 September 1993, a year and five days after the alleged rape, Bahveri Devi's supporters won their first victory when the Delhi Central Bureau of Investigation (CBI) was finally forced to issue arrest warrants for the five accused. When the men disappeared from the village the CBI threatened to confiscate their property, and on 24 January 1994 all five gave themselves up to the police. A fortnight later, a second and even more important victory was won when the men's bail applications were thrown out by Justice N.M. Tibrewal, the High Court judge who was hearing the case. In his summing-up he made it clear what he believed to have happened:

'From the above details it is quite clear to me that Bahveri Devi was gang-raped, and that despite her appeals for help the local villagers did not come to her aid for fear of the accused. *Prima facie* it is a case of gang-rape which was done to take revenge against Bahveri for her success in preventing the child-marriage.' The judge was also highly critical of the police response to the case, which he termed 'highly dubious'.

So, a year later, at the end of February, Sanjeev and I again took a car down the dusty Rajasthani roads to talk to the inhabitants of village Batteri.

This time none of the villagers insulted Bahveri Devi when we asked for directions; instead they politely pointed out the way without comment. I remarked on this when we found Bahveri Devi on her verandah, again chopping up vegetables for her lunch.

'Since those people were arrested, everything has changed,' she said. 'Earlier everything was falling apart. Now it is much more peaceful. The villagers have started to talk to me again. It is not back to normal, but it is getting better. And the government has given me some money. Look!'

Bahveri showed us her new shoes and *choli*, and pointed out the new coat of paint on the side of her house, the fruit of a fifteen-thousand-rupee gift awarded to her by her employers, the Indian Women and Children's Development Fund.

'Are you surprised by what has happened?' asked Sanjeev.

'No,' said Bahveri. 'The truth had to prevail. Even though the police have taken money from the accused, it looks now as if we will win the case. Those men will be jailed for good. Before, rapes like this were very common. Now powerful men will be afraid to touch even a *kumar* woman. If we win the case it will have a very good effect.'

Bahveri shrugged her shoulders: 'Everything is in the hands of God.'

'Have you had any word from Badri's family?' asked Sanjeev.

'Yes,' replied Bahveri. 'Last month some mediators came from his family. They said Badri admitted he had made a mistake and asked me to withdraw the case. They said that without their menfolk their family would starve.'

'What did you reply?'

'That they must go through their jail term. They must be punished for what they have done. Unless they are suitably punished, it won't be a lesson and they will return to their old ways.'

'Will their women go hungry?' I asked.

'I hope the Gujjar women will not suffer too much,' said Bahveri. 'But did they feel bad when their husbands did this to me?'

Before we left the village we went over to the Gujjars' house. There we found Badri's womenfolk—four wives and two old grandmothers—as well as a scattering of filthy, half-naked children covered with flies, all squatting together on the verandah. The situation of the previous year had been reversed; the wheel had turned. The buffaloes had disappeared—presumably sold—and it was now the turn of the Gujjars to be wearing torn, soiled clothes.

'It's all a lie,' insisted Badri's grandmother, a wrinkled old woman who said she had forgotten her age. 'We have been framed. Bahveri was prompted to lie by all those educated women from Jaipur who didn't want us to marry off our children. For the last three months we have been crying. All my sons have been locked up. Badri has been beaten in prison. Now there is no one in the house who works. The only man who is left is my husband, and he is eighty. Who will cut the crops? Who will look after the animals? We are all ruined.'

The old lady began to sob.

'Where will these children go?' she cried, pointing to the infants around her. 'Who will feed them? Oh Maharaj! Look at them!'

We wished her well and turned to go, the old lady still shuddering with grief. As we got in to the jeep she shouted behind us: 'That woman Bahveri Devi,' she called. 'That bitch! She made it all up! Now she's ruined us all.'

# Sati Mata

On 22 October 1996, thirty-two men trooped out of a courtroom into the bright desert sunlight of the small Rajasthani town of Neem Ka Thana. After a trial lasting ten years and a controversy which profoundly divided the people of India, the thirty-two men were finally cleared of ritually burning to death an eighteen-year-old widow, and attempting to revive the ancient Hindu practice of *sati*.

In Rajasthan, like many of the more traditional parts of India, different centuries, even different millennia manage to exist side by side. In the larger towns, advertisements for cellular phones and satellite television now score a skyline once dominated by the spires of temples. But head out into the countryside and you soon have the unnerving sensation of the twentieth century simply slipping away.

Turning off the Jaipur–Delhi highway and driving north into the arid thorn-scrub, you leave the modern world far behind you. Cars and trucks disappear, to be replaced by camel and bullock carts. Women carry water from wells in bulbous brass pots balanced carefully on their heads. Occasionally at road junctions you pass small domed cenotaphs commemorating the site of some long-forgotten *sati*: a memorial put up to mark the place where a living, breathing widow chose to climb atop her husband's burning funeral pyre, sacrificing herself to ensure her husband's successful rebirth. In this way she is believed to join her soul with the goddess Sati Mata and to bring good luck to her family and her village for seven generations. Under the domes of the cenotaphs stand a series of stone stelae, some dating back to the sixth century A.D. On these are carved small, primitive sculptures of a husband and wife standing side by side, sometimes with the husband's arm over his wife's shoulders. The cenotaphs—known as *chattries*—are cool,

peaceful spots, and standing beside them listening to the
cooing of Rajasthani rock doves, it is easy to forget the
violence and brutality of the events they commemorate.

*Sati* is still deeply engrained in the culture of many parts
of rural India, and nowhere more so than in Rajasthan, which
is now the centre of the cult of the goddess Sati Mata.
Historically, of course, widow-burning is not unique to India:
Greek myths record its presence in Europe, and there is
archaeological evidence for its existence among the Scythian
tribes of the Central Asian steppe. Moreover, the practice has
links to the widespread ancient belief that a man needed his
companions in the afterlife as much as in this world. But its
presence in India is recorded from at least the first century
B.C.—*sati* appears in the *Mahabharata* and in the Indian writings
of the Greek historian and traveller Diodorus Siculus—and
from the third century A.D. onwards it became increasingly
common, with the very greatest reverence being paid to
those women who (in the eyes of the Hindu faithful) sacrificed
themselves for their family's well-being. In Rajasthan the cult
came to be particularly associated with the warrior Rajput
caste, who saw *sati* as an expression of their martial valour:
while the men showed their bravery by fighting the Muslim
sultans of Delhi, the women showed theirs by opting to die
on their husbands' funeral pyres.

*Sati* began to die out elsewhere in India after the British
banned it in 1829, but astonishingly, in Rajasthan it has
lingered on to the present day in some of the more distant
villages, with around forty cases thought to have taken place
since Independence. The most recent—and much the most
controversial—of these *satis* took place in the village of
Deorala. There, on 4 September 1987, Roop Kanwar, an
exceptionally beautiful eighteen-year-old Rajasthani girl, was
burned to death on her husband's pyre.

Roop was the youngest of six children in a middle-class
Rajput family, and had grown up in the Rajasthani state
capital of Jaipur, where her father ran a trucking company.
She was well educated, and had finished ten years of schooling
by the time her parents arranged for her to marry Maal
Singh, the son of a Rajput landowning family from Deorala,
where many of Roop's cousins lived.

In the photographs Roop has large, sensuous eyes and finely chiselled cheekbones. Some newspaper reports talked of her painting her nails—the mark of an outrageously modern girl in conservative Rajasthan—but her family says that she was always unusually religious. She had been married only eight months when her husband, Maal Singh, began to complain of stomach pains. On 2 September 1987 he was taken by Roop to the local hospital at Sikar, north of Jaipur. The doctors said his condition was not serious, so Roop returned home that evening. That night, however, Maal's appendix burst, and he died in the early hours of the morning. The body was brought back to Deorala by Maal's father. Roop had no children. Now she was faced with the prospect of spending the rest of her life as a childless widow. In a traditional Indian village this is regarded as the lowest form of life. High-caste widows like her would be expected to shave their heads, sleep on the floor, wear only simple white clothes and to perform menial tasks; for a woman of Roop Kanwar's caste there would be no possibility of remarriage.

The following morning, the young widow appeared at the door of the family's eighteenth-century *haveli*. She was dressed in her finest wedding sari, decked in jewellery, with her hands brightly painted with bridal henna. Word had already spread about what was going to happen, and the young widow soon found herself leading a procession of over six hundred villagers through the narrow lanes of Deorala, past a line of crumbling *havelis* and some abandoned camel carts, past the village shops and the village well.

On reaching the cremation ground the procession wound its way through a cluster of centuries-old cenotaphs erected to commemorate three *satis* which had taken place in the village in the Middle Ages. There Roop Kanwar split off from the crowd, and three times circled the funeral pyre that had been erected in the shade of a wide-spreading peepul tree. As she did this her in-laws raised Maal Singh's body—wrapped in a white shroud, but with his face showing—on to the logs. Then Roop climbed up on to the pyre, put her husband's head on her lap and commanded her sixteen-year-old brother-in-law to light the kindling. Brahmin priests intoned Sanskrit prayers, drums began to beat and the crowd took up the chant *'Sati Mata ki jai!'* Long live Sati Mata! *'Jab tak suraj chand rahega, Roop Kanwar tera nam rahega!'* As long as there is a sun and a moon, Roop Kanwar's name will live!

The pyre was apparently slow to catch alight, and when a police constable arrived some fifteen minutes later Roop Kanwar may still just have been alive. But the constable did not intervene, and eventually the flames did their work. Within half an hour Roop Kanwar and her husband had both been reduced to ashes.

On these events there is general agreement. But beyond the bare facts there is profound dissent about what happened in Deorala on the day of Roop Kanwar's *sati*; indeed, the controversy soon grew into a major national debate, splitting the country in two.

Roop's own family, her in-laws and the whole of the village maintain that the young widow voluntarily gave herself up to the pyre. They say she firmly resisted all attempts, by both her in-laws and the village Brahmins, to dissuade her from becoming a *sati*. They say an almost supernatural calm came over her as she proceeded through the village, blessing passers-by who fell at her feet to touch her robes, and performing a miracle on the way by healing the bleeding of an elderly relative. They say she smiled beatifically from the pyre as the flames danced around her. This is the version that is uncritically accepted by the Hindu faithful of rural Rajasthan, who quickly turned Roop into both a saint and a goddess: within a fortnight of her burning, three quarters of a million people had turned up to worship at the site of her pyre.

But the police, the state government, Indian feminist organisations and most of the English-language Indian media will have none of this. There was deep embarrassment in both Jaipur and New Delhi when the news broke about the survival of such a primeval tradition, and within a few days the Jaipur police had started to leak stories to the papers which implied that what had happened in Deorala was not *sati*, but a barbaric public execution in which the entire village was implicated. Roop's marriage was said to have been a failure, and it was hinted that she might even have been conducting an affair; it was also pointed out that she was well educated and not particularly religious. The chances of such a woman voluntarily jumping on her husband's funeral pyre were—so the reports implied—next to zero. It was suggested that Roop had been pressurised into the *sati* by her in-laws, then drugged with opium; and that her 'beatific calm' was not due to spiritual ecstasy, but to the mesmeric effects of the opium poppy.

In 1829 the British Governor General Lord William Bentinck had passed a law making it an offence to aid or abet a *sati*, and the offence remains on the Indian statute books. But in the case of Deorala the police chose not to invoke this law. Instead they charged no fewer than thirty-seven villagers—ranging in age from sixteen to seventy—with a more straightforward charge: murder.

Taking their lead from the police, the Indian papers began to send teams of reporters to the village, with the intention of proving that Roop Kanwar's *sati* was involuntary. Soon stories began to appear offering increasingly grisly versions of the event to the Indian public. The Bombay *Sunday Observer* quoted an unnamed farmer who said that Roop Kanwar had attempted three times to get off the funeral pyre, and was each time forced back on to it by irate villagers. The Calcutta *Telegraph* reported that Roop had tried to avoid being burned by hiding in the home of her aunt; the source for this story was given as 'some Deorala women'. The Women and Media Committee of the Bombay Union of Journalists sent a task force to the village who came up with an even more lurid version of the incident. According to an unnamed 'Congress Party worker', Roop had in fact been dragged screaming through the streets by six hundred fanatical villagers, a version of events that has gone down in the feminist literature on the subject as gospel truth, endlessly requoted, though the anonymous Congress worker has never been named, and certainly never surfaced at the subsequent trial. Finally, the *Hindustan Times* published a story which announced that Roop's husband was both impotent and a manic depressive, that the marriage was a sham and that Roop had spent little time with him after the wedding.

If the 'village sources' on which these stories were based ever existed, none of them came forward during the trial to give evidence, and despite the police applying considerable pressure on the accused and allegedly attempting to extract confessions by torture, the prosecution failed to produce a single witness who would testify to having seen Roop Kanwar compelled to become a *sati*.

The trial ground on for nearly a decade before the judge finally reached his verdict at the end of October 1996. To the astonishment of middle-class India, which had long assumed that Roop Kanwar was brutally executed, the judge decided that the villagers were innocent of murder, and characterised the police case as a tangle of inconsistencies and fabrications.

But this has not closed the case. For three months following the trial the Indian papers were full of articles expressing outrage at the acquittal, until at the beginning of January 1997 the state government of Rajasthan announced that it was appealing against the verdict. A new prosecution is now soon due to begin in the Jaipur High Court.

When I went to see the Chief Secretary of Rajasthan, who took the decision to appeal, I asked him why he thought the session judge's verdict was unsatisfactory. He replied quite frankly that he believed a voluntary *sati* was impossible in modern India: 'It is a preposterous idea,' he said. 'We live in 1997, not 2000 B.C. All our villages have televisions. Newspapers reach there. You think a literate woman would choose to go from her house in a procession to have herself burned to death? It is so unlikely that it is next to impossible to believe. The balance of probability is definitely against it.'

The same conviction drove M.M. Mehrishi, who at the time was the Superintendent of Police charged with investigating the *sati*. Now retired from the police, he told me he had never believed for a minute that there was any chance that Roop Kanwar could have freely chosen to go to her death; he always assumed the burning was forced: 'I thought it was extremely improbable that today, in modern India, a woman could commit *sati*. This led me to investigate the situation very closely.' Mehrishi also hinted that after the story hit the headlines, he came under extreme pressure to get quick results. When I asked him if his men had used torture to extract confessions from the accused he replied: 'I will not pretend the police are saints. You have to make these people feel the law has force.'

Yet what both the Chief Secretary and the Superintendent of Police found impossible to conceive is quite unsurprising to the ordinary villagers of Rajasthan. For them *sati* is not only possible, but actually a cause for celebration. While most urban Indians regard *sati* with horror, seeing it as a primeval custom unthinkable in contemporary India, in rural Rajasthan the villagers are quite unrepentant, and continue piously to revere past *satis*. The women in particular remain visibly proud of the courage and loyalty of their ancestors who, as they see it, abandoned life to join their husbands in the afterworld. In daily usage the word *sati* simply means 'a good woman', and Rajasthani women, particularly those from the Rajput caste, are brought up to see *satis* as the paradigm of the ideal woman and the perfect wife. In most Rajasthani villages the goddess Sati Mata is actively venerated, and the *sati* stones which litter the Rajasthani countryside are annually adorned with vermilion and silver foil, and are visited by every family after a birth or before a marriage.

Indeed, however much urban India would prefer it otherwise, the awful truth is that in the countryside *satis* are actually popular with both men and women. Not only did 750,000 people turn up to worship at the site of Roop Kanwar's pyre within a fortnight of the *sati*, but seven months later, long after the event had faded from the headlines, four hundred visitors were still visiting it every day to offer prayers. When Rajiv Gandhi's government passed a law in November 1987 making the 'glorification of *sati*' a criminal offence, a hundred thousand villagers took to the streets of Jaipur to protest. By contrast, the feminist rallies calling for the conviction of the menfolk of Deorala attracted only three thousand middle-class Indians, many of them bussed in from Delhi. The issue highlights a national divide in India, showing the growing mental gulf that now separates the towns from the villages of the subcontinent, a gulf into which all discussion of the Deorala *sati* has become lost. Most secular urban Indians, and especially the feminist lobby, have started from the assumption that in the late twentieth century no educated woman could possibly commit *sati*, and that Roop Kanwar's *sati* could only have been forced. The villagers of Rajasthan, male and female, have a very different perspective.

It seems unlikely now that it will ever be firmly established what actually did happen that day in Deorala. Either the *sati* was forced, in which case there has been a terrible miscarriage of justice and a barbarous crime has—so far—gone unpunished. Or else, if you accept the session judge's verdict—which on the face of it seems an eminently informed and impartial one, based not on political sensitivities but on the weakness and internal contradictions of the prosecution case—we are dealing with a Salem witch-hunt where, to satisfy the secular incredulity of India's middle-class urban élite, the menfolk of an entire peasant village have been rounded up, forced confessions have been extracted, and thirty-seven men have been unjustly hounded for a decade for a crime they did not commit.

To get to Deorala, you drive north from Jaipur into ever more arid territory. Except for the occasional herdsman leading his goats across the flat, desert planispheres, the landscape is harsh and empty and primitive.

You become aware of both the reverence for *sati* and the deep defensiveness of the villagers on the subject immediately you enter the village. Mention it casually, and the answer will be evasive: we were not here the day of the *sati*, it was long ago, who knows what happened? But talk a little longer, scratch the surface, and the answer you receive will be very different.

Kripal Singh Shekhawat is one of the best-educated men in the village, a middle-class engineer now living and working in Madras. He was on holiday when I visited the village, and

I found him sitting unshaven in his pyjamas, reading the paper on his doorstep. Like everyone else in Deorala, he claims to have been away on the day of the *sati*, but admits he was proud of what Roop Kanwar had done: 'Our Rajput women are very valorous,' he said. 'What she did has made the whole village respect her, and the whole of Rajasthan respect this village. It's complete nonsense that she was forced. Can a murder be committed in front of five hundred people? My wife saw the whole thing from the roof of our house. She says that Roop came through the village with a smiling face, blessing the people as she went. Even today my wife worships her as a goddess.'

Kripal's next-door neighbour is the retired village schoolteacher, Narayan Singh. Like his neighbour I found him sitting outside his brightly painted *haveli* enjoying the pale winter sun; from the top of the arched gateway of his house a peacock was calling to its mate. When I asked him why everyone was pretending they were away on the day of the *sati* he laughed.

'Of course people are hiding things,' he said. 'Who wants to get into this confusion? I'm seventy-five, and I was arrested by those thugs in the police. They picked up everyone: the shopkeepers, the old men, even the boys playing in the street. The bastards booked the entire village. For three weeks there was hardly a man left in Deorala. Sixty-six of us were bundled off to jail and interrogated.'

'Violently?'

'Of course. The police here know no other way. Even at the best of times they treat villagers like animals. Many of us were beaten. Bodu Ram the carpenter had his arms broken. Several old men were put into iced baths and had their heads held under water. They used electric shocks on others. It is you journalists that caused the problem. The journalists and the women's organisations.'

'In what sense?'

'You people come here and write what you want. You all assume that Roop Kanwar was forced. But sixty of her relatives are here in this village. Would they allow it to happen? You are from a big city. I don't know you. But if someone here tried to beat you up, I and everyone else would run to help. So much more so with our own relatives. How would we allow one of our own to be murdered? The family tried to dissuade the girl, but she was obstinate.'

'Has the *sati* brought any benefits to the village?' I asked.

'On the contrary,' said Narayan Singh. 'It has been a terrible thing for us. People are now so afraid none of them dare to go to funerals any more. Even the priests are careful. If a Rajput dies, first the priest will ask, "Is the widow intending to become a *sati*?" Only then will they agree to attend the cremation.'

It was only after many hours of interviews in and around Deorala that I found one eyewitness who was prepared to come on the record and admit that he had been present at the *sati*. Inder Singh said that he was the oldest man in the village, although he was unsure exactly what his age was: well over ninety, he thought. In his youth he had fought for the British, first in the thirties at Kandahar and Kabul (where he lost his thumb), then, during the Second World War, in North Africa and Italy. He had seen action at Tobruk and had been decorated for being among the first ashore at the Salerno landings. He had leathery skin and a grey walrus moustache. On his head he wore a bright orange turban.

'Of course I was here,' he said. 'And not just me: the whole village. Everyone was here, no matter what they say now. Yes, I saw the whole *sati* with my own eyes. She was not forced. Absolutely not. So many people saw her. Can you force somebody to sit on a funeral pyre in front of five hundred people?'

'But didn't you feel you should have stopped her?' I asked.

'No one can stop a *sati*,' replied Inder Singh. 'We believe that if anyone stops a *sati* they will be cursed. Something will definitely happen to them.'

'And she didn't try to get off the pyre?'

'No,' said Inder. 'It was her own choice. *Sati* is something from inside. It is no *sati* if it is forced. When the fire was lit she just sat there with her husband's head on her lap. She seemed to feel no pain. You see, *satis* have a special power. When the gods want something they can do anything. In the past, when the gods willed it the great warriors of India fought on even when their heads had been cut off. Compared to that, what is a *sati*?'

'What do you think of the law banning the glorification of *sati*?' I asked.

'These are ungodly times,' said Inder Singh. 'These ladies from the women's organisations come here unveiled, without their husbands, wearing trousers. They tell us we burn our daughters by force. Do they think we are animals? When Lord Ram was the ruler he allowed *sati*. So who are these people in Delhi to ban it?'

Inder Singh moved closer to me and whispered in his cracked voice: 'This is the *Kaliyuga*, the Age of Kali, the epoch of disintegration. Ungodly things are happening all around us. Publicly these people from the towns have stopped us worshipping the goddess Sati Mata. But in our hearts we still do. Who can stop us?'

# 3

# The North

# The Age of Kali

On the night of 13 February 1992 two hundred armed Untouchables surrounded the high-caste village of Barra in the northern Indian state of Bihar. By the light of burning splints, the raiders roused all the men from their beds and marched them out into the fields. Then, one after another, they slit their throats with a rusty harvesting sickle.

Few of my Delhi friends were surprised when I pointed out the brief press report of the massacre, buried somewhere in the middle pages of *The Indian Express*: it was the sort of thing that was always happening in Bihar, they said. Two thousand years ago, it was under a bo tree near the Bihari capital of Patna that the Buddha had received his enlightenment; that, however, was probably the last bit of good news to come out of the state. These days Bihar was much more famous for its violence, corruption and endemic caste-warfare. Indeed, things were now so bad that the criminals and the politicians of the state were said to be virtually interchangeable: no fewer than thirty-three of Bihar's State Assembly MLAs had criminal records, and a figure like Dular Chand Yadav, who had a hundred cases of dacoity and fifty murder cases pending against him, could also be addressed as Honourable Member for Barh.

Two stories I had first noticed in the news briefs of the Indian press give an idea of the seriousness of the crisis in the state.

The first was a tale of everyday life on the Bihar railways. One morning in October 1996, the Rajdhani Express from New Delhi to Calcutta made an unscheduled stop at Gomoh, a small station in southern Bihar. Mumtaz Ansari, the local Member of Parliament, got into the first-class compartment. With him were three security guards. Neither Ansari nor his henchmen had tickets, but they nevertheless turfed out of their seats four passengers with reservations. When one of them, a retired government official, had the temerity to protest at his eviction, Ansari answered that it was he who made the laws, so he had the right to break them. When the old man continued to protest, the MP waved his hand and ordered the guards to beat him up. At the next stop Ansari was received by a crowd of supporters, including another MP and ten of his armed retainers. They dragged the retired official out of the carriage and continued the work begun by Ansari's guards. As the train pulled out, the old man was left bleeding on the platform.

The second story was a tale of life in the Bihar civil service. In October 1994, a young graduate named G. Krishnaiah received his posting as District Magistrate of Gopalganj, a remote and anarchic district of northern Bihar. It was not exactly a dream assignment: Gopalganj was renowned as one of the most lawless areas in India, and only two weeks before, Krishnaiah's predecessor as District Magistrate had been killed by a bomb hidden in a briefcase in his office. Nevertheless, Krishnaiah was energetic and idealistic, and he set about his new job with enthusiasm, giving a brief interview to Doordarshan, the Indian state television network, in which he announced a series of measures intended to turn the area around: to control crime, generate employment and uplift the Untouchables of Gopalganj.

Watching the clip now, with the young official speaking so blithely about his intention of rooting out violence, the manner of his end seems all the more horrifying. Two months later, Krishnaiah was driving along a road at dusk when he ran into the funeral procession of a local mafia don who had been killed in a shoot-out the day before. The procession was being led by the local MP, Anand Mohan Singh, who prior to entering politics had spent most of the previous two decades as an outlaw with a price on his head: in that time the police had registered nearly seventy charges against him, ranging from murder and criminal conspiracy to kidnapping and the possession of unlicensed arms. According to statements collected by the police, Singh 'exhorted his followers to lynch the upstart official', whereupon the mourners surrounded Krishnaiah's car, and one of Singh's henchmen fired three shots at him. Krishnaiah was badly wounded but still alive. So, encouraged by Singh, the mourners pulled him from his car and slowly stoned him to death.

That a sitting MP could be arrested for ordering a crowd to lynch and murder a civil servant was bad enough, but what happened next reveals quite how bad things have become in Indian politics in recent years. Anand Mohan Singh was arrested, but from his prison cell he contested and retained his seat in the 1996 general election, later securing bail to attend Parliament. He recently distinguished himself during a parliamentary debate by snarling, 'Say that again and I'll come and break your teeth' at an opponent on the other side of the Lok Sabha debating chamber. Justice in India being what it is, few believe that the police now have much chance of bringing a successful prosecution.

Over the years, my friends explained, violence had come to totally dominate almost every aspect of life in Bihar. It was said that in Patna no one bothered buying second-hand cars any more; instead armed gangs stopped vehicles in broad daylight, then forced the drivers to get out and sign pre-prepared sale deeds. As the Bihar government was too poor to pay the contractors who carried out public works, the contractors had been compelled to start kidnapping the government's engineers and bureaucrats in order to get their bills paid. Other contractors, desperate for business, had taken to wreaking violence on each other: one report I had seen described a shoot-out in Muzaffarpur between the *goondas* of competing engineering companies after tenders had been put out to build a minor bridge in an obscure village. In some upper-caste areas, the burning of Untouchables had become so common that it was now almost an organised sport. Various lower-caste self-defence forces had formed in reaction, and were said to be busily preparing for war in villages they had rechristened with names like Leninnagar and Stalinpur. There were now estimated to be ten major private armies at work in different parts of Bihar; in some areas the violence had spun completely out of control, and was approaching a situation of civil war.

Bad things went on in Bihar, my friends told me: that was just the way it was. But the singularly horrific nature of the Barra massacre stuck in my mind, and a year later, when I found myself in Patna, I decided to hire a car and go and visit the village.

The road leading to Barra from Patna was much the worst I had ever travelled on in five years of living in India: although it was one of the principal highways of Bihar, potholes the size of bomb craters pitted its surface. On either side, the rusting skeletons of dead trucks lined the route like a succession of *mementi mori.*

As we drove, I had the feeling that I was leaving the twentieth century far behind. First the electricity pylons came to a halt. Then cars and trucks disappeared from the road; even the rusting skeletons vanished. In the villages, wells began to replace such modern luxuries as hand-pumps. We passed the odd pony trap, and four men carrying a palanquin. The men flagged us down and warned us about highwaymen. They told us to be off the roads by dark.

Eventually, turning right along a dirt track, we came to Barra. It was a small, ancient village raised above the surrounding fields on an old earthen tell. Its population was entirely Bhumihar: Brahmins who had converted to Buddhism at the time of the Emperor Ashoka, around 300 B.C., and who had then been denied readmittance to the priestly caste when Indian Buddhism was wiped out by an aggressive Hindu revival a thousand years later. Bhumihars were still high-caste, but they had never quite regained the top place in the caste pyramid they had lost 250 years before the Romans first arrived in Britain.

I was taken around Barra by Ashok Singh, one of the two male survivors of the massacre. He walked me over to an embankment where a small white monument had been erected to the memory of the forty-two murdered villagers. A hot wind blew in from the fields; dust-devils swirled in the dried-out paddy. I asked: 'How did you escape?'

'I didn't,' he said. And pulling off a scarf, he showed me the lurid gash left by the sickle which had sliced off the back of his neck. 'They cut me then left me for dead.'

Ashok began to describe, in detail, what had happened. He said that, as normal, he had gone to bed after eating his supper at eight-thirty. The week before, there had been an atrocity when the Savarna Liberation Front, the (upper-caste) Bhumihar militia, had gang-raped and killed ten Harijan women in the next district; but Barra was far from there, and no one was expecting trouble. Ashok, his brothers, father and uncle were all asleep on their *charpais* when they were woken by the sound of explosions at ten-thirty. They were frightened, and went to the women's part of the house to alert their wives and mothers. The explosions and the sound of gunfire came closer. Then a burning splint was thrown on to the thatch of their roof. At the same time there was a shout from outside that everyone should come out and give themselves up, or else burn to death.

'As soon as the roof caught fire my uncle and I began trying to put out the blaze. We didn't take any notice of what was being shouted, so eventually these low people had to break down the door and drag us all out. There were hundreds of them, armed with guns, spears, bows, lathis and sickles. They left the women by our house, but they tied the men up with lengths of cloth.'

'Did they say where they were from? What militia they were part of?'

'No, but they were local men. We could tell by their accents. At first they left us lying where we were as they destroyed all the village houses with fire and dynamite. Then they said, "There is a meeting," and they dragged us men to the edge of the village. There they made us sit in the middle of a circle. Then, one by one, they started killing us, right there where we were sitting. A great crowd was watching, but only two people were doing the killing, so it took a long time. I was very frightened. My mind went blank.

'They killed all my brothers. They killed my father and they killed my uncle and my cousins. Eventually my turn came. One of the men pushed me forward and the other got his sickle and took three swipes. It made deep cuts on the back of my neck and head. I was senseless. The next thing I knew I woke up in hospital in Gaya. It was three weeks before I could get out of bed.'

'You were very lucky.'

'How can you say that? I lost eight of my kin.'

Ashok's face crumpled, and he looked down. After some time, he again met my eyes: 'I would like to take revenge,' he said quietly, 'but I don't have the capacity.'

Ashok showed me the houses he and the widows of the village had erected with the compensation money they had been awarded by the government. They were miniature castles: tall and square, with no windows except for thin arrow-slits on the third storey. Unwittingly, they were almost exact miniature copies of the Peel Towers erected across the Scottish borders in the sixteenth century, when central authority had completely broken down. There could be no better illustration of Bihar's regression into the Dark Ages.

Ashok rubbed the huge scar on his neck and said: 'Now the Harijans refuse to work on our fields, and there are not enough Bhumihar men left to till them ourselves. When the Harijans pass us on the road, they pass comments at us: "We have not finished with you yet," or "You will meet the same fate as your brothers." These low people are enjoying what has happened. They have grown fat and behave like they are Brahmins. But us Bhumihars, every night after sunset we are frightened. Every night I have nightmares. They may come again. What is to stop them? The police and the government of Laloo Prasad Yadav are on their side. This massacre was his handiwork.'

'In what sense?'

'Laloo is from a low caste,' said Ashok. 'He is always encouraging these *nichla* (oiks) to rise up against us. When Laloo came here after the massacre we threw stones at him. Every day we pray for his downfall.'

'But don't your new houses give you some protection?' I asked.

'Our houses are strong,' replied Ashok, 'but we are vulnerable. We cannot stay in our houses all day. We have to move around.'

Cowherds were now leading the buffalo back to the village for milking. Around where we were standing, women were lighting dung fires and beginning to cook supper. The afternoon was drawing in. I thought of the warnings we had received to be back in Patna and off the roads by the fall of darkness.

'The government will not protect us,' said Ashok as we walked back to the car, 'so we are left at the mercy of God. This is the *Kaliyuga*, the epoch of disintegration. The lower castes are rising up. Everything is falling apart.'

After living in India for five years, I finally left Delhi in 1994. I dismantled my flat and set off to write a book in the Middle East. Returning to the subcontinent two and a half years later, I found that a quiet social revolution had taken place in my absence, with lower-caste politicians seizing power in state after state across India. This process seemed to have started in Bihar, in the person of Laloo Prasad Yadav, the man the villagers of Barra had blamed for their massacre. Laloo in many ways seemed to personify much that was happening in India, and I decided to return to Bihar to try and meet him.

Although a similar revolution was taking place at the same time in Uttar Pradesh, when he first came to power in 1991 Laloo was still a relatively unlikely figure in north Indian politics. The Indian establishment was then still firmly dominated by the higher castes: Nehru, his daughter Mrs Gandhi and her son Rajiv were all Brahmins, as was Rajiv's successor as head of the Congress Party and Prime Minister, Narasimha Rao. Brahmins had ruled India for forty-four of fifty years of independence. Kshatriyas (the second rung in the caste pyramid) ruled for two more years, in the persons of V.P. Singh (1989–90) and Chandra Shekhar (1990–91). Lower- or intermediate-caste Prime Ministers had been in power for fewer than four years of the half-century since the British left India.

Laloo was the son of a low-caste village cowherd. In the Bihar of the 1960s and 70s it was against all the odds that a man like him would manage to get educated and attain even a foothold in politics. Despite the fact that the lower castes, the Untouchables and tribesmen together formed a full

seventy-three per cent of the population of Bihar, in the 1962
Bihar Legislative Assembly over sixty per cent of MLAs were
from the top two castes, while less than seven per cent were
from low-caste backgrounds. But from the early 1980s onwards
the lower castes had been on the rise, while the upper castes
were in rapid retreat. In the 1984 general election, Bihar
returned twenty-five upper-caste MPs to the national
Parliament, including seven Brahmins. By 1989 this number
had sunk to eighteen, with the Brahmins still retaining their
quota of seven. In 1991, the year Laloo came to power,
replacing a Kshatriya Chief Minister, the number of upper-
caste MPs had shrunk to ten, with only one Brahmin among
them. From 1989 to 1991, the Congress Party was unable to
field even one Brahmin who could win a parliamentary seat
in Bihar. In the Bihar Legislative Assembly there has been an
equally dramatic shift. Today only 10.2 per cent of Bihar
MLAs are from the top two castes, while 52.5 per cent are
from low-caste backgrounds.

Laloo's political views were formed by his childhood
experience of being kicked around by the higher castes of his
village. From the beginning of his career he spoke out bitterly
against the Brahmins and the Hindu revival that in many
areas was bringing about a new hardening in the caste
system. 'Our fight is against the wearers of the Sacred Thread'
he told his audiences. 'For centuries the priests have made
fortunes by fooling villagers. Now I tell them they should
learn to milk cattle and graze them, otherwise they will
starve.' On other occasions he publicly voiced his disbelief in
the Hindu gods: 'Ram should punish these murderous
fundamentalists—if he exists, that is. But he is nowhere. If he
was there, so many poor people would not have died, there
would not have been such poverty, such fights...'

In a country as obsessed with religion as India, such
brazen anti-Brahminical atheism was a completely new
message, at least in the north. But, to many people's surprise,
it worked. In the 1991 general election, Laloo—supported by
the combined votes of the poor, the casteless and the
oppressed Muslim community—was swept into power with
an unprecedented majority. Since then, in the 1996 election
Laloo's vote fell back slightly, but he managed to retain his

hold on power, despite increasingly clear evidence that his government—and indeed his own family—were deeply corrupt, and were presiding over the looting of the state treasury. One act had brought him into particular disrepute: the alleged embezzlement of vast sums of agricultural subsidies, referred to in the Indian papers as 'the multi-crore fodder scam'.

Yet, notwithstanding the fall in his share of the vote, Laloo had gained greatly increased national power, as he now formed part of the ruling coalition government. For what had happened in Bihar in 1991 happened elsewhere in northern India in the 1996 election, with the rural lower castes seizing control of state governments across the country, and candidates from the upper-caste élite losing their seats *en masse*. H.D. Deve Gowda, a middle-caste farmer from Karnataka, was sworn in as Prime Minister to replace the Brahmin Narasimha Rao, propped up by a variety of regional parties, many of whom represented the lower castes. Where Bihar had led, the rest of the country had followed.

There are two theories about the effects of this social revolution. Pessimists point out that while the Anglicised Brahmin élite produced leaders of the calibre of Jawaharlal Nehru and Indira Gandhi, the rise of the rural lower castes has resulted in the emergence of a cadre of semi-literate village thugs, men like Laloo and his counterpart in Uttar Pradesh, Mulayam Singh Yadav, a small-time wrestler and alleged mafia don who rose to become India's Defence Minister. Many such rustics can barely write their names, and they certainly have no hope of mastering the finer points of international diplomacy and economics.

On the other hand, the last decade of Brahmin rule brought to power a man like Rajiv Gandhi, who for all his polish was barely able to speak Hindi, and certainly had no grasp of the realities of life for the eighty per cent of Indians who lived in villages. Ten years ago every second person at Delhi drink-parties seemed to be either an old schoolfriend of the Prime Minister or a member of his cabinet. Now, quite suddenly, no one in Delhi knows anyone in power. A major democratic revolution has taken place almost unnoticed, leaving the urban Anglicised élite on the margins of the

Indian political landscape. As Mulayam Singh Yadav put it on his elevation to the national cabinet, 'For the first time, power has come to the underprivileged and the oppressed, and we will use it to ensure that their lot is bettered.'

This is also the stated intention of Laloo. So far his political success may have done little in concrete terms to boost the welfare of the lower-caste poor, but what it certainly has done is to boost their confidence. The lower castes are no longer content to remain at the bottom of the pile and be shoved around by the Brahmins. Laloo has given them a stake in power and made them politically conscious: exactly as the Civil Rights Movement did for American blacks in the 1960s.

The rise of lower-caste politicians has also done something to slow the rise of the Hindu revivalist movement, by demonstrating to the masses how little they have to gain by voting in a Hindu theocracy dominated by the same castes which have oppressed them for millennia. In the dying days of 1992, when India was engulfed in the bloody chain of Hindu–Muslim riots that followed the destruction of the Babri mosque at Ayodhya, even the previously peaceful commercial capital of Bombay was burning. Yet Bihar remained uncharacteristically—indeed almost miraculously— peaceful. With a series of unambiguous threats to the more excitable elements in the Bihar police force, Laloo had been able to contain the anti-Muslim pogroms which elsewhere in India left two thousand dead.

Indian politics are rarely predictable, but it was certainly one of the more unexpected developments in modern Indian history that led to the low-caste and semiliterate Chief Minister of India's most corrupt and backward state becoming the custodian of the crumbling Nehruvian ideal of a secular, democratic India.

The more I read about Bihar, the more it became clear that Laloo was the key to what was happening there. But ringing

Bihar proved virtually impossible from Delhi: it was much easier to get through to Britain, ten thousand miles further away. Unable to contact Laloo, I was forced to take pot luck and book a flight to Patna without having arranged an interview. But by remarkable good fortune, it turned out that Laloo had been speaking at a rally in Delhi, and was returning to Patna on the same flight as myself.

The first I learned of this was when the Bihar flight was delayed for half an hour while it waited for Laloo to turn up. When he eventually did so, striding on board like a conquering hero, he brought with him half his cabinet.

Laloo turned out to be a small, broad-shouldered, thick-set man; his prematurely grey hair was cut in a boyish early-Beatles mop. He had reserved the whole of the first row of seats for himself; his aides, MPs and bodyguards filled up the next seven tiers. They were all big, slightly sinister-looking men. All, including Laloo himself, were dressed in white homespun cotton pyjamas, once the symbol of Mahatma Gandhi's identification with the poor, but now (when synthetic fibres are far cheaper) the unmistakable insignia of political power.

The delay, the block-booking and the extravagant manner in which Laloo sprawled lengthwise along the first row of seats like some degenerate Roman Emperor, graphically illustrated all I had heard about Laloo being no angel of political morality. To get to the top, he had had to play politics the Bihar way: at the last election, one MP had gone on record to declare: 'Without one hundred men armed with guns you cannot hope to contest elections in Bihar.' To become Chief Minister you would need to have more toughs and more guns than your rivals. Laloo was no innocent.

Yet, in the most ungovernable and anarchic state in India, his government had been at least relatively effective. A retired senior Bihar civil servant quoted Chanakya, the ancient (c.300 B.C.) Indian Machiavelli, when he described the administration of the new Chief Minister: 'Chanakya said that to rule India you must be feared. Laloo is feared. He likes to play the role of the simple villager, but behind that façade he is nobody's fool. He is a violent man. No one would dare ignore his orders.'

Certainly the entourage at the front of the plane seemed bewitched by their leader. They circled the Chief Minister, leaning over the seats, squatting in front of him on their haunches and laughing at his jokes. When I eventually persuaded one of the MPs to introduce me to his leader, the man literally knelt down in front of Laloo while he explained who I was.

Laloo took it all in his stride. He indicated that I should sit down on the seat beside him—leaving the MP on his knees to one side—and asked how he could help. I asked for an appointment to see him. With a nonchalant wave of his hand he called over a secretary, who fixed the interview for five-thirty that afternoon.

'But,' he said, 'we could begin the interview now.'

'Here? In the plane?'

'Why not? We have ten minutes before we arrive.'

I asked Laloo about his childhood. He proved only too willing to talk about it. He lolled back against the side of the plane, his legs stretched over two seats.

'My father was a small farmer,' he began, scratching his balls with the unembarrassed thoroughness of a true yokel. 'He looked after the cows and buffaloes belonging to the upper castes; he also had three acres of his own land. He was illiterate, wore a dhoti and never possessed a pair of shoes in his life. My mother sold curds and milk. She also was illiterate. We lived in a mud-thatch cottage with no windows or doors: it was open to the dog, the cat and the jackal.

'I was one of seven. I had five brothers and one sister. There was never enough money. When we were old enough we were all sent out to graze the buffaloes. Then my two elder brothers went to the city (Patna) and found a job working in a cattle farm near the airport. They earned ninety-four paise a day. When they had saved enough money, my brothers called me to Patna and sent me to school. I was twelve. Until that time I did not know even ABC.'

I asked: 'How were you treated by the upper castes in your village?'

Laloo laughed. The other MPs—who had all gathered around and were listening reverently to the words of their leader—joined in with a great roar of canned laughter.

'All my childhood I was beaten and insulted by the landlords,' said Laloo. 'For no reason they would punish me. Because we were from the Yadav caste we were not entitled even to sit on a chair: they would make us sit on the ground. I remember all that humiliation. Now I am in the chair and I want those people to sit on the ground. It is in my mind to teach them a lesson. I don't hate them,' he added. 'But their minds have to be...' He paused, searching for the right word: 'Their minds have to be changed. We have been an independent country for fifty years, but there has been no alteration in the caste system, no social justice. I want to end caste. I want intercaste marriages. But these Brahmin priests will not allow it.'

'But how can you hope to destroy a system that has been around for three and a half thousand years?' I asked. 'Isn't caste the social foundation of Hinduism?'

'It is an evil system,' said Laloo simply. 'It must go.'

The plane was now wheeling above Patna. Below I could see the grey ribbon of the Ganges threading its way along the edge of the city, past the *ghats* and out into the fertile floodplains of Bihar.

'Go back to your seat now,' said Laloo curtly. 'I will talk to you again this afternoon.'

No one has ever called Patna a beautiful city; but revisiting it I found I had forgotten how bad things were. As you drive in through the outskirts, the treeless pavements begin to fill with occasional sackcloth shacks. The shacks expand into slums. The slums are surrounded by garbage heaps. Around the garbage heaps goats, pigs, dogs and children compete for scraps of food. The further you go, the worse it becomes. Open drains line the road. Beside them lie emaciated migrants from famine-hit villages. Sewer-rats the size of cats scamper among the rickshaws.

Bihar is in fact one of the last areas of the subcontinent which really conforms to the image of India promoted by well-meaning Oxfam advertisements, all beggars, cripples and overpopulated leper hospitals: 'Send £10 and help Sita regain her sight...' For the reality after fifty years of independence is that India is now the seventh industrial power on earth, with a large, prosperous and entrepreneurial middle class.

Yet while much of the southwest of India seems to be surging purposefully towards a future of modest prosperity, health and full literacy, Bihar has begun to act as a kind of leaden counterweight, dragging the north of the country back towards the Middle Ages. One of the state's few really profitable industries is the manufacture of counterfeit pharmaceuticals—salt pills dressed up as aspirins, sugar tablets pretending to be antibiotics—a field in which it apparently leads South Asia. Recently an enterprising Bihari counterfeiter expanded his operations to include the manufacture of great quantities of a fake chalk-based toothpaste called Colfate. Otherwise, despite exceptionally rich mineral deposits and fertile soil, the state remains the poorest in India.

Not only is the economy stagnant, crime is completely out of control: 64,085 violent offences (such as armed robbery, looting, rioting and murder) took place between January and June 1997. This figure includes 2,625 murders, 1,116 kidnappings and 127 abductions for ransom, meaning that Bihar witnesses fourteen murders every day, and a kidnapping every four hours. Whatever index of prosperity and development you choose, Bihar comes triumphantly at the bottom. It has the lowest literacy, the highest number of deaths in police custody, the worst roads, the highest crime, the fewest cinemas. Its per capita income is less than half the Indian average. Not long ago it even had a major famine. The state has withered; Bihar is now nearing a situation of anarchy.

The day I flew back into Patna, there were six stories vying for attention on the front page of the Bihar edition of the *Hindustan Times*; each in its own way seemed to confirm the collapse of government in the state.

The paper led with a report about a group of tribals who were demanding an independent state in the hills of southern Bihar. They had just carried out a raid on a mine and successfully got away with 'almost six hundred kilograms of gelignite, over a thousand detonators and fifteen hundred metres of igniting tape'.

Below this was a report of a shoot-out in which the Patna police killed 'a notorious criminal wanted in several cases of dacoity including the kidnapping of the Gupta Biscuit Company's proprietor'.

Next, a political piece carried a statement from the Congress opposition accusing the Bihar government of 'ignoring the famine-like situation prevailing in the state'.

Another report, headlined 'Crime on the Rise in Muzaffarpur', detailed the arrest over the previous three months of '1,437 criminals' during the '116 riots' that the town had apparently suffered since the New Year.

At the bottom of the page was an item announcing an initiative to resuscitate the moribund Bihar tourist industry: a paramilitary Tourist Protection Force was to be set up, providing a heavily armed escort for any Japanese tourists wishing to brave a visit to the site of the Buddha's enlightenment at Bodh Gaya.

But the most astonishing story concerned the goings-on at Patna University. There angry examinees had 'torched a police jeep and damaged the car of the Vice-Chancellor'. What had caused this? A cut in student grants? Nothing of the sort. 'According to reports, the Vice-Chancellor, in a surprise visit to the (exam) centre found all the examinees adopting unfair means. He ordered a body search and seized two gunny bags full of notes, chits and books from the examinees...In a brazen move the examinees then walked out of the examination hall and resorted to wanton vandalism.'

That afternoon I called on the Vice-Chancellor, to see if the reports were exaggerated. Professor Mohinuddin was a small, wiry man with heavy black glasses. He maintained that, on the contrary, the press had played down the violence. On being caught red-handed the students had attacked him, hurling desks and chairs, and forced him to take shelter in a sandbagged police post. There, despite a valiant defence by the six policeman on duty, the mob had succeeded in driving the Vice-Chancellor from his refuge with the help of a couple of crude firebombs. Later, for good measure, the students had issued a death threat against him. 'It is lucky I am a widower,' said the Professor. 'I only have my own safety to worry about.'

Not far from Professor Mohinuddin's house was the home of Uttam Sengupta, the editor of the Patna edition of the *Times of India*. Like his academic neighbour, Mr Sengupta had had a somewhat upsetting week. Two days previously, someone had taken a potshot at him with a sawn-off shotgun. The pellets had lodged themselves in the back door of his old Fiat. Sengupta had escaped unscathed but shaken.

According to Sengupta, what was happening in Bihar was nothing less than the death of the state. Much of the problem, he said, derived from the fact that the Bihar government was broke and unable to provide the most basic amenities. The National Thermal Power Corporation, the Indian national grid, had recently threatened to cut off Bihar's electricity supply unless its dues were paid. In the Patna hospital there were no bedsheets, no drugs and no bandages. The only X-ray machine in the city had been out of order for a year; the hospital could not afford to buy the spare parts. Patna went black at night, as there were no lightbulbs for the street lamps. (According to the writer Arvind Das, who researched the problem in some detail, the city apparently required six thousand bulbs. On one occasion during Diwali, the Hindu festival of light, the administration managed to muster as many as 2,200; but normally only a fraction of that number were available. Occasionally businesses clubbed together to light a single street; otherwise, every day at sunset, Patna, a city of over a million people, was plunged into medieval darkness.)

What was bad in Patna, said Sengupta, was much, much worse in rural areas. Outside the capital, electricity had virtually ceased to be supplied—this despite the fact that Bihari mines produce almost all of India's coal. Without power, industry had been brought to a grinding halt. No roads were being built. There was no functioning system of public transport. In the villages, education had virtually packed up and literacy was rapidly declining: since 1981 the number of adult illiterates had actually risen from thirteen to fifteen million.

There were two principal effects of this breakdown, Sengupta told me. Firstly, those who could—the honest, the rich and the able—had migrated elsewhere. Secondly, those who had stayed had made do. This involved a sort of unofficial wave of privatisation. As the government no longer provided electricity, health care or education, those who could had to provide them for themselves. Middle-class residents in blocks of flats had begun to club together to buy generators. There had been a mushrooming of private coaching institutes and private health clinics.

This privatisation had not been limited just to the towns. In rural areas, the richer villagers had begun to build their own roads to link them to the markets. In the absence of state buses there had even been a revival of the use of palanquins. The four men I had met on the road to Barra on my last visit were brothers, who were returning from carrying a woman to her relatives in a nearby village. They had made their palanquin themselves, they said, and were now bringing in more money from it than they were from their fields.

All this was very admirable, but the situation became more sinister when people took into their own hands the maintenance of law and order. It was the landlords who were the first to recruit armed gangs, initially to deal with discontented labourers. In response, the poor had fought back, organising themselves into amateur guerrilla groups and arming themselves with guns made by local blacksmiths. Great swathes of countryside were now controlled by the private armies of landlords or their rival Maoist militias.

When Delhi newspapers publish articles on Bihar's disorders and atrocities, they tend to make a point of emphasising the state's 'backwardness'. What is needed, they say, is development: more roads, more schools, more family-planning centres. But as the ripples of political and caste violence spread from Patna out into the rest of north India, it seems likely that Bihar could be not so much backward as forward: a trend-setter for the rest of the country. In a very real sense, Bihar may be a kind of Heart of Darkness, pumping violence and corruption, pulse after pulse, out into the rest of the subcontinent. The first ballot-rigging recorded in India took place in Bihar in the 1962 general election. Thirty years later, it is common across the country. The first example of major criminals winning parliamentary seats took place in

Bihar in the 1980 election. Again, it is now quite normal all over India.

So serious and infectious is the Bihar disease that it is now throwing into question the whole notion of an Indian economic miracle. The question is whether the prosperity of the south and west of the country can outweigh the moral decay which is spreading out from Bihar and the east. Few doubt that if the 'Bihar effect'—corruption, lawlessness, marauding caste armies and the breakdown of government— does prevail and overcome the positive forces at work, then, as Uttam Sengupta put it: 'India could make what happened in Yugoslavia look like a picnic.'

Everyone I talked to that week in Patna agreed on one thing: behind much of Bihar's violence lay the running sore of the disintegrating caste system.

One of the worst-affected areas was the country around Barra: the Jehanabad District, to the south of Patna. There, two rival militias were at work: the Savarna Liberation Front, which represented the interests of the high-caste landowning Bhumihars, and the Maoist Communist Centre, which took the part of the lower castes and Untouchables who farmed the Bhumihars' fields. Week after week, the Bhumihars would go 'Harijan hunting', setting off in convoys of jeeps to massacre 'uppity Untouchables', 'to make an example'; in retaliation, the peasants would emerge from the fields at night and silently behead an oppressive landlord or two. The police did little to protect either group.

Similar battles take place across the width of Bihar, and this caste warfare has provided great opportunities for criminals wishing to gain a foothold in Bihar's political arena. Anand Singh Mohan first made his name as the protector of the upper castes against a rival low-caste outlaw-MP, Pappu Yadav. In the same way, Pappu Yadav first gained his seat in Parliament by leading a low-caste guerrilla army against high-caste landlords and attempting a Bihari variant of ethnic cleansing, emptying his constituency of Rajput and Brahmin families. In June 1991, whilst he was engaged in this work, three cases of murder were lodged against him, and he was also booked under the National Security Act for creating a 'civil war situation'. In the current Parliament he remains the MP for the north Bihar district of Purnea.

The closer you look, the more clear it becomes that caste hatred and, increasingly, caste warfare lie at the bottom of most of Bihar's problems. The lower castes, so long oppressed, have now begun to assert themselves, while the higher castes have begun to fight back in an attempt to hold on to their ground. Moreover, job reservations for the lower castes have begun to be fitfully introduced around the country, reawakening an acute awareness of caste at every level of society. The proportion of reserved jobs varies from state to state—from two per cent in Haryana to sixty-five per cent in Tamil Nadu—but all over India a major social revolution is beginning to take place. This is particularly marked in institutions like the Indian Administrative Service, where prior to the introduction of reservations the Brahmins, who make up just five per cent of the population, filled fifty-eight per cent of the jobs.

In the 1960s and 70s most educated Indians believed that caste was beginning to die out. Now it has quite suddenly become the focus of national attention, and arguably the single most important issue in the country's politics.

Later that afternoon when I turned up at the Chief Minister's residence I found Laloo sitting outside, his legs raised on a table. He was surrounded by the now familiar circle of toughs and sycophants. Their appearance reminded me of the incident on the train when the civil servant had been beaten up by one of Laloo's MPs, and I asked him if the press reports had been accurate.

'Why don't you ask the man responsible?' replied Laloo. He waved his hand at one of the MPs sitting to his left. 'This is Mumtaz Ansari.'

Ansari, a slight, moustachioed figure in white pyjamas, giggled.

'It is a fabricated story,' he said, a broad grin on his face. 'A baseless story, the propaganda of my enemies.'

'It was only his party workers who beat the man up,' explained Laloo. 'Ansari had nothing to do with it.'

'So the man *was* beaten up?'

'A few slaps only,' said Ansari. 'The fellow was misbehaving.'

'What action have you taken?' I asked Laloo.

'I told my MPs: "You must not behave like this. A citizen is the owner of the country. We are just servants."'

'That's all you did?'

'I have condemned what happened,' said Laloo, smiling from ear to ear. 'I have condemned Mr Ansari.'

Both Laloo and Ansari burst out laughing. Laloo then finished the cup of tea he was drinking, threw the dregs over his shoulder and dropped the cup on the grass, calling for a turbaned bearer to pick it up. 'Come,' he said, standing up and indicating that I should do the same. 'This was a small incident only. Let me show you my farm.'

Before I could argue, Laloo had taken my arm. He led me around what had once been the neat rose garden of the British Governor's residence. Apart from a small patch of lawn at the back of the house, the whole plot had been ploughed up and turned into a series of fields. In one corner stood Laloo's fishpond and beehives; in another his dairy farm, rabbit hutches, cattle and buffalo sheds. In between were acres of neat furrows planted with chillies, spinach and potatoes. 'This is *sattoo*,' he said. 'Very good for farting.'

'Who eats all this?' I asked.

'I do—along with my wife and family. We villagers like fresh produce. The rest we distribute to the poor.'

While we examined a new threshing machine manned by one of Laloo's cousins, Laloo talked of the Brahmin political establishment.

'The Bharatiya Janata Party and the Congress are both Brahminical parties,' he said. 'The backward castes have no reason to vote for them. Already they have realised this in Bihar. In time they will realise this everywhere. The support of these parties will dry up like a dirty puddle on a summer's day.

'The backward castes will rise up,' he said as he led me back to my car. 'Even now they are waking up and raising their voices. You will see: we will break the power of these people...'

In the darkness of the *porte-cochére*, Laloo was declaiming as if at a public rally: 'We will have a flood of votes,' he said. 'Nobody will be able to check us.'

The driver was itching to be off: it would soon be dark, and he wanted to be back at the hotel before sunset. Even in Patna, he said, it was madness to be on the roads of Bihar after dark.

*Postscript*: Despite many of the key witnesses suffering mysterious fatal 'accidents' before the police could interview them, the Indian Central Bureau of Investigation gradually closed in on Laloo during the spring of 1997, as the full scale of the amount embezzled by his administration in the 'Fodder Scam' became clear: around a thousand crore rupees, a large sum anywhere, but a truly colossal figure by Bihar standards. In May 1997 Laloo was finally arrested, but when pressure on him to step down became insupportable, he pulled off a *putsch* of characteristic audacity: he resigned as Chief Minister of Bihar, only to hand over the reigns of government to his illiterate wife, Rabri Devi. She continues to rule Bihar at the time of writing.

Despite these scandals, in the 1998 general election Laloo's party performed much better than anyone had expected. Indeed, he was one of the few senior Janata Dal figures not to suffer electoral disaster, proving once and for all (if it still needed proving) that the Indian electorate regards all politicians as equally dishonest, and thus remains oddly immune to revelations of misconduct, however damaging. Standing for election while on bail awaiting trial, Laloo was returned to his seat with a reduced but comfortable majority, while his—or rather, technically, his wife's—government returned to power in alliance with the Congress.

During polling, despite the deployment of whole regiments of the Indian Army, violence in Bihar reached spectacular new levels, with mortars and landmines being deployed to assist the ballot-stuffing manoeuvres, prompting the memorable *Statesman* headline 'Many Dead in Bihar: Police Party Blown to Smithereens'. The true scale of the fatalities will probably never be known, but certainly well over fifty died on polling day, including one of the candidates. The accused in the murder, one Brij Behari Prasad, was rewarded with the post of Power Minister in Laloo's government, though there are reports that he has recently 'absconded' in order to avoid arrest.

Meanwhile, the anarchy in Bihar grows worse month by month. This winter, a friend of mine tried driving from Patna to the north Bihari district of Purnea to inspect a series of obscure Mughal monuments. On the first day of his trip, in broad daylight, his car was stopped on a national highway by dacoits armed with an assortment of spears, swords and automatic weapons. My friend was robbed of everything he had with him—money, cameras and baggage. He had, however, anticipated just such an eventuality, and bravely continued on his journey with the dollars he had secreted in his socks. Twenty miles later he was stopped by a second hold-up, and in the ensuing strip-search his dollars, shoes, socks and car were taken too. He was forced to return to Patna barefoot.

# In the Kingdom of Avadh

On the eve of the Great Mutiny of 1857, Lucknow, the capital of the Kingdom of Avadh, was indisputably the largest, most prosperous and most civilised precolonial city in India. Its spectacular skyline—with its domes and towers and gilded cupolas, its palaces and pleasure gardens, ceremonial avenues and wide *maidans*—reminded travellers of Constantinople, Paris or even Venice. The city's courtly Urdu diction and baroque codes of etiquette were renowned as the most subtle and refined in the subcontinent; its dancers admired as the most accomplished; its cuisine famous as the most flamboyantly elaborate. Moreover, at the heart of the city lay Lucknow's decadent and Bacchanalian court. Stories of its seven-hundred-women harems and numberless *nautch* girls came to epitomise the fevered fantasies of whole generations of Orientalists; yet for once the fantasy seems to have been not far removed from the swaggeringly sybaritic reality.

'But look at it now,' said Mushtaq, gesturing sadly over the rooftops. 'See how little is left...'

We were standing on the roof of Mushtaq's school in Aminabad, one of the oldest quarters of the city and the heart of old Lucknow. It was a cold, misty winter's morning, and around us, through the ground mist, rose the great swelling, gilded domes of the city's remaining mosques and *imambaras*. A flight of pigeons wheeled over the domes and came to rest in a grove of tamarind trees to one side; nearby a little boy flew a kite from the top of a small domed Moghul pavilion. It was a spectacular panorama, still one of the greatest skylines in the Islamic world; but even from our vantage point the signs of decay were unmistakable.

'See the grass growing on the domes?' said Mushtaq, pointing at the great triple dome of the magnificent Jama

Masjid. 'It hasn't been whitewashed for thirty years. And at the base: look at the cracks! Today the skills are no longer there to mend these things: the expertise has gone. The Nawabs would import craftsmen from all over India and beyond—artisans from Tashkent and Samarkand, masons from Isfahan and Bukhara. They were paid fantastic sums, but now no one ever thinks to repair these buildings. They are just left to rot. All this has happened in my lifetime.'

A friend in Delhi had given me Mushtaq Naqvi's name when he heard I was planning to visit Lucknow. Mushtaq, he said, was one of the last remnants of old Lucknow: a poet, teacher and writer who knew Lucknow intimately, and who— slightly to everyone's surprise—had chosen never to leave the city of his birth, despite all that had happened to it since Independence. Talking with my Delhi friends, I soon learned that this qualification—'despite all that has happened to Lucknow'—seemed to be suffixed to any statement about the place, as if it were a universally accepted fact that Lucknow's period of greatness lay long in the past.

The city's apogee, everyone agreed, was during the eighteenth century, under the flamboyant Nawabs of Avadh (or Oudh)—a time when, according to one authority, the city resembled an Indian version of '(pre-Revolutionary) Teheran, Monte Carlo and Las Vegas, with just a touch of Glyndebourne for good measure'. Even after the catastrophe of 1857 and the bloody reprisals of the vengeful British, Lucknow had been reborn as one of the great cities of the Raj.

It was Partition in 1947 that finally tore the city apart, its composite Hindu-Muslim culture irretrievably shattered in the unparalleled orgy of bloodletting that everywhere marked the division of India and Pakistan. By the end of the year, Lucknow's cultured Muslim aristocracy had emigrated *en masse* to Pakistan, and the city found itself swamped instead with non-Muslim refugees from the Punjab. These regarded the remaining Muslims with the greatest suspicion—as dangerous fanatics and Pakistani fifth-columnists—and they brought with them their own very different, aggressively commercial culture. What was left of the old Lucknow, with its courtly graces and refinement, went into headlong decline. The roads stopped being sprinkled at sunset, the buildings ceased to receive their annual whitewash, the gardens decayed, and litter and dirt began to pile up unswept on the pavements.

Fifty years later, Lucknow is renowned not so much for its refinement as for the coarseness and corruption of its politicians, and the crass ineptitude of its officials. What was once regarded as the most civilised city in India, a city whose manners and speech made other Indians feel like oafish rustics, is rapidly becoming notorious as one of the most hopelessly backward and violent, with a burgeoning mafia and a notoriously thuggish and corrupt police force.

'You must have seen some sad changes in that skyline,' I said to Mushtaq as we turned to look eastwards over the charmless tower-blocks which dwarfed and blotted out the eighteenth-century panorama in the very centre of the city.

'In thirty years all sense of aesthetics has gone from this town,' he replied. 'Once Lucknow was known as the Garden of India. There were palms and gardens and greenery everywhere. Now so much of it is eaten up by concrete, and the rest has become a slum. See that collapsing building over there?'

Mushtaq pointed to a ruin a short distance away. A few cusped arches and some broken pillars were all that was left of what had clearly once been a rather magnificent structure. But now shanty-huts hemmed it in on three sides, while on the fourth stood a fetid pool. At its edge a cow munched on a pile of chaff.

'It is difficult to imagine now,' said Mushtaq, 'but when I was a boy that was one of the most beautiful *havelis* in Lucknow. At its centre was a magnificent *shish mahal*. The *haveli* covered that whole area where the huts are now, and that pool was the tank in its middle. Begums from all over Aminabad and Hussainabad would go there to swim. There were gardens all around. See that tangle of barbed wire? That used to be an orchard of sweet-smelling orange trees. Can you imagine?'

I looked at the scene again, trying to picture its former glory.

'But the worst of it,' continued Mushtaq, 'is that the external decay of the city is really just a symbol of what is happening inside us: the inner rot.'

'What do you mean?' I asked.

'Under the Nawabs Lucknow experienced a renaissance that represented the last great flowering of Indo-Islamic genius. The Nawabs were profoundly liberal and civilised figures: men like Wajid Ali Shah, author of a hundred books, a great poet and dancer. But the culture of Lucknow was not just limited to the élite: even the prostitutes could quote the great Persian poets; even the tonga-drivers and the tradesmen in the bazaars spoke the most chaste Urdu and were famous across India for their exquisite manners.'

'But today?'

'Today the grave of our greatest poet, Mir, lies under a railway track. What is left of the culture he represented seems hopelessly vulnerable. After Partition nothing could ever be the same again. Those Muslims who left were the second rung. They simply don't have the skills or education to compete with the Punjabis, with their money and business instincts and brightly-lit shops. Everything they have has crumbled so quickly: the owners of palaces and *havelis* have become the *chowkidars*. If you saw any of the old begums today you would barely recognise them. They are shorn of all their glory, and their *havelis* are in a state of neglect. They were never brought up to work—they simply don't know how to do it. As they never planned for the future, many are now in real poverty. In some cases their daughters have been forced into prostitution.'

'Literally?'

'Literally. I'll tell you one incident that will bring tears to your eyes. A young girl I know, eighteen years old, from one of the royal families, was forced to take up this work. A rickshaw driver took her in *chador* to Clarke's Hotel for a rich Punjabi businessman to enjoy for five hundred rupees. This man had been drinking whisky, but when the girl unveiled herself he was so struck by her beauty, by the majesty of her bearing, that he could not touch her. He paid her the money and told her to go.'

Mushtaq shook his head sadly: 'So you see, it's not just the buildings: the human beings of this city are crumbling too. The history of the decline of this city is written on the bodies of its people. Look at the children roaming the streets, turning to crime. Great-grandchildren of the Nawabs are pulling rickshaws. If you go deeply into this matter you would write a book with your tears.'

He pointed at the flat roof of a half-ruined *haveli*: 'See that house over there? When I was a student there was a nobleman who lived there. He was from a minor Nawabi family. He lived alone, but every day he would come to a *chaikhana* and *gupshup*. He was a very proud man, very conscious of his noble birth, and he always wore an old-fashioned *angurkha*. But his properties were all burned down at Partition. He didn't have a job and no one knew how he survived.

'Then one day he didn't turn up at the *chaikhana*. The next day and the day after that there was no sign of him either. Finally on the fourth day the neighbours began to smell a bad smell coming from his house. They broke down the door and found him lying dead on a *charpai*. There was no covering, no other furniture, no books, nothing. He had sold everything he had, except his one set of clothes, but he was too proud to beg, or even to tell anyone of his problem. When they did a postmortem on him in the medical college they found he had died of starvation.

'Come,' said Mushtaq. 'Let us go to the *chowk*: there I will tell you about this city, and what it once was.'

At the height of the Mughal Empire during the early seventeenth century, said Mushtaq, Shah Jahan, the builder of the Taj Mahal, had ruled over a kingdom that stretched from the Hindu Kush in the north almost to the great diamond mines of Golconda in the south. But during the eighteenth century, as the empire fell apart, undermined by civil war and sacked by a succession of invaders from Persia and Afghanistan, India's focus moved inexorably eastwards, from Delhi to Lucknow. There the Nawabs maintained the fiction that they were merely the provincial governors of the

Mughals, while actually holding a degree of real power and wealth immeasurably greater than the succession of feeble late-Mughal monarchs who came and went on the throne of Delhi.

Gradually, as the Mughals' power of patronage grew ever smaller, there was a haemorrhage of poets and writers, architects and miniature-painters from Delhi to Lucknow, as the Nawabs collected around them the greatest minds of the day. They were men such as Mir, probably the greatest of all the Urdu poets, who in 1782, at the age of sixty-six, was forced to flee from his beloved Delhi in an effort to escape the now insupportable violence and instability of the Moghul capital.

The Nawabs were great builders, and in less than fifty years they succeeded in transforming the narrow lanes of a small medieval city into one of the great capitals of the Muslim world: 'Not Rome, not Athens, not Constantinople, not any city I have ever seen appears to me so striking and beautiful as this,' wrote the British war correspondent William Russell in the middle of the Great Mutiny. 'The sun playing on the gilt domes and spires, the exceeding richness of the vegetation and forests and gardens remind one somewhat of the view of the Bois de Boulogne from the hill over St Cloud...but for the thunder of the guns and the noise of the balls cleaving the air, how peaceful the scene would be!'

After six hundred years of Islamic rule in India, what the Nawabs achieved at Lucknow represented the last great swansong of Indo-Islamic civilisation, a final burst of energy and inspiration before the onset of a twentieth century holding little for Indian Muslims except division, despair and inexorable decline.

Since I had arrived in the city I had spent a couple of bright, chilly winter days jolting around the old city on a rickshaw, visiting a little of what was left. The architecture of the Nawabs has sometimes been seen as a decadent departure from the pure lines of the great Moghul golden age, and there is some truth in this: there is nothing in Lucknow, for example, to compare to the chaste perfection of the Taj. Moreover, in the years leading up to the Mutiny some of the buildings erected in Lucknow did indeed sink into a kind of florid, camp voluptuousness which seems to have accurately reflected the mores of a city whoring and dancing its way to extinction. To this day a curtain covers the entrance to the picture gallery in Lucknow, after a prim British memsahib fainted on seeing the flirtatiously bared nipple of the last Nawab, Wajid Ali Shah, prominently displayed in a portrait of the period. The same feeling of overripe decadence is conveyed in late-Nawabi poetry, which is some of the most unblushingly fleshy and sensual ever written by Muslim poets:

> I am a lover of breasts
> Like pomegranates;
> Plant then no other trees
> On my grave but these.

> *Nasikh*

Confronted with such verses, Mir expressed his view that most Lucknavi poets could not write verse, and would be better advised to 'stick to kissing and slavering'.

He may well have thought the same of late-Nawabi architecture, with its similarly unrestrained piling on of effects. For by the end Lucknow's builders had developed a uniquely blowsy Avadhi rococo whose forms and decorative strategies seem to have borrowed more from the ballrooms and fairgrounds of Europe than from the austere shrines and fortresses of Babur and Timur the Lame. There was no question of sobriety or restraint: even in monuments built to house the dead, every inch of the interior was covered with a jungle of brightly coloured plasterwork intertwining promiscuously with gaudy curlicues of feathery stucco.

Nevertheless, the best of the buildings in Lucknow— those that date from the late eighteenth century—are evidence of a remarkable silver age which in sheer exuberance has no equal in India. The Great Imambara complex was constructed by Asaf ud-Daula for Shiite religious discourses in 1784. One of the largest vaulted halls in the world, it was built in order to create employment during a famine. Here there is none of the camp doodling that would be seen on later Nawabi buildings. Instead the Imambara is a vast and thoroughly monumental building: long, echoing arcades of cusped arches rise to great gilded onion-domes and rippling lines of pepperpot semidomes; at the corners soaring minarets culminate in solid, well-designed *chattries*. The whole composition surrounded by the Great Mosque and the Rumi Darwaza exudes a bold, reckless and extravagant self-confidence. Lucknow was consciously aiming to surpass the glories of late-Mughal Delhi, and the Great Imambara shows it could do so with dashing panache.

Driving today through the melancholic streets of modern Lucknow, the massive buildings dating from the days of the Nawabs rear out of the surrounding anarchy like monuments from some lost civilisation, seemingly as disconnected from the present as the pyramids are from modern Egypt. At times it seems almost impossible to believe that they date from less than two hundred years ago, and that at that period Lucknow was famed as one of the richest kingdoms in Asia. For today the city is as shabby and impoverished as anywhere in India. Waves of squabbling cycle-rickshaw drivers pass down the potholed roads, bumping in and out of the puddles. Rubbish lies uncollected by the roadside, with dogs competing with rats to snuffle in the piles of garbage. Beside them, lines of desperate street-vendors squat on dirty rush-mats, displaying their tawdry collections of cheap plastic keyrings and fake Rolex watches. There is no grass in the parks and no flowers in the beds; barbed wire hangs limply around what were once beautiful Mughal gardens alive with the sound of parakeets and peacocks. Above the crumbling ruins of the old city of the Nawabs rise the monsoon-stained tower-blocks erected since Independence, and now, like the ruins, showing signs of imminent collapse, with deep fissures running up their sides.

The contrast between the magnificent follies of the Nawabs and the decayed, impoverished postcolonial intrusions which stand among them is almost unbearably painful: everywhere, it seems, there has been a universal drop in standards and expectations.

Yet even as the greatest buildings of Nawabi Lucknow were being erected, the Kingdom of Avadh was acutely conscious that it was living on borrowed time. In 1764, before the Nawabs had even established their capital at Lucknow, their armies had already been defeated in battle by the East India Company, and over the course of the early nineteenth century the Company ate like a cancer into the territories of Avadh: in less than fifty years the British annexed more than half the kingdom. But the Nawabs remained surprisingly well disposed towards Europeans, and delighted in the trinkets and amusements Westerners could provide for their court: European jugglers, portrait painters, watch menders, piano tuners and even fashionable London barbers were all welcomed to Lucknow, and were well paid for their services.

If the Nawab sometimes amazed foreign visitors by appearing dressed as a British admiral, or even as a clergyman of the Church of England, the Europeans of Lucknow often returned the compliment. Miniature after miniature from late-eighteenth-century Lucknow shows Europeans of the period dressed in long white Avadhi gowns, lying back on carpets, hubble-bubbles in their mouths, as they watch their *nautch* girls dance before them. Even those who never gave up European dress seem to have taken on the mores of Nawabi society: Major General Claude Martin, for example, kept a harem which included his favourite wife Boulone as well as her three sisters. Nor was this sexual curiosity one-way: at least two British memsahibs were recruited to join the royal Avadhi harem, and a mosque survives which was built by the Nawab for one of them, a Miss Walters.

Much of the surviving architecture of the city reflects this unique moment of Indo-European intermingling. Constantia, Claude Martin's great palace-mausoleum, now the La Martiniere school, is perhaps the most gloriously hybrid building in India, part Nawabi fantasy and part Gothic colonial barracks. Just as Martin himself combined the lifestyle of a Muslim prince with the interests of a renaissance man— writing Persian couplets and maintaining an observatory, experimenting with map-making and botany, hot-air balloons and even bladder surgery—so his mausoleum mixes Georgian colonnades with the loopholes and turrets of a medieval castle; Palladian arcades rise to Mughal cupolas; inside, brightly-coloured Nawabi plasterwork encloses Wedgwood plaques of classical European gods and goddesses.

For while Martin designed Constantia to be the most magnificent European funerary monument in India, the East India Company's answer to the Taj Mahal, it was also intended to be defensible. The eighteenth century was an anarchic and violent time in India, and during an uprising in the 1770s Martin had to defend his residence with a pair of cannon filled with grapeshot. It was a lesson he never forgot, and he built Constantia to be his last redoubt in case of danger. Lines of cannon crowned the façade, and thick iron doors sealed off the narrow spiral staircases which connected the various 'bomb-proof' floors. On the façade Martin erected two colossal East India Company lions which were designed to hold flaming torches in their mouths. The sight of these illuminated beasts belching out fire and smoke on a dank night was intended to terrify would-be intruders.

In its willful extravagance and sheer strangeness, Constantia embodies like no other building the opulence, restlessness and open-mindedness of the city on the faultline between East and West, the old world of the Nawabs and the new world of the Raj. To this day the whole extraordinary creation stands quite intact, still enclosed in acres of its own parkland. As you approach on your rickshaw you proceed along a superb avenue of poplar and tamarind, eucalyptus and casuarina, at the end of which you pass the perfect domed Mughal tomb which Martin built for his beloved Boulone. As he rather touchingly wrote in his will: 'She choosed never to quit me. She persisted that she would live with me, and since we lived together we never had a word of bad humour one against another.'

Not far from Constantia, a short rickshaw ride over the railway crossing, I stumbled across a smaller but equally remarkable building from the same period. It turned out to be the ruins of one of the Nawabs' most lovely pleasure palaces, named Dilkusha, or Heart's Delight. Yet despite this very Persian name, Dilkusha was in fact closely modelled on one of the great English country houses, Seaton Delaval in

Northumberland—but with four gloriously ornate octagonal minarets added to the otherwise austere Palladian design.

The whole period was an extraordinary moment of Indo-European fusion—a moment pregnant with unfulfilled possibilities, and one which is often forgotten in the light of Lucknow's subsequent history. For this process of mutual enrichment did not last. As the nineteenth century progressed, the British became more and more demanding in their exactions on the Nawabs, and more and more assured of their own superiority. They learned to scoff at the buildings and traditions of Lucknow, and became increasingly convinced that they had nothing to learn from 'native' culture. Relations between the Nawabs and the British gradually became chilly: it was as if the high-spirited tolerance of courtly Lucknow was a direct challenge to the increasingly self-righteous spirit of evangelical Calcutta. In 1857, a year after the British forcibly deposed the last Nawab, Lucknow struck back, besieging the British in their fortified residency.

In the event, after nearly two years of siege and desperate hand-to-hand fighting in the streets of Lucknow, the British defeated the Mutineers and wreaked their revenge on the conquered city. Vast areas of the capital of the Nawabs were bulldozed, and for half a century the administration of the region moved to Allahabad. Every site connected to the Mutiny was lovingly preserved by the British—the pockmarked ruins of the besieged residency, the tombs of the fallen British leaders, every point in the town where the relieving forces were ambushed or driven back—turning much of Lucknow into a vast, open-air Imperial war memorial, thickly littered with a carapace of cemeteries and spiked cannons, obelisks and rolls of honour. But shorn of its court and administrative status, preserved only for the curiosity of British visitors, Lucknow gradually turned into the melancholic backwater it is today.

'Yet even in my childhood something of Lucknow's old graces survived,' said Mushtaq. 'I'll show you what I mean.'

We walked together through the *chowk*, the narrow, latticed bazaar-labyrinth which was once the centre of Lucknow's cultural life. Above us, elaborately carved wooden balconies backed on to latticed windows. Figures flitted behind the wooden grilles. Every so often we would pass the arched and pedimented gateway of a grand *haveli*: the gateway still stood magnificently, but as often as not the old mansion to which it led had been turned into a godown or warehouse. A bird's nest of electricity wires was strung down the side of the *chowk*, often brutally punched through the walls and arcades of the old mansions.

Below the latticed living quarters was a wonderful collection of tiny, boxlike shops, all arranged in groups by trade: a row of stores selling home-made fireworks would be followed by another row piled high with mountains of guavas or marigold garlands; a group of ear-cleaners—whose lives revolved around the patient removal of wax from their customers' inner ears—would be followed by a confraternity of silver-beaters who made their living from hammering silver into sheets so fine they could be applied to sticky Lucknavi sweets.

'When I was a boy, before Partition, I came here with my brother,' said Mushtaq. 'In those days the *chowk* was still full of perfume from the scent shops. They had different scents for different seasons: *khas* for the hot season, *bela* for the monsoon and *henna* for the cold. Everywhere there were stalls full of flowers: people brought them in from gardens and the countryside roundabout. The bazaar was famous for having the best food, the best kebabs and the best women in north India.'

'The best women?' Looking around now, all I could see was the occasional black beehive flitting past in full *chador*.

'Ah,' said Mushtaq. 'You see, in those days the last courtesans were still here.'

'Prostitutes?'

'Not prostitutes in the Western sense, although they could fulfil that function.'

'So what was it that distinguished them from prostitutes?' I asked.

'In many ways the courtesans were the guardians of the culture,' replied Mushtaq. 'Apart from anything else they preserved the traditions of Indian classical music for centuries. They were known as *tawwaif*, and they were the incarnation of good manners. The young men would be sent to them to learn how to behave and deport themselves: how to roll or accept a *paan*, how to say thank you, how to *salaam*, how to stand up, how to leave a room—as well as the facts of life.

'On the terraces of upper-storey chambers of the *tawwaif*, the young men would come to recite their verses and *ghazals*. Water would be sprinkled on the ground to cool it, then carpets would be laid out and covered with white sheets. Hookahs and candles would be arranged around the guests, along with *surahis*, fresh from the potters, exuding the monsoon scent of rain falling on parched earth. Only then would the recitations begin. In those days anyone who even remotely aspired to being called cultured had to take a teacher and learn how to compose poetry.'

We pulled ourselves on to the steps of a kebab shop to make way for a herd of water-buffaloes which were being driven down the narrow alley to the market at the far end. From inside came the delicious smell of grilled meat and spices.

'Most of all the *tawwaif* would teach young men how to speak perfect Urdu. You see, in Lucknow language was not just a tool of communication: it was a projection of the culture—very florid and subtle. But now the language has changed. Compared to Urdu, Punjabi is a very coarse language: when you listen to two Punjabis talking it sounds as if they are fighting. But because of the number of Punjabis who have come to live here, the old refined Urdu of Lucknow is now hardly spoken. Few are left who can understand it— fewer still who speak it.'

'Did you ever meet one of these *tawwaif*?'

'Yes,' said Mushtaq. 'My brother used to keep a mistress here in the *chowk*, and on one occasion he brought me along too. I'll never forget her: although she was a poor woman, she was very beautiful—full of grace and good manners. She was wearing her full make-up and was covered in jewellery which sparkled in the light of the oil lamps. She looked like a princess to me—but I was hardly twelve, and by the time

I was old enough to possess a *tawwaif* myself, they had gone. That whole culture with its poetic *mehfils* and *mushairas* went with them.'

'So is there nothing left?' I asked. 'Is there no one who can still recite the great Lucknavi poets? Anyone who remembers the old stories?'

'Well, there is one man,' said Mushtaq. 'You should talk to Suleiman, the Rajah of Mahmudabad. He is a remarkable man.'

The longer I lingered in Lucknow, the more I heard about Suleiman Mahmudabad. Whenever I raised the subject of survivors from the old world of courtly Lucknow, his name always cropped up sooner or later in the conversation. People in Lucknow were clearly proud of him, and regarded him as a sort of repository of whatever wisdom and culture had been salvaged from the wreck of their city.

I finally met the man a week later at the house of a Lucknavi friend. Farid Faridi's guests were gathered around a small sitting room sipping imported whisky and worrying about the latest enormities committed by Lucknow's politicians. A month before, in front of Doordarshan television cameras, the MLAs in the State Assembly had attacked each other in the debating chamber with microphone stands, desks and broken bottles. There were heavy casualties, particularly among the BJP politicians who had come to the Assembly building marginally less well-armed than their rivals: around thirty had ended up in hospital with severe injuries, and there was now much talk about possible revenge attacks.

'Power has passed from the educated to the illiterate,' said one guest. 'Our last Chief Minister was a village wrestling champion. Can you imagine?'

'All our politicians are thugs and criminals now,' said my neighbour. 'The police are so supine and spineless they do nothing to stop them taking over the state.'

'We feel so helpless in this situation,' said Faridi. 'The world we knew is collapsing, and there is nothing we can do.'

'All we can do is to sit in our drawing rooms and watch these criminals plunder our country,' said my neighbour.

'The police used to chase them,' said the first guest. 'But now they spend their time guarding them.'

Mahmudabad arrived late, but was greeted with great deference by our host, who addressed him throughout as 'Rajah Sahib'. He was a slight man, beautifully turned out in traditional Awadhi evening dress of a long silk sherwani over a pair of tight white cotton pyjamas. I had already been told much about his achievements—how he was as fluent in Urdu, Arabic and Persian as he was in French and English, how he had studied postgraduate astrophysics at Cambridge, how he had been a successful Congress MLA under Rajiv Gandhi—but nothing prepared me for the anxious, fidgety polymath who effortlessly dominated the conversation from the moment he stepped into the room.

Towards midnight, as he was leaving, Mahmudabad asked whether I was busy the following day. If not, he said, I was welcome to accompany him to the *qila*, his ancestral fort in the country outside Lucknow. He would be leaving at eleven a.m.; if I could get to him by then I could come along and keep him company on the journey.

Suleiman's Lucknow *pied à terre*, I discovered the following morning, turned out to be the one surviving wing of the Kaiserbagh, the last great palace of the Nawabs. Before its partial destruction during the Mutiny, the Kaiserbagh had been larger than the Tuileries and the Louvre combined; but what remained more closely resembled some crumbling Sicilian *palazzo*, all flaking yellow plasterwork and benign baroque neglect. An ancient wheelless Austin 8 rusted in the palace's *porte-cochère*, beside which squatted a group of elderly retainers, all dressed in matching white homespun.

Suleiman was in his study, attending to a group of petitioners who had come to ask favours. It was an hour before he could free himself and call for the driver to come round with the car. Soon we had left the straggling outskirts of Lucknow behind us and were heading on a raised embankment through long, straight avenues of poplars. On either side spread yellow fields of mustard, broken only by clumps of palm and the occasional pool full of leathery water-buffaloes. As we drove Suleiman talked about his childhood, much of which, it emerged, had been spent in exile in the Middle East.

'My father,' he said, 'was a great friend of Jinnah and an early supporter of his Muslim League. In fact he provided so much of the finance that he was made the treasurer. But despite his admiration for Jinnah he never really seemed to understand what Partition would entail. The day before the division, in the midst of the bloodshed, he quietly left the country and set off via Iran for Kerbala (the Shias' holiest shrine) in Iraq. From there we went to Beirut. It was ten years before he took up Pakistani citizenship, and even then he spent most of his time in London.'

'Did he regret helping Jinnah?'

'He was too proud to admit it,' said Suleiman, 'but I think yes. Certainly he was profoundly saddened by the bitterness of Partition and the part he had played in bringing it about. After that he never settled down or returned home. I think he realised how many people he had caused to lose their homes, and he chose to wander the face of the earth as a kind of self-imposed penance.'

Mahmudabad lay only thirty miles outside Lucknow, but so bad were the roads that the journey took over two hours. Eventually a pair of minarets reared out of the trees—a replica of the mosque at Kerbala built by Suleiman's father—and beyond them, looking on to a small lake, towered the walls of the *qila* of Mahmudabad.

It was a vast structure, built in the same Lucknavi Indo-Palladian style I had seen at La Martiniere and Dilkusha. The outer wall was broken by a ceremonial gateway or *naggar khana* (drum house), on which was emblazoned the fish symbol of the Kingdom of Avadh. Beyond rose the ramparts of a medieval fort on to which had been tucked an eighteenth-century classical bow front; above, a series of balconies were surmounted by a ripple of Moghul *chattries* and cupolas.

It was magnificent; yet the same neglect which had embraced so many of the buildings of Lucknow had taken hold of the Mahmudabad *qila*. The grass had died on the lawn in front of the gateway, and the remaining flowers in the beds were twisted and desiccated; bushes sprouted from the fort's roof. In previous generations the chamber at the top of the *naggar khana* would have been full of musicians announcing the arrival of the Rajah with kettle drums and shenai. It was empty now, of course, but there was certainly no shortage of servants to fill it. As we drove into the *qila's* courtyard a crowd of between twenty and thirty retainers was massed to greet the Rajah, all frantically bowing and *salaaming*; as Suleiman got out of the car the foremost ones dived to touch his feet.

I followed him into the *qila* and up through the dark halls and narrow staircases of the fort; the troop of servants followed behind me. Dust lay thick underfoot, as if the *qila* was some lost castle in a forest in a child's fairy tale. We passed through a splintered door into an old ballroom, empty, echoing and spacious. Once its floor had been sprung, but now many of the planks were missing, and others were littered with pieces of plaster fallen from the ceiling. A torn family portrait of some bejewelled Rajah hung half in, half out of its frame. It looked as if no one had entered the room for at least a decade.

Suleiman threw back a door and led the way into what had once been the library. Cobwebs hung like sheets from the walls; the chintz was literally peeling off the armchairs. Books were everywhere, great piles of 1920s hardbacks, but you had to wipe them with a handkerchief to read their spines and to uncover lines of classics—*The Annals of Tacitus*, *The Works of Aristotle*—nestling next to such long-forgotten titles as *The Competition Wallah* and *The Races of the North-West Provinces of India*.

'This library was my ancestors' window on the world,' said Suleiman. 'But, like everything, it's fast decaying, as you can see.'

I looked around. There were no carpets on the floors, which, uncovered, had become stained and dirty. Above there were holes in the ceiling, with the wooden beams showing through the broken plaster like bones sticking out of wounded flesh. Suleiman was at the window now, pressing the shutters to try to open them; pushing too hard, he nearly succeeded in dislodging the whole window frame. Eventually the shutter gave way and hung open, precariously attached to the frame by its one remaining hinge.

A servant padded in and Suleiman ordered some cold drinks, asking when lunch would be ready. The servant looked flustered. It became apparent that the message had not reached them from Lucknow that we would be expecting lunch; probably the telephone lines were not working that day.

'It wasn't always like this,' said Suleiman, slumping down in one of the mothreaten armchairs underneath a single naked lightbulb. 'When the 1965 Indo-Pakistani war broke out, the *qila* was seized by the government as enemy property. My father had finally made the decision to take Pakistani citizenship in 1957, and although he had never really lived there, it was enough. Everything was locked up and the gates were sealed. My mother—who had never taken Pakistani citizenship—lived on the verandah for three or four months before the government agreed to allow her to have a room to sleep in. Even then it was two years before she was allowed access to a bathroom. She endured it all with great dignity. Until her death she carried on as if nothing had happened'.

At this point the bearer reappeared and announced that no cold drinks were available. Suleiman frowned and dismissed him, asking him to bring some water and to hurry up with the lunch.

'What was I saying?' he asked, distracted by the domestic chaos.

'About the sealing off of the palace.'

'Ah, yes. The Indian Armed Constabulary lived here for two years. It wasn't just neglect: the place was looted. There were two major thefts of silver—they said ten tons in all...'

'Ten tons? Of silver?'

'That's what they say,' replied Suleiman dreamily. He looked at his watch. It was nearly three o'clock and his absent lunch was clearly on his mind. 'Ten tons...though it's probably exaggerated. Certainly everything valuable was taken: even the chairs were stripped off their silver backing.'

'Were the guards in league with the robbers?'

'The case is still going on. It's directed against some poor character who got caught: no doubt one of the minnows who had no one to protect him.'

Suleiman walked over to the window and shouted some instructions in Urdu down to the servants in the courtyard below.

'I've asked them to bring some bottled water. I can't drink the water here. My stomach—you've no idea the hell I've been through with it, the pain. I have to keep taking these terrible antibiotics. I've been to specialists, but they can't do anything.'

Shortly afterwards the bearer reappeared. There was no bottled water, he said. And no, Rajah Sahib, the *khana* was not yet ready. He shuffled out backwards, mumbling apologies.

'What are these servants doing?' said Suleiman. 'They can't treat us like this.'

He began to pace backwards and forwards through the ruination of his palace, stepping over the chunks of plaster on the floor.

'I get terrible bouts of gloom whenever I come here,' he said. 'It makes me feel so tired—exhausted *internally*.'

He paused, trying to find the right words: 'There is...so much that is about to collapse: it's like trying to keep a dike from bursting. Partly it's because I don't live here enough...But it preys on my mind wherever I am. I feel overwhelmed at even the thought of this place.'

He paused again, raising his hands in a gesture of helplessness: 'I simply can't see any light at the end of *any* of the various tunnels. Each year I feel that it is less and less worth struggling for. Sometimes the urge just to escape becomes insupportable—just to leave it all behind, to take a donkey and some books and disappear.'

'Come,' he said, suddenly taking my arm. 'I can't breathe. There's no air in this room...'

The Rajah led me up flight after flight of dark, narrow staircases until we reached the flat roof at the top of the fort. From beyond the moat, out over the plains, smoke was rising from the early-evening cooking fires, forming a flat layer at the level of the treetops. To me it was a beautiful, peaceful Indian winter evening of the sort I had grown to love, but

Suleiman seemed to see in it a vision of impending disaster. He was still tense and agitated, and the view did nothing to calm him down.

'You see,' he explained, 'it's not just the *qila* that depresses me. It's what is happening to the people. There was so much that could have been done after Independence, when they abolished the holdings of the *zamindars* who were strangling the countryside. But all that happened was the rise of these criminal politicians: they filled the vacuum and they are the role models today. Worse still, theirs are the values—if you can call them values—to which people look up: corruption, deception, duplicity, and crude, crass materialism. These are seen to be the avenues to success.

'The world that I knew has been completely corrupted and destroyed. I go into fits of depression when I see the filth and dirt of modern Lucknow and remember the flowers and trees of my youth. Even out here the rot has set in. Look at that monstrosity!'

Suleiman pointed to a thick spire of smoke rising from a sugar factory some distance away across the fields.

'Soft powder falls on the village all day from the pollution from that factory. It was erected illegally and in no other country would such a pollutant be tolerated. I spoke to the manager and he assured me action was imminent, but of course nothing ever happens.'

'Perhaps if you went back into politics you could have it closed down?' I suggested.

'Never again,' said Suleiman. 'After two terms in the Legislative Assembly I came on record saying I would leave the Congress Party if it continued to patronise criminals. The new breed of Indian politician has no ideas and no principles. In most cases they are just common criminals, in it for what they can plunder. Before he died I went and saw Rajiv and told him what was happening. He was interested but he didn't do anything. He was a good man, but weak, unsure of himself. He did nothing to stop the rot.'

'Do you really think things are that bad?' I asked

'There has been a decline in education, in health, in sanitation. There is a general air of misery and suffering in the air. It's got much, much worse in the last fifteen years.

Last week, a few miles outside Lucknow, robbers stopped the traffic and began robbing passers-by in broad daylight. Later, it turned out that the bandits were policemen.

'When I first joined the Legislative Assembly I was elected with an unprecedented majority. Perhaps you are right: perhaps I should have stayed in politics. But what I saw just horrified me. These people...In their desire to get a majority, the rules are bent, the laws broken, institutions are destroyed. The effects are there for anyone to see. You saw the roads: they're intolerable. Twenty years ago the journey here used to take an hour; now it takes twice that. Electricity is now virtually nonexistent, or at best very erratic. There is no health care, no education, nothing. Fifty years after Independence there are still villages around here which have no drinking water. And now there are these hold-ups on the road. Because they are up to their neck in it, the police and the politicians turn a blind eye.'

'But isn't that all the more reason for you to stay in politics?' I said. 'If all the people with integrity were to resign, then of course the criminals will take over.'

'Today it is impossible to have integrity or honesty and to stay in politics in India,' replied Suleiman. 'The process you have to go through is so ugly, so awful, it cannot leave you untouched. Its nature is such that it corrodes, that it eats up all that is most precious and vital in the spirit. It acts like acid on one's integrity and sincerity. You quickly find yourself doing something totally immoral, and you ask yourself: "What next?" '

We fell silent for a few minutes, watching the sun setting over the sugar mill. Behind us, the bearer reappeared to announce that the Rajah's *dal* and rice was finally ready. It was now nearly five o'clock.

'In some places in India perhaps you can still achieve some good through politics,' said Suleiman. 'But in Lucknow it's like a black hole. One has an awful feeling that the forces of darkness are going to win here. It gets worse by the year, the month, the week. The criminals feel they can act with impunity: if they're not actually Members of the Legislative Assembly themselves, they'll certainly have political connections. As long as they split ten per cent of their takings between the local MLA and the police, they can get on and plunder the country without trouble.

'Everything is beginning to disintegrate,' said Suleiman, still looking down over the parapet. 'Everything.'

He gestured out towards the darkening fields below. Night was drawing in now, and a cold wind was blowing in from the plains. 'The entire economic and social structure of this area is collapsing,' he said. 'It's like the end of the Moghul Empire. We're regressing into a dark age.'

# Warrior Queen: The Rajmata of Gwalior

GWALIOR, MADHYA PRADESH, 1993

The Inspector General of Police had thick tufts of black hair growing out of his earlobes; his sunglasses glinted in the bright winter sunlight. He looked out over the dusty airstrip towards the heavily armed guards lining the perimeter fence. Facing them, at the end of the strip, a group of local dignitaries sat waiting in the shade of a tarpaulin. The IG looked up into the sky, down at his watch, and then felt at his hips for the reassuring hilt of his carbine.

'So,' I said. 'You're expecting trouble?'

'Trouble?' he replied. 'What is trouble?'

'Protests? Demonstrations? Riots?'

'Antisocial elements are there,' said the IG, patting his carbine again. 'But we can deal with them.'

Suddenly the dignitaries rose from their chairs; from the sky came the faint buzz of a distant plane. The small jet circled lower and lower then came into land, throwing up clouds of dust in its wake. After a pause, the door opened and the guards stiffened to attention.

From the dark aperture on the side of the plane emerged the figure everyone had been waiting for. It was no peak-capped general or briefcase-carrying government minister. Instead, an old, grey-haired woman tottered down the steps of the private jet, clutching a small white handbag. She wore a white sari, and as she emerged into the sunlight she covered her head with a thin muslin veil. Waiting for her at the bottom of the steps was a thickset figure in a leather jacket and rollneck pullover. He was bald and slightly sinister-looking: not dissimilar to Blofeld in *Goldfinger*.

As the woman stepped off the bottom rung, the assembled reception committee ran up and threw themselves to the ground, competing with each other to be the first to touch her feet. The woman acknowledged the scrabbling dignitaries with a slight nod of the head, then handed her bag to Blofeld and walked on towards the waiting limousine. A liveried bearer slammed the door. Blofeld got in the other side, and the chauffeur drove off.

Behind the car followed a convoy of open-topped police jeeps. Each was filled with paramilitary troops armed with assault rifles and submachine-guns. With a screeching of tyres, the convoy passed through the gates of the airstrip and disappeared past the bullock carts and bicycle rickshaws into the dusty heat-haze of the Indian evening.

If you ask people in India what they think of Rajmata Vijayaraje Scindia—the Dowager Maharani of Gwalior, Vice-President of the World Hindu Council and doyenne of India's growing army of militant Hindu revivalists—you will get many different replies. All of them will, however, be forceful. Like Lady Thatcher— whose unshakeable convictions and sense of destiny she shares— the Rajmata provokes the strongest of responses.

In her time the Rajmata has been called a madwoman and a saint; a dangerous reactionary and a national saviour; a stubborn and self-righteous old lunatic and a brave and resilient visionary. At the age of seventy-nine she is still an enigma. Though her father was born to an ordinary smallholding family in an anonymous Indian village, she managed to win the hand of one of the subcontinent's premier Maharajahs, and for many years ruled with him over an area the size of Portugal. Her vast baroque palace contained— among other treasures—the second-largest chandelier in the world; but her kingdom was dissolved at independence in 1947, and by the mid-Seventies her politics led to her spending months in a filthy Indian prison, sharing a cell with prostitutes, gangsters and murderers.

The Rajmata is very religious, and spends at least two hours every day deep in prayer. Few, even among her enemies, would deny that she is one of the most remarkable politicians in India, and for nearly fifty years she has ceaselessly fought and suffered for what she believes in: the toppling of the increasingly corrupt and power-hungry Congress Party and its replacement by the right-wing Hindu nationalist Bharatiya Janata Party.

Yet it is far from impossible that the political revolution the Rajmata hopes to effect could in the long term change India from a tolerant secular democracy to some sort of ultra-nationalist Hindu state. Moreover, if she succeeds in her aims, India's largest minority—its 150 million Muslims—will effectively find themselves second-class citizens in their own country. Although the Rajmata may personally be a good and even a holy woman, many aspects of her party's agenda remain deeply troubling.

For the BJP is not like other Indian political parties, in that it was founded as the political arm of a neofascist paramilitary organisation, the secretive Rashtriya Swayamsewak Sangh (Association of National Volunteers, or RSS). To this day most senior BJP figures have RSS backgrounds, and several hold posts in both organisations. The RSS and the BJP both believe, as the centrepiece of their ideology, that India is in essence a Hindu nation, and that the minorities, especially the Muslims, may live there only if they acknowledge this.

Like the Phalange in Lebanon, the RSS was founded in direct imitation of 1930s European fascist movements; and like its models it still makes much of daily parading in khaki drill. The RSS views this as an essential element in the creation of a corps of dedicated and disciplined paramilitary followers who, so the theory goes, will form the basis of a revival of some long-lost golden age of national strength and purity.

It is easy to laugh at the RSS as they line up every morning in shabby *mofussil* towns across northern India to drill with their Boy Scout shorts and bamboo swagger-sticks, but their founding philosophy is anything but comical. Madhav Gowalkar, the early RSS leader still known simply as 'the Guru', took direct inspiration from Hitler's treatment of Germany's religious minorities: 'To keep up the purity of the nation and its culture, Germany shocked the world by the purging of its Semitic race, the Jews,' Gowalkar wrote admiringly in *We, or Our Nationhood Defined*. 'National pride in its highest has been manifested there. Germany has also shown how well-nigh impossible it is for races and cultures having differences going to the root to be assimilated... The non-Hindu people in Hindustan must learn...to revere the Hindu religion, must entertain no idea but the glorification of the Hindu nation, claiming nothing, deserving nothing.'

During Partition, the RSS was responsible for many of the most horrifying atrocities against India's Muslims, and it was a former RSS member, Nathuram Godse, who assassinated Mahatma Gandhi in 1948, for 'pandering to the minorities'. Today, both the RSS and the BJP have moved a long way since the time when they were little more than a vehicle for an extreme form of neo-fascist Hindu fundamentalism, and the BJP in particular now embraces a wide spectrum of conservative and nationalist opinion. Moreover, the rise of the BJP has taken place, at least partly, due to Indian Muslims' increasing distrust of the Congress, which despite claiming to be a secular party has, since the 1980s, done less and less to protect India's minorities.

Nevertheless, the BJP and its Hindu nationalist allies have been consistently implicated across northern India in the almost monthly anti-Muslim pogroms which are becoming such a defining feature of India at the close of the twentieth century. However respectable its leaders have become, and however inured the Indian élite have become to its message, when communal riots break out the local cadres of the RSS and the BJP are rarely far away. Indeed, as the Rajmata's BJP gathers momentum, and its ideology grows in popularity and respectability, India has seen communal conflict assume a scale and significance not witnessed since the massacres of Partition half a century ago.

Yet for all this, to meet the Rajmata, and to sit listening to her over breakfast, you would never guess she could be capable of anything more sinister than winning an award for Most Loveable Granny at an English village fete.

'Please, Mr William,' she said, 'you must have one more guava. This is the height of the season.'

'I mustn't. I've got to watch my weight.'

'When I was a girl I always thought it better to have a little extra round the middle. In those days we thought it a sign of good health.'

'No. Really. Thank you.'

'Never mind. I'll keep it for you for tea.'

She clapped her hand, and the small green piece of fruit was carried away on an escutcheoned plate by a liveried bearer.

The Rajmata was sitting at the top of the table in the grand dining room of the Jai Vilas Palace in Gwalior. As she nibbled at pieces of fruit from the huge crystal bowl in front of her, she chatted happily about the progress of her day. Although it was only eight o'clock in the morning, the old lady had already been up for two and a half hours performing her lengthy morning *puja*.

'Everyone gets very angry,' she said, 'because before I do *anything* in the morning I must spend at least two hours bathing my little Krishna, putting on his clothes and decorating him with garlands. I do it just the particular way he likes it.'

'Really?'

'Oh yes.'

'You have a...close relationship with Krishna?' I asked.

'I can't really describe what it's like,' said the Rajmata. 'I mean, I really shouldn't: it's so personal. It's...it's like two lovers: you can't say to them, "Describe how you behave when you are together."'

Sitting silently beside me, still in his leather jacket, was Sardar Angre, the Blofeld-figure I had seen the day before at the airport. He kept out of the conversation about the Rajmata's *puja*, and for its duration appeared absorbed in his omelette.

When the Rajmata's husband died in July 1961 and the Dowager Maharani became estranged from her son Madhav

Rao Scindia, the new Maharajah, Sardar Angre stepped into the breach and began acting as her constant companion and adviser. A nobleman whose family has served the Gwalior Maharajahs since the eighteenth century, the Sardar holds the Rajmata in an awe and respect which has not dimmed with time. She in turn looks to him for advice and guidance. They make a good team: he is as dry, sober and practical as she is mystical and quixotic.

As the conversation at the breakfast table turned, inevitably, to politics, the Rajmata commented that the recent dramatic rise in the popularity of the BJP seemed to be almost supernaturally guided.

'Really,' she said, 'it is nothing short of a miracle.'

'No, no, Highness,' said Sardar Angre in his measured tone. 'It is the will of the people.'

'This is your view,' said the Rajmata firmly. 'But I see the hand of God. I believe it is the doing of Hanuman.'

'You really think the BJP is somehow...divinely propelled?' I asked.

'I have a feeling so,' said the Rajmata, turning to me with an excited conspiratorial whisper. 'Miracles can happen even these days.'

Seeing me scribble the Rajmata's comments into my pocket notebook, Sardar Angre sensed danger, and whispered sharply to the Rajmata in Hindi: 'The modern world does not believe in miracles.'

'You are wrong, Sardar,' said the Rajmata, holding her ground. 'Only yesterday I was reading in the Reader's Digest about a great miracle in America: some invalids being healed— I can't remember the details. But if these people are believing...'

Sardar Angre frowned.

'If you are on the right path,' persisted the Rajmata, 'truth will always prevail. My Hanuman is always on the side of truth. I have taken His protection, and Hanuman will always sort out our problems. He will remove all obstacles from our path.'

Seeing the Sardar's expression, I said: 'I don't think Sardar Angre likes you to talk about religion.'

'No, no—you are quite wrong,' said the Rajmata. 'He also is very religious. One day I was looking for him and he would not answer my calls. So I went to his room and there he was sitting cross-legged in front of his Krishna idol...'

Sardar Angre was visibly blushing, but the Rajmata was in full flight.

'...and tears were running down his face. I would not have thought—such a practical man...'

Sardar Angre was spared more embarrassment by one of the bearers bringing in a great pile of the morning's papers. He and the Rajmata began scanning the headlines.

'Riots, riots, riots,' said the Rajmata. 'Every day it is the same.'

Sardar Angre was however engrossed in a report in a Hindi newspaper concerning the latest episode of his own long-standing feud with the Rajmata's son. The dispute, which had been going on for some fifteen years—and which had, since its outset, been closely followed by the whole country— was currently enjoying one of its periodic flare-ups. Sardar Angre read the report out to the Rajmata.

'This is all my fault,' said the Rajmata, shaking her head. 'A mother's weakness.'

I must have looked a little confused by all this, for I was immediately treated to a résumé of the whole celebrated affair. In 1975, when Mrs Gandhi locked up the Opposition, suspended the Constitution and declared the Emergency, the Rajmata found herself transferred from the splendours of Gwalior to the less familiar surroundings of the infamous Tihar jail near Delhi. Her son, however, did a deal with the Congress and escaped to Nepal, leaving the Rajmata to fester in prison. She has never forgiven him. Moreover, as a minister in the current Congress government, the Maharajah remains a political as well as a personal adversary, the battle within the divided family mirroring the political divide of the nation at large.

'He did not fight the people who imprisoned his own mother,' growled Sardar Angre. 'He should have gone underground and joined the resistance against Mrs Gandhi. Instead he totally surrendered. Nobody in this great family has ever done that. He betrayed his own ancestors.'

'When he was in power Sardar Angre's house was attacked (by the police, apparently acting on Madhav Rao's orders). Half his possessions were taken, photographs were smashed...'

'My two Rottweillers were shot dead...'

'But worst of all,' continued the Rajmata, 'in the Emergency he left me inside that jail with the criminals and prostitutes. Imagine it: one of the inmates had *twenty-four* cases against her, including four murders. These were the companions he thought suitable for his mother.'

'How did you cope in jail?' I asked.

'I had faith in my Hanumanji,' replied the Rajmata. 'He sent help.'

'Hanuman came to you in person?' I asked.

'No,' replied the Rajmata, sighing and shaking her head sadly. 'But he spoke within me and showed me that all human beings—even the most hardened criminals—will respond if you show them affection.'

The Rajmata raised her eyes to heaven: beatific smile. 'And he was quite right, you know: they did. One murderer became my cook—I don't think I've ever had such a faithful servant. I wept when I finally left the prison—I was leaving so many close friends.'

From the front hall a bearer appeared and whispered in the Rajmata's ear. She nodded, dabbed her mouth with a napkin and got up.

'I have to go,' she said. 'There are some ladies here to see me.'

She added: 'Sardar Angre would, I'm sure, be pleased to show you around.'

Sardar Angre duly took me around the palace.

I followed him through room after room, hall after hall—great prairies of marble reflected back and forth by tall Victorian pier-glass mirrors.

Upstairs, all was rotting chintz and peeling plaster: a faint but unmistakable scent of decay hung in the air. Several of the rooms were unlit and seemed to be unused. They were visited only by the sparrows nesting in the wooden hammerbeams of the roof; a heavy lint of old cobweb formed fan-vaults in the corner-angles. When the shutters were opened the intruding beams of light illuminated thick snowstorms of swirling dust motes.

Only the Rajmata's bedroom really seemed loved and cared for. In a corner was a little silver shrine, full of idols. In front, a line of incense sticks were still smouldering. Every surface in the room was heavily loaded with other pieces of devotional clutter: photographs of Hindu saints and sadhus; a pair of Shiva lingams and a black mirrorwork image of the boy Krishna playing his flute.

By the bed, somewhat surprisingly, stood a photograph of the Rajmata's son taken on his wedding day. Despite all the hurt of their disagreements and public wrangling, the Rajmata's maternal ties still remained strong.

'Come,' said Sardar Angre, seeing where my eyes were resting.

He opened the double doors and stepped out on to the balcony. Together we looked out over the long lawns of the garden leading up, past groves of palm trees, to a delicate Mughal pavilion at the end.

Then I noticed that to one side of the palace, a few hundred yards away, lay another, even larger, edifice. Suddenly I realised that the vast building I had just toured was only a small, detached wing—a kind of garden cottage— tucked off to the side of the main bulk of the Jai Vilas Palace. This far larger palace was the home of the Sardar's enemy, the Maharajah. Like the building we were standing in, it was a late-nineteenth-century construction built in an Italian baroque style: a kind of massive Milanese wedding cake air-dropped into the jungles of central India.

It was here, in the larger palace, that lay the two most celebrated follies of India's nineteenth-century Maharajahs. Upstairs glittered the great chandelier, said to be rivalled only by that in the Tsar's Winter Palace in St Petersburg. So heavy was it that before it was hoisted in to place, a ramp a mile long was built, allowing twelve elephants to climb up on to the roof. Only after it was confirmed that the vaults could indeed bear the weight of all twelve of these massive beasts did the architect feel confident enough to order the chandelier to be raised in to place.

Meanwhile, downstairs in the dining room, the palace's other great eccentricity was being constructed: a solid silver model railway that took the port around to the Maharajah's male dinner guests. When a guest lifted the decanter from its carriage, the train would stop until it was replaced. Then it would hoot and shunt its way around the table to the next guest.

Both of these follies, and indeed the entire palace complex, were built for the ill-fated visit of the Prince and Princess of Wales to Gwalior in 1875. Realising that his present palace was ill-suited for entertaining European royalty, the Scindia of the day had given orders that work should begin on the grandest and most modern palace in Asia. A fortune was spent on the new building. In its nine-hundred-odd rooms gold leaf covered every dado, while solid marble flagged every floor. Everything was to be of the best: a warehouseful of Bruges tapestries, Chippendale chairs and huge Louis XIV mirrors was imported from Europe. Only one thing was lacking: it never occurred to the Maharajah to take the trouble to find a proper architect.

Instead, he turned to a jobbing amateur, and instructed a local Indian Army Colonel to knock something up. Colonel Michael Filose had no formal architectural training—in fact, prior to starting work on Jai Vilas he had worked on only one building: the Gwalior jail. But the Maharajah saw this as no obstacle: he packed Filose off to Paris to see Versailles, instructing him to come back quickly and build something similar in Gwalior before the Prince of Wales arrived.

It is not clear exactly what went wrong, but on the night the Prince of Wales came to stay, the silver train braked suddenly and toppled the port decanter right into his lap. Later that night there was another disaster. Before she went to bed, the future Queen Alexandra decided to have a bath. As the vast marble tub slowly filled with water, it quivered imperceptibly, then slowly sunk out of sight through the floor.

As we were leaving Jai Vilas, Sardar Angre and I bumped into a couple of other elderly sardars, or noblemen, from the old Gwalior kingdom. Brigadier Pawar was in the lead, accompanied by his wife, Vanmala, and another old gentleman who was addressed throughout merely as 'the Major'. As

Angre and Vanmala stood chatting, I asked the two old
sardars what they missed most about the old days when the
Maharajah and Rajmata ruled Gwalior.

'Well actually,' said Brigadier Pawar, 'the old days we
miss altogether. We miss them so much you can't pinpoint
any one thing: *everything* is missed.'

'In the old days everybody had time,' said the Major.
'There was time for processions, for riding, for tiger
shooting...'

'There was not much competition,' continued the Major.
'Things were just there. Now you have to struggle for each
achievement.'

'Before it was a very much sheltered life. Now it's more
competitive.'

'Unless you pull someone down you can't go up.'

The two old men looked at each other sadly.

'You cannot imagine the splendour and affluence of those
days,' said Vanmala, filling the moment's silence. 'If I started
telling you, you would feel it is a story I am making up.'

'In those days every sardar had fifteen horses and an
elephant,' said the Major. 'But now we cannot afford even a
donkey.'

'But it's not just the sardars who are nostalgic,' said
Vanmala. 'The entire population is nostalgic. That's why the
Rajmata—and all Scindias—are still so popular. Whenever
any of them stands for election they are voted in by the people.'

'But why is that?' I asked. 'Don't people prefer
democracy?'

'No,' said the Pawars in unison.

'Absolutely not,' said the Major.

'You see, in those days there was no corruption,' said the
Brigadier. 'The Maharajahs worked very hard on the
administration. Everything was well run.'

'The city was beautifully kept up,' said the Major. 'The
Maharajah would himself go around the city, you know, at
night, incognito, and see how things were being managed.
He really did believe his subjects were his children. Now
wherever you go there is corruption and extortion.'

'Today,' said Vanmala, 'every *babu* in the civil service
thinks he is a Maharajah, and tries to make difficulties for the

common man. But in those days there was just one King. The people of Gwalior had confidence that if they told their story he would listen and try to redress them.'

'The Maharajah and the Rajmata were like a father and mother to them,' said the Major.

'Now all of that is no more,' said Brigadier Pawar.

'That world has gone,' said the Major.

'Now only our memories are left,' said Brigadier Pawar. 'That's all. That's all we have.'

When they died, the mortal remains of the Maharajahs were cremated at a sacred site not far from the Jai Vilas Palace. After saying goodbye to the Pawars and the Major, Sardar Angre took me over in his jeep to see the place.

The memorials—a series of freestanding marble cenotaphs raised on the site of the original funeral pyres—were dotted around an enclosure dominated by a huge cathedral-like temple.

'The complex has its own staff,' said Sardar Angre as we drove in. 'In each of the shrines is a small bust of one of the Maharajahs. The staff changes the clothes of the statues, prepares them food and plays them music, just as if they were still alive.'

He jumped out of the jeep and led me towards one of the cenotaphs.

'The same will happen to the Rajmata when she dies,' he said. 'You see, in Gwalior the people still believe the Maharajahs are gods—or at least semidivine. They think the departed Maharajahs are still living in the form of the statues.'

'You believe this?' I asked.

'No,' said Sardar Angre.

I laughed, but soon realised I had missed the point: 'No, actually I believe in reincarnation,' said Sardar Angre. 'I think the Maharajahs are alive somewhere else in a different body, not in some statue.'

Sardar Angre removed his shoes and led the way into one of the shrines. In the portico stood a small marble Shiva lingam; ahead, in the main sanctuary—the part of the temple normally reserved for the image of the god—sat a statue of a large, rather jolly-looking lady in 1930s Indian dress.

'This is the mother of Her Highness's late husband,' said Sardar Angre. 'Look! She has a new pink sari.'

She had, but that was not all. What looked like a diamond necklace had recently been hung around her marble neck; someone had also placed a sandalwood tikka mark on her forehead, between her eyes. A small cot with a mosquito-net canopy and a full complement of blankets and pillows had been left to one side of the statue; beside it, on the bedside table, stood a framed photograph of the old Maharani and her husband.

Sardar Angre explained the statue's daily routine. It woke up in the morning to the sound of musicians. Then the priest gave it a discreet ceremonial bath, after which its clothes were changed by a maidservant. Later, the statue had lunch, followed by an afternoon siesta. In the evening, after tea, it was treated to a small concert before being brought dinner: dal, rice, two vegetables, chapattis and some sticky Indian pudding. Then the bed was put out and made ready—the corners turned back—and the lights turned off. The statue was allowed to make its own way between the sheets.

Grave goods—everything the Maharani would need for the afterlife—lay scattered all around. I felt rather as if I had stumbled into a pyramid twenty years after the death of Ramses II.

'Death is nothing to us,' said the Rajmata later, as we went in to lunch. 'For us it is only a change of circumstance.'

'Like moving house?'

'Exactly.'

I knew then, before it arrived, exactly what we were going to have to eat: dal, rice, two vegetables and chapattis, followed by some sticky Indian pudding. The same meal as the statues, cooked by the same kitchen, just the way the old Maharajahs liked it.

I left Gwalior that day, both charmed and amazed by the Rajmata: it seemed impossible to reconcile the old-fashioned, slightly batty Dowager Maharani I had met with the fire-breathing fascist depicted by her detractors in the Indian press. Her eccentricities seemed weird but endearing; there was absolutely nothing sinister about her.

I put my notebooks away in a bottom drawer, and forgot all about them.

Then, eleven months later, on 6 December 1992, the Rajmata hit the headlines again, this time in the most unsavoury circumstances.

For the previous five years Indian politics had been dominated by the Babri Masjid dispute. This concerned a sixteenth-century mosque in the town of Ayodhya, reputedly built by invading Muslims over a temple marking the site of the birthplace of the Hindu god Ram.

Every year since 1989, various of the Rajmata's Hindu organisations had held an annual rally at the disputed mosque. There they had performed sacred rites to indicate their wish to rebuild a temple on the site. In November 1992 the rally was called as normal, but things did not proceed as expected.

Instead, having been whipped up into a frenzy by the Rajmata and other BJP leaders, the vast crowd of two hundred thousand militant Hindus stormed the barricades. Shouting slogans like 'Victory to Lord Ram!' 'Hindustan is for the Hindus!' and 'Death to the Muslims!' they began tearing the mosque apart with sledgehammers, ropes, pickaxes and their bare hands.

One after another, like symbols of India's time-honoured traditions of tolerance, democracy and secularism, the three domes of the mosque fell to the ground. In little more than four hours the entire structure had been reduced not just to ruination but—quite literally—to rubble.

By the time the last pieces of the mosque's masonry had been brought tumbling down, one group of Hindu militants had begun shouting 'Death to the journalists!' and attacked a group of foreign correspondents with knives and iron bars, smashing cameras and television equipment. Having tasted blood, the mob set off to murder as many local Muslims as they could find. They finished off the job by torching the Muslims' houses.

While all this was happening, Rajmata Scindia—who had earlier signed a written pledge to the Indian High Court guaranteeing the mosque's safety—stood on the viewing platform, cheering as enthusiastically as if she was a football fan watching her team win the World Cup. As the demolition proceeded, she grabbed a microphone and encouraged the militants over the Tannoy.

Later that afternoon, a party of journalists stopped her limousine as she was leaving the town. They asked her whether she at least condemned the attacks on the correspondents. She replied in just two words: 'Acha hoguya'— it was a good thing.

Over the next fortnight, unrest swept India: crowds of angry Muslim demonstrators came out on to the streets, only to be massacred by the same police force that had earlier stood by and allowed the Hindu militants to destroy the mosque without firing a shot. In all, about two thousand people were killed and eight thousand injured in the violence that followed the demolition of the mosque.

Bombay was the scene of some of the worst rioting, but—as elsewhere—the trouble had pretty well died down by Christmas. Then, on the night of 7 January 1993, a Hindu family was brutally roasted alive when petrol bombs were thrown into their shanty hut. It is still unclear who was responsible for the killings—the evidence seems to point to criminal gangs working for unscrupulous property developers—but the local Hindu fundamentalists assumed it was the work of the Muslims, and set to work orchestrating a bloody and brutal revenge.

For the next week Bombay blazed as Muslims were hunted down by armed mobs, burned in their homes, scalded by acid bombs or knifed in the streets by mobile hit-squads. A few prominent middle-class Muslims—factory owners, the richer shopkeepers, newspaper editors—were also singled out for attack. Some of the poorer Muslim districts of the city were completely gutted by fire. In several places the municipal water pipes were turned off, and when the Muslims began to creep out of their ghettos with buckets in their hands, they found themselves surrounded by thugs who covered them with kerosene and set them alight, burning hundreds alive. In all, an estimated forty thousand Hindu activists went on a meticulously planned rampage, with the tacit support of the (96 per cent Hindu) police force. For a fortnight Bombay, India's effervescent commercial capital, was transformed in to a subcontinental version of Beirut or Sarajevo.

When the army was finally brought in, a curfew declared and the acid bombs, flick-knives and AK-47s had been put back in their hiding places, at least fourteen hundred people— the overwhelming majority impoverished Muslims—had been slaughtered. Many more were injured and disfigured. Hundreds of thousands of others fled from the city to the shelter of their ancestral villages. According to a memorandum prepared by Citizens for Peace, a pressure group formed by Bombay's business élite, the violence was 'nothing short of a deliberate plan to change the ethnic composition of what was hitherto regarded as a cosmopolitan city'.

Behind the mass murder and ethnic cleansing was the local Hindu nationalist party allied to the Rajmata's BJP: the Shiv Sena. Their leader, a former cartoonist named Bal Thackeray, made no secret of the fact that the mobs were under his control, and boasted in a magazine interview that he aimed to 'kick out' India's 110 million Muslims and send them to Pakistan'. 'Have they behaved like the Jews in Nazi Germany?' he was quoted as asking. 'If so, there is nothing wrong if they are treated as Jews were in Germany.'

Yet according to one newspaper report that I read, the Rajmata, far from attacking the bloodshed, let it be known that she regarded Thackeray and the Shiv Sena as close allies of the BJP: their aims were right, she said; only some of their methods were a little questionable.

Her position on this, and her apparent lack of concern at the bloody massacre of several thousand Indian Muslims— indeed the whole country's gradual slide towards communal anarchy—seemed irreconcilable with the impression I had formed of her in Gwalior as a cosy old grandma. Baffled, I decided to revisit the Rajmata, to try to understand how one woman could behave so very differently in different circumstances.

I telephoned her aides in Delhi and discovered that the seventy-nine-year-old was now busy campaigning in the jungles and villages of central India: after the recent upheavals, she expected the government to fall by March, and wanted to be ready for the general election when it was called. The Rajmata was uncontactable, said her aides: she was campaigning in the remotest corners of her old kingdom, far from any working telephone. But, I was told, if I went to the town of Shivpuri the following weekend I might be able to catch her on her way through.

I did as I was told. By Sunday morning I had tracked the Rajmata down to the house of the local sardar in Shivpuri. She was heading south towards Bhopal in half an hour, she said. She did not have time to speak to me now, but if I could come with her in her car I could interview her on the way.

'Oh!' she said as we headed down the driveway in the limo. 'I wish you had been there at Ayodhya when the mosque fell! When I saw the three domes come down I thought: "This is what God wanted. It was His will."'

'But what about all the murders? What about the massacres in Bombay?' I said. 'You wouldn't say Bal Thackeray's Shiv Sena thugs were the hand of God as well, would you?'

'I won't criticise Thackeray,' said the Rajmata benignly. 'For so long the Muslims have been appeased by the Congress. What happened was a reaction. Thackeray is a bit extreme, but...'

'No,' said Sardar Angre. 'He is quite right. The Muslims must be made to understand that they should be proud of Hindustan. We cannot tolerate Muslims in this country if they don't feel themselves Indian. Look what happens at cricket matches: the Muslims always support Pakistan.'

I wondered whether Angre realised he was unconsciously echoing the sentiments of Lord Tebbit, but decided not to complicate the issue. I simply said: 'You can hardly justify murdering people because they support the wrong cricket team.'

'Hindus are docile people,' said the Rajmata. 'They always welcome anyone—even the Jews.' She nodded her head as if to emphasise what she clearly regarded as an extreme feat of tolerance. 'They are not violent.'

'They don't seem to be very docile at the moment,' I said.

'The Muslims have been appeased for so long,' repeated Angre.

'The police don't seem to appease them much,' I said. 'They always take the side of the Hindus.'

'Well, naturally birds of a feather will flock together,' replied the Rajmata brightly. 'You cannot expect Hindu policemen to attack their own Hindu brethren.'

'And what about the police raping Muslim women? There have been many reports of that.'

The Rajmata considered this for a minute then replied: 'I think that maybe those policeman who do that have seen some similar atrocity done to Hindu women by the Muslims. That would make them mad with anger and grief.'

She looked across at me, smiling benignly as if she had just solved the whole problem.

'Anyway,' she said, 'if only the Muslims followed the Hindu ideology there would be no more trouble.'

'But you can hardly expect a hundred million Muslims to abandon their faith and convert to Hinduism.'

'That's just the trouble,' she replied. 'The Muslims should realise that they are Indians. Babur was not their ancestor, Ram was. They should accept our common culture and unite with us in the name of God. This must be the answer. Anyway,' she added with a frown, 'they are too many to drive out.'

What can one make of a brave, pious, sweet-natured old woman who can close her eyes to the massacre and murder of innocent people carried out by her own supporters? Who can wilfully fail to make the connection between the emotions she whips up and the garrotted corpse lying in the dirt of a narrow alleyway? In her blindness, the Rajmata remains an unsettling reminder that you need not be personally objectionable to subscribe to the most deeply objectionable political creeds: charm and sweetness are clearly not guarantees against either violent nationalism or the most xenophobic religious fundamentalism and bigotry.

My last image of the Rajmata was the sight of her addressing an adoring crowd in a remote district in central India. After she had finished speaking and the crowds were cheering and clapping, the drums were beating and marigold garlands were being thrown over her neck, she slowly made her way through a police cordon towards her waiting helicopter. Already the rotor blades were beginning to turn.

'Who is going and who is not?' asked an aide.

'I have no idea. I am going. That much I know,' replied the Rajmata, looking at the helicopter with some misgiving.

'Are you frightened of flying?' I asked.

'No, no,' she replied. 'Flying I am absolutely at home. But it has to be with wings.'

Then she smiled.

'My Hanuman can fly too. He flew to Lanka to rescue Sita. But of course, he does not need a helicopter...'

The aides were waiting. Bending low beneath the rotor blades, the old lady scuttled into the cockpit, ready for another bout of campaigning in some other district of her old kingdom.

As the crowd of villagers looked on, the blades turned quicker and quicker. There was a noise like a great wind, and clouds of dust blew over the podium where the Rajmata had been speaking just minutes before.

Some of the villagers, terrified, ran for cover; others prostrated themselves on the ground. When they raised their heads they saw that the Rajmata had risen like a Hindu goddess into the heavens, carried, as it were, on the wings of Garuda, the great winged vehicle of the immortals.

*Postscript* : In 1997 the Rajmata suffered a major heart attack, but following bypass surgery she has returned undaunted to full-time politics at the age of eighty-four. In the 1998 general election she retained her seat, albeit by a slightly reduced margin.

Ever since the destruction of the mosque at Ayodhya, the BJP has continued to grow in popularity and influence. In 1992 it took 113 seats in Parliament, up from eighty-nine in the previous election. In 1996 the number rose to 161, making it the largest single party in the Lok Sabha. It succeeded in forming a short-lived coalition government which survived only two weeks before losing a crucial vote of confidence. Finally, the BJP won the 1998 general election with a record 179 seats, but this still fell short of a majority, and its administration was forced to rely on a hotchpotch of minority parties, some of which were strongly opposed to its more extreme pro-Hindu policies.

Moreover, the BJP's entry in to the political mainstream from the mid-Nineties onwards was largely achieved by toning down much of its more inflammatory Hindu rhetoric. The party's leading moderate, Atal Bihari Vajpayee, was appointed as its leader, and many of its more extreme figures, including the Rajmata, were sidelined. It remains to be seen, however, if this new, relatively acceptable face of the BJP represents a fundamental change in the party, or merely a disguise with which to woo the credulous voter. The decision to explode the 'Hindu' nuclear bomb, the hawkish anti-Pakistan rhetoric that followed it, and the call by some BJP activists to erect a temple at the site of the blast, would seem to indicate that the extremists and bigots in the party are still far from defeated.

# East of Eton

Just before dawn on 7 March 1997, two figures made their way to a small classical bungalow on the perimeter of La Martiniere College in Lucknow, India's oldest and once its most distinguished public school.

Walking silently to the back of the building, they found a broken windowpane looking into the bedroom of the school's Anglo-Indian PT instructor, Frederick Gomes. The two took aim and, at a signal, fired at the sleeping figure with a .763 Mauser and .380 pistol. One shot missed, but the other hit Gomes in the leg. The schoolmaster immediately leaped out of bed and hobbled into the corridor.

According to the police reconstruction, the two killers then ran round to the front of the building, kicked open the front door and took some more shots at the terrified man, wounding him in the back as he tried to run back to his bedroom. Bleeding heavily, Gomes succeeded in shutting the door and barricading it with a chair. But the killers returned to the back and fired a random hail of bullets into the room through the window. When Gomes' body was later discovered by another schoolmaster, the PT instructor was found to have sustained no fewer than eight hits: four in the chest, one in the leg, two in his back and the fatal one on his temple.

The murder, which remains unsolved, created a sensation in India, particularly when several guns (though not the murder weapons) were found to be circulating among the school's pupils. For La Martiniere is an institution of legendary propriety and distinction, as *pukka* as Kipling himself, who appropriately sent his fictional hero Kim to a Lucknow school—St Xavier's—clearly modelled on La Martiniere. During the Raj, the school produced generations of District Magistrates, Imperial civil servants and Indian Army officers, and the names of many of these Victorian pupils—Carlisle, Lyons, Binns, Charleston, Raymond—are still carved on the front steps of the school. Since then La Martiniere has educated several members of the Nehru-Gandhi dynasty, as well as producing great numbers of cabinet ministers, industrialists and newspaper editors. If India's increasingly endemic violence and corruption could creep into such an institution, it was asked, what was the hope for the rest of India? 'The killing is a metaphor of our times,' I was told by Saeed Naqvi, one of the country's most highly regarded political commentators and an old boy of the school. 'For such a level of violence to reach the groves of academe and the sacred precincts of La Martiniere is symbolic of the way the country of Mahatma Gandhi has completely ceased to be what it once was.'

In Britain there may have been widespread celebrations marking fifty years of Indian Independence, but in India there has been much less rejoicing. As *The Times of India* acknowledged in an editorial to mark the 1997 Republic Day, 'in this landmark year not much remains of the hope, idealism and expectations that our founding fathers poured into the creation of the Republic. In their place we now have a sense of abject resignation, an increasing sense of drift. We are ostensibly on the verge of a global breakthrough; yet the truth is that the deprived India is eating voraciously into the margins of the prosperous India.'

If decay and corruption have set into many of the old institutions of the Raj, the public schools that the English left dotted around the subcontinent have always vigorously resisted any accommodation with the postcolonial world outside their walls: however much India and Britain may both have moved on since 1947, India's public schools have, for better or worse, maintained intact the ways and attitudes of early-twentieth-century England. 'Independence changed nothing at La Martiniere,' I was told by one old boy. 'The curriculum didn't change, the boys didn't change, the games didn't change, the discipline didn't change. They kept the Union Jack flying from the roof well into the mid-Sixties. Diwali continued to be celebrated as Guy Fawkes Day. Even today they teach the history of the First War of Independence (the Indian Mutiny) from the British point of view.'

'The literature, poetry and music are still English,' I was told by another old La Martinian. 'The manners, tastes and customs are English, even the sports are English. In my day there was very little about the history or culture of Continental Europe, and nothing at all about the history and culture of India. In fact we were encouraged to forget all the Urdu culture we had learned at home. Instead, we were always taught about all the brilliant things that British civilisation was about, and how we *paan*-chewing Indians were basically degenerate and we'd never get anywhere. Look how far the British had come, they told us; the sun never sets on the British Empire. We were indoctrinated into believing that talking in Hindi, reciting Urdu poetry, wearing khadi, chewing *paan* and spitting into spittoons—all this was vulgar and obscene, and after a while it really did seem like that to us. Still does sometimes.'

La Martiniere was founded in 1845 by Major General Claude Martin, an enigmatic Frenchman in the service both of the East India Company and the Nawabs of Lucknow, the last Muslim dynasty to rule India. In life Martin lived like a Moghul; in death he adopted the Mughal practice of building a tomb to commemorate his achievements. But in his will he broke with tradition by leaving the somewhat bizarre instruction that a school for children of all religions should be established in his vast mausoleum.

So it was that within this strange Indo-baroque necropolis complex, India's first English public school opened in 1845. Here, everything that might be expected in a school on the banks of the Thames was exactly reproduced on the banks of the Gomti, right down to the statutory inedible food and the oddball cast of eccentric schoolmasters. Of these, according to Saeed Naqvi, none was more memorable than Mr Harrison.

'Harrison had a huge moustache which he used to wax,' remembers Saeed, 'and he also had a talking parrot which used to say things like, "Rise and shine, rise and shine"—you know, the usual public school nonsense. Chaufin, a friend of mine in school who hated Waxy for a variety of very valid reasons, used to get up in the morning at five o'clock and tried teaching the parrot to say, "Waxy is a bastard, Waxy is a bastard".

'He did this with such an absolute sense of dedication and purpose that in a year's time the parrot picked up the line, and every time Waxy walked past he'd squawk, "Waxy is a bastard, Waxy is a bastard".

'Now, Waxy thought this was a joke, but then one day he was taking Doutre, the headmaster, on a tour of all the wonderful things he was doing to the dormitories, and as he walked past the parrot recited the famous line. So the story had a very macabre ending, because Waxy in his temper twisted the neck of the parrot; and that was the end of Waxy's parrot.'

On the surface, little appears to have changed at La Martiniere since Saeed left thirty years ago. Now, as then, boys of all religions still attend chapel every day, listening to a choir made up of Muslims and Hindus dressed in white surplices sing the *Te Deum*, *Jerusalem* and *The Lord is my Shepherd*. The masters still wear black academic gowns, the curriculum and uniform remain firmly those of the English public school of the 1930s, and khaki drill, cricket, the works of John Buchan and furtive schoolboy homosexuality are apparently all still ery much *de rigueur*. Urdu or Hindi literature is never ught; instead pupils still learn by heart great swathes of V.ordsworth, Tennyson and Byron.

One morning, after the boarders had attended chapel and the whole school had massed at assembly to sing the school hymn, *Bright Renown*, I talked to some of the boys who were doing their prep in the spectacular Mughal-Gothic school library. At the rear of the room, the form mistress, Mrs Faridi (who earlier in the morning had doubled up as organist on the old manually-pumped organ in the chapel), was looking around her, scowling through her hornrims and shouting out: 'Settle down now, boys! Settle down!'

Obediently, I sat at a table next to three seventeen-year-olds: Samir, Pradeep and Tony, a Muslim, a Hindu and an Anglo-Indian Christian respectively. I asked them whether they knew about La Martiniere being the model for St Xavier's, the boarding school in *Kim*.

'We all know,' said Samir. 'But I've never read the book myself.'

'I saw the film on Star TV,' said Pradeep, referring to Murdoch's satellite venture in India. 'It was good. I mean, I was very proud when I saw it had been filmed at La Martiniere.'

'What other British books have you come across?' I asked.

'*All* the books we are taught are British,' said Tony.

'It's true,' said Samir. 'We still have Shakespeare, *Great Expectations*, Emily Brontë, Charlotte Brontë—all those novels.'

'Can you recite any British poetry?'

'Of course,' said Pradeep. ' "The wind was a torrent of darkness among the gusted trees, the moon was a ribbon of moonlight tossed among cloudy seas..." We know all that stuff.'

'And what about the great Urdu poets of Lucknow and Delhi: Ghalib, Mir Taqi Mir, Dagh and so on. Are you taught those?'

'No,' said Pradeep. 'We haven't been taught about the culture of Lucknow at all. Or about the culture of India. We only study British poets and novelists.'

'Does that seem odd?'

'Perhaps,' said Samir uncertainly. 'I've never really thought about it.'

'What about 1857—the Indian Mutiny?' I asked. 'How is that taught?'

There was an anxious pause.

'Well, you know fifty La Martiniere boys fought in the defence of the British residency?' said Samir. 'So as far as the school is concerned, we are with the British. We feel very proud of the boys when we go to the residency and see La Martiniere's name on the wall.'

'But in other parts of India,' added Pradeep, 'we support the Indians, of course. Don't we?' The three boys looked at each other and giggled nervously.

'But if you'd been there,' I persisted, 'which side would you have been on: with your school or with your countrymen?'

'Um...' said Samir.

'I don't know,' said Pradeep.

'It's a difficult question,' said Tony.

Despite the extraordinary survival of such Anglophile sympathies, the recent murder at La Martiniere has shattered the notion that the subcontinent's public schools can forever remain an archipelago of Englishness floating untroubled in an increasingly choppy Indian sea. Although they remain wholly English in outlook and style, schools like La Martiniere are beginning to realise quite how fragile is the bubble in which they exist.

Lucknow is the capital of India's largest state, Uttar Pradesh, which with its 120 million inhabitants forms the very heart of the country, but is also a symbol of much that is most worrying about modern India. The terrifying speed of the corruption and decay of the state's politics over the last decade can perhaps be best measured by charting the number of criminals among members of the State Assembly. In 1985, there were thirty-five MLAs with criminal cases registered against them. By 1989 the number had grown to fifty. In 1991, only two years later, that total more than doubled to 103. In the 1993 elections, a grand total of 150 Uttar Pradesh MLAs had criminal records.

The symbol of this new style of north Indian politician is Mulayam Singh Yadav, a semiliterate village wrestler who quickly rose to be, for two successive terms, the Chief Minister of Uttar Pradesh, and has since been India's Defence Minister. Prior to this elevation into high politics Mulayam had had over two dozen criminal cases registered against him, including charges of wrongful confinement, rioting, provoking breaches of the peace and criminal intimidation.

Mulayam's time as Chief Minister of Uttar Pradesh saw the state's politics sink to new lows. At one stage a group of his MLAs, supported by the Lucknow University Students' Union— around two hundred people, all armed with home-made guns and grenades—tried to murder Mayawati, the leader of a rival party, while she and her associates slept in the State Guest House. Following a shoot-out between the two groups of politicians and the police—all of which was caught on film by a television camera-crew—Mulayam's government fell from power.

According to Mohan Sohai, the Lucknow correspondent of the Calcutta *Statesman*, who has been monitoring the decay of UP for more than a decade, 'There is intense rivalry between the leaders of the different political parties to recruit the state's biggest criminals and gangsters. Of course, the criminals are delighted. Once they become politicians, the police who used to hunt them down have to protect them instead, while the cases which are pending against them—murder, abduction, banditry—will either be dropped, or else investigated so slowly they will not make it to the courts for decades. Moreover, if they are already in prison, and win their seat from behind bars, they will almost certainly be released on bail to attend parliament. It's just getting worse and worse. Democracy is badly under threat.'

Against such a background, perhaps it was only a matter of time before the violence and corruption seeped into the precincts of La Martiniere: if anything, it is surprising that some sort of atrocity did not take place earlier. After all, the children of many of Lucknow's most notorious politicians are pupils at the school, including a nephew of Mulayam. Moreover, on the edge of the school's immaculate cricket pitches lie two villages which are said to be the headquarters of the Lucknow drug mafia, led by a caste-brother of Mulayam, Suraj Pal Yadav, one of the most wanted men in north India. One theory has it that Yadav's gang had Gomes assassinated after he accidentally witnessed some mafia action.

The Lucknow police, however, believe that the murder may well have been carried out by some of La Martiniere's own pupils, and there certainly seems to be no shortage of suspects with motives. As well as being La Martiniere's PT instructor, Gomes was in charge of administering beatings and punishments, a job which made him many enemies. A month before his murder, he had discovered a pistol in the locker of one of the school's boarders. He beat the boy up, and made sure that he was expelled. Off-the-record police sources indicate that a student is one of the principal suspects.

'Of course, it's very unsettling and shocking when a murder has been committed,' said the headmaster, Elton de Souza. 'But what can we do? By and large the children and the staff have all pulled together, and somehow we seem to have overcome what happened. I don't know whether it's a reflection of what's going on in the town, but the murder has certainly left a deep impression on the school, the boys, the masters—everyone concerned.'

Many old boys have blamed de Souza himself for the decline of the school—a decline that the murder can only accelerate. But Saeed Naqvi believes that La Martiniere's troubles are part of a much wider change that is affecting all that is left of Britain's legacy in India: 'The old Anglophile élite of India is being pushed into the margins,' he says. 'In their place a new, lower-caste, Hindi-speaking élite—men like Mulayam—are rising up, and bringing a very different set of values with them. There is a change in the schoolmasters too: in my day they had an almost missionary zeal to propagate English values. Now that has all gone. The standard of teaching has gone right down, and so has the quality of the intake.'

As evidence, Naqvi points to the figures: the Anglo-Indian community which dominated the school in his day has now largely emigrated and almost completely disappeared from the classrooms, while as many as a quarter of the present intake is from the newly empowered lower castes. These are often not from English-speaking or even literate backgrounds.

'They are less well educated when they come in and they're less well educated when they come out,' says Naqvi. 'It's taken fifty years, but what is happening now is really the final twilight of the Raj. La Martiniere was a wonderful survival from a vanished world, and I still regard the place with great affection: I had a very good time there, and am none the worse for the corporal punishment or the bullying or the learning by rote. But in the long term the school just can't go on. Already it's no longer the school it used to be. It's an ailing institution, in fast decay. In fifty years the culture and the society which sustained it have simply disappeared.'

If I really wanted to see how bad the future of La Martiniere could look, Saeed told me, I should meet some of the Lucknow University students' leaders. They were notorious, he said, for running protection rackets in the bazaars of the city, taking 'donations' from the shopkeepers and beating up any who refused to make the appropriate contribution. A recalcitrant photographer's shop had apparently been reduced to ashes by the students only a week before.

But protection rackets were not the worst of it, I later learned. Rival wings of the Lucknow University Students' Union, all of which were competing for political patronage from the government, had declared war on each other, and there were now open street battles between different factions armed with guns and grenades. So far thirty-odd students had been wounded; eight were dead. Both of the last two student union leaders had been given 'tickets' to stand for one of the political parties in the UP Legislative Assembly; both were now in jail on murder charges. There could not be a more grim—or geographically closer—model of what can happen when a great educational institution plummets into catastrophic decline.

I went over to the Habibullah Hostel—the most notorious student hall of residence—early one morning; it lay in a leafy campus a few miles from La Martiniere. With me came the son of the Lucknow Inspector General of Police, who said he knew some of the student leaders. We sat in front of the imposing Indo-Saracenic façade, once no doubt the pride of some high-minded Victorian Vice-Chancellor. College servants brought out benches on to the overgrown front lawn, once a cricket pitch, and as we sat sipping small cups of milk tea, the student politicians crowded around and excitedly told me about their little war.

It had begun three years earlier, apparently, when two student leaders had got into a petty argument over who should sit in a particular seat during an exam: both had identified it as the best place in which they could get away with cheating. After the exam had finished there had been a fight outside, and several Habibullah students had been badly beaten up. The squabble quickly escalated into a full-scale feud between two different halls of residence. When a group from the rival hostel ambushed and badly injured two students from Habibullah Hostel, they decided to counterattack.

'About fifty of us attacked the Victoria Hostel one night,' said Veeru Singh. He looked a nice boy: shy, polite, well dressed. He was standing for Student Union President in the summer, he said, and was hoping that, like his predecessors, the position would enable him to receive a nomination from one of the political parties the following year. 'We had about twenty guns and a lot of home-made grenades, but the first time we attacked them we were over-excited and began shooting off our guns as soon as we left here. By the time we got to Victoria we had no ammunition left. So we lodged a charge of attempted murder against the Victoria boys with the police, and managed to get two of them arrested. The second time we were more organised. We wanted to kill their leader, Abhay Singh.'

At this point I interrupted: 'I'm sorry,' I said. 'Did you say you wanted to kill him?'

'Why not kill?' replied one of the boys at the back of the group. 'It's not difficult.'

'Anyway,' continued Veeru. 'We surrounded the hostel in silence then barged in. We went from room to room and wounded five or six of them, but in the dark Abhay escaped. Then the police raided here and arrested a couple of us. They also discovered half of our arms in Praveen Verma's room.'

Veeru indicated Praveen at one side of the crowd. He was a small, sly-looking boy of about nineteen with a downy adolescent moustache.

'What happened?' I asked.

'They found sixteen country-made pistols, one proper grenade and eight home-made bombs,' said Praveen. 'But I said they belonged to my roommate, so they arrested him instead. He didn't dare say they were mine. He knew what would happen to him if he did.'

'But where do you get all this weaponry?' I asked.

'The guns we buy in the bazaar,' replied Praveen. 'The grenades we make ourselves.'

'After that Abhay began to get rattled,' said Veeru, determined not to be sidetracked. 'So on 7 January 1996 he shot one of my best friends, Bablu. Six people attacked him on motorbikes when he was sitting in the tea stall on the main road. They shot him in the back. Praveen was sitting next to him. Since then they've been trying to shoot Praveen. He is the only witness. He has to be armed twenty-four hours a day.'

'Are you carrying a gun now?' I asked.

'Of course,' replied Praveen. He unbuttoned his trousers and lifted a home-made pistol from his Y-fronts. It was a horrible thing: crude and ugly, with a barrel made from the steering shaft of a rickshaw. Praveen flicked a catch and opened it up. Inside was a small red shotgun cartridge.

'What about grenades?' I asked. 'Are you carrying any of them?'

'I've got some in my room: country-made ones. Would you like to see them?'

I said I would, so Praveen sent off one of the college servants to fetch one. The servant returned five minutes later with an innocent-looking bundle of white gauze about the size of a tangerine.

'They're quite effective,' said Praveen proudly. 'We fill them with glass and nails. But be careful: if you drop them they go off. I injured my leg with one once.'

'Shall I continue?' asked Veeru.

'Please.'

'The night they killed my friend, we attacked the Victoria Hostel properly. We managed to get some assault rifles and about fifty bombs. We did a lot of damage but they were expecting us, and two of our people were badly wounded.'

'We took them to the hospital,' said Praveen, 'but the doctors wouldn't operate. They said it was a police case and they couldn't touch them. So we beat the place up. We trashed the emergency ward and burned an ambulance. We hit the doctors and tore the clothes off the nurses and shoved injections up the doctors' backsides. We said, "Save them," but the doctors said, "They're dying. Let them die." In the end the police came and thirteen of us were arrested.'

For forty more minutes the students continued with their story unabashed: the attacks on the courthouse when Abhay was brought to trial; the attempts to kill him in prison; the police raids; the ambushes and the murders. At the end of it, when they were reviewing the death toll—four dead on each side—I asked them: 'And do you think this is a good way to spend your lives?'

'The situation is like this,' replied Veeru, shrugging his shoulders. 'What can we do about it?'

'We can't make peace,' said Praveen. 'If we do, they'll double-cross us.'

'But you're turning into *goondas*,' I said.

'No: we're students. We've only become *goondas* because of the situation. If we stop now we'll be shot dead. We regret that politics is getting more violent and that we have to use guns for self-protection. But the psychology here is such that people without muscle-power can't do anything. If it's necessary to use muscle-power, then that is what we will have to do.'

'It's true,' said Praveen. 'Right now you can't fight an election without a pistol. Naturally we are sad. But that is the situation. Whatever the situation is, you must adjust to it.'

'And you think you'll continue in politics?'

'I'm already in,' said Veeru. 'I'm standing as an independent in the next state election. I've always wanted to be an MLA.'

'Why?'

'I'd fight for society. At the moment I'm fighting for the students. But I suppose everyone starts like that: idealistic.'

Veeru giggled innocently: 'But you know, in the end all our politicians are just the same,' he said, smiling a sweet smile. 'They just want more power.'

# The City of Widows

The eye of faith can often see much that is hidden from the vision of the nonbeliever. To most secular visitors, Vrindavan appears to be nothing more than a rundown north Indian bazaar town, its dusty streets clogged with cows, beggars, bicycles and rickshaws. But to the pious pilgrim it is the dwelling place of Krishna, and thus—in that sense at least—an earthly paradise fragrant with the scent of tamarind and Arjuna trees.

Devout Hindus believe that Krishna is still present in this temple town with its crumbling palaces and swarming ashrams, its open sewers and its stalls selling brightly coloured lithographs of the God Child. Listen carefully in Vrindavan, I was told by an old sadhu on the riverbank, for if you are attentive you can still catch the distant strains of Krishna's flute. In the morning, said the sadhu, the god can sometimes be glimpsed bathing at the *ghats*; while in the evening he is often seen walking with Radha along the bank of the Yamuna.

Every year, hundreds of thousands of Hindu devotees come to Vrindavan, making their way barefoot to the Yamuna along the *parikrama* which links all the town's most holy temples and shrines. Most then head on to another neighbouring pilgrimage site: the mountain of Govardhan, which, according to legend, Krishna used as an umbrella, lifting it with his little finger. It is now not much more than a hillock, but this does not worry the pilgrims; they know the legend that the more sin proliferates in the world, the more the mountain is diminished.

Some who come to Vrindavan, however, never leave the town again. For many Hindus believe that there is nowhere more holy in all India, and therefore that there is nowhere better to spend your final days, nowhere better to prepare for death.

The pilgrims come from many different castes and communities, from amongst the rich and the poor, from the north and south; but one group in particular predominates: the widows. You notice them the minute you arrive in Vrindavan, bent-backed and white-saried, with their shaven heads and outstretched begging-bowls; on their foreheads they wear the tuning-fork-shaped ash-smear that marks them out as disciples of Krishna. Some of them have slipped out of their homes and left their families, feeling themselves becoming an encumbrance; others have fled vindictive sons and daughters-in-law. Most have simply been thrown out of their houses. For in traditional Hindu society, a woman loses all her status the minute her husband dies. She is forbidden to wear colours or jewellery or to eat meat. She is forbidden to remarry (at least if she is of reasonably high caste; low-caste and Untouchable women can do what they want) and she is forbidden to own property. She may no longer be expected to commit *sati* and throw herself on her husband's funeral pyre, but in many traditional communities, particularly in the more remote villages, she *is* still expected to shave her head and live like an ascetic, sleeping on the ground, living only to fast and pray for her departed spouse.

This practice receives a certain legitimacy in the ancient Hindu tradition that old people who have seen the birth of their grandchildren should disappear off into the forest and spend their last days in prayer, pilgrimage and fasting. In modern India the custom has largely died out, but in some parts, notably rural Bengal, a form of it has survived that involves simply kicking bereaved grandmothers out of their houses and sending them off to the City of Widows.

Every day widows from all over India arrive in Vrindavan. They come to seek the protection of Krishna, to chant *mantras* and to meditate on their own mortality. They live in great poverty. In return for four hours of chanting, the principal ashram will give a widow a cupful of rice and two rupees. Otherwise the old women, a surprising number of them from relatively wealthy, high-caste, landowning families, subsist on what they can beg. They have no privacy, no luxuries, no holidays. They simply pray until they keel over and die.

There are eight thousand of them at present in the town, and every year their number increases.

'If I were to sit under a tree,' said Kamala Ghosh, a local women's rights activist, 'and tell you the sadness of the widows of Vrindavan, the leaves of that tree would fall like tears.'

'My husband died when I was seventeen years old,' said Kanaklatha. 'He had some sort of stomach disorder. I took him to lots of hospitals in Calcutta but he did not recover. He suffered for a month. Then he died.'

The old lady looked past me, her clouded eyes focused towards the *ghats* and the course of the holy river Yamuna.

'I still remember his face when they brought him to me,' she said. 'He was very fair, with fine, sharp features. When he was alive his eyes were unusually large, but now they were closed: he looked as if he was sleeping. Then they took him away. He was a landlord in our village, and greatly respected. But we had no children, and when he died his land was usurped by the village strongmen. I was left with nothing.

'For two years I stayed where I was. Then I was forced to go to Calcutta to work as a maid. I wasn't used to working as a servant, and every day I cried. I asked Govinda (Krishna), "What have I done to deserve this?" How can I describe to anyone how great my pain was? After three years Krishna appeared to me in a dream and said that I should come here. That was 1955. I've been here forty years now.'

'Do you never feel like going back?'

'Never! After my husband died and they took away everything I owned, I vowed never to look at my village again. I will never go back.'

We were standing in the main bazaar of Vrindavan. Rickshaws were rattling past us along the rutted roads, past the tethered buffaloes and the clouds of bees swarming outside the sweet shops. Behind us rose the portico of the Shri Bhagwan Bhajan *ashram*. Through its door came the sound of bells and clashing cymbals and the constant rising, falling eddy of the widows' incessant chant: 'Hare Ram, Hare Krishna, Hare Ram, Hare Krishna...' Occasionally, above the chant of two thousand women, you could hear snatches of the soaring Bengali verses of the lead singer:

Mare Keshto rakhe ke?
Rakhe Keshto mare ke?

Whom Krishna destroys, who can save?
Whom he saves, who can destroy?

It was ten in the morning and Kanaklatha had just finished her four-hour shift. In her hand she held her reward: a knotted cloth containing a single cupful of rice and her two rupees. 'We try to remember what we are chanting,' said Kanaklatha, following my gaze, 'but mostly we carry on so that we can eat. When we fall ill and cannot chant, the ashram doesn't help: we just go hungry.'

Kanaklatha said she had got up at four-thirty, as she did every day. She had bathed and dressed her Krishna idol, spent an hour in prayer before it, then performed her ablutions at the ghat. Then from six until ten she chanted her mantras at the ashram. After that, a day of begging in the bazaars of Vrindavan stretched ahead.

'I stay with my mother,' said Kanaklatha. 'She is ninety-five. My father died when I was sixteen and she came here then. We have to pay a hundred rupees rent a month. It is my main worry in life. Now I'm two months in arrears. Every day I ask Govinda to help us make ends meet. I know he will look after us.'

'How can you believe that after all you've been through?'

'If Govinda doesn't look after us who will?' said Kanaklatha. 'If I didn't believe in him how could I stay alive?'

The widow looked straight at me: 'All I want is to serve him,' she insisted. 'Whatever we eat and drink is his gift. Without him we would have nothing. The way he wants things to be, that is how they are.'

'Come,' she said, her face lighting up. 'Come and see my image of Govinda. He is so beautiful.'

Without waiting to see if I would follow, the old lady hobbled away along the street at a surprising pace. She led me through a labyrinth of lanes and alleys, past roadside shrines and brightly-lit temples, until eventually we reached a small courtyard house near the *ghats*. There, on the floor of a cramped, dark, airless room, lay Kanaklatha's mother. She was shaven-headed and smeared with ash like her daughter, but she was toothless and shrunken, lying curled up like an embryo on a thin cotton sheet. Around her were scattered a few pots and pans. Kanaklatha squatted on the floor beside her and gently stroked her head.

'My mother was a strong woman,' she said. 'But she had a haemorrhage two years ago and after that she just withered away. Now she just lies on this bed. If I could afford to give her just one glass of fruit juice she would be better than she is. I want her to die without pain, but I am consumed by the thought that if something bad happens we could not afford medical treatment.'

'It is all fate.' It was the mother speaking. 'When we were young we never imagined this would be our end.'

'We were a landowning family,' explained Kanaklatha. 'Now we have to beg to survive. Even now I'm full of shame when I beg, thinking I am from a good family. It is the same with all the widows. Our usefulness is past. We are all rejects. This is our *karma*.'

'Only Govinda knows our pain and misery,' said her mother. 'No one else could understand.'

'Yet compared to some of the others...'

'What do you mean?' I asked.

'Some of the other widows. At least we are together. But many women I know were thrown out of their houses by their own children. When their sons discover that they are begging on the streets of Vrindavan they are forbidden from writing to their grandchildren.

'We haven't committed a crime,' said the old lady. 'Why should we go through all this?'

'Sometimes I think even *sati* would have been preferable to the life of a widow,' said Kanaklatha. 'At the time, burning on my husband's pyre seemed horrible. But after living through so much pain and misery, I wonder whether *sati* would not have been the better option. Now all I want is to serve Govinda and my mother, and spend the rest of the time in prayer. Here, come inside, see my little Krishna.'

Kanaklatha indicated that I should step over her mother. She pointed to the end of her tiny room. There, raised up on a wooden bench beside a small paraffin stove stood a pair of small brass idols of Krishna, each dressed in saffron dolls' clothes. One figure showed Krishna as a child; the other as a youth, dancing with a flute in his hands.

'Look at his beauty!' said Kanaklatha. 'Every day I bathe him and change his clothes and give him food. Krishna is my protector. He cannot resist the entreaties of any woman.'

She walked over to the shrine and bowed her head before the images.

'Sometimes when I am asleep he comes to me,' she said. 'I tell him my sorrows and he tells me how to cope. But the moment I awake, he disappears...'

That evening, in a nearby temple, I met Kanaklatha's landlord, a Brahmin priest named Pundit Krishna Gopal Shukla.

'If those women die tomorrow,' he said, spitting on the floor, 'I will have to bear the expense of cremation. It should be the ashram's responsibility. They get so much money from pilgrims. I do so much for these widows already. I rent them a room. I even give them free water.'

According to Shukla, the widows' ashrams in Vrindavan were increasingly set up by Delhi businessmen as a means to launder black money. They would give donations to their ashrams and receive receipts stating that they had given much larger amounts, which would be written off against tax. As far as the ashram owners were concerned, the widows were just a means to a financial end, a quick route to a clever tax dodge.

There was no doubting the very considerable funds the ashrams of Vrindavan receive. One medium-sized one attracted donations by undertaking to erect an inscribed

marble plaque recording the name of any devotee who gave
at least two thousand rupees, and promising that the widows
would sing *bhajans* for the donor 'for the next seven
generations'. The resulting plaques covered not only every
wall in the hangar-sized building, but also its floor and
ceiling. Many of the donors turned out to be British Hindus:
next to plaques recording donations from Agra, Varanasi and
Calcutta were a number from rather less exotic centres of
Hindu culture such as Southall, Northolt and Leicester.

'They treat the old women very badly,' said Shukla.
'They show them no respect. They give them less than the
minimum on which they can survive. Some of the ashrams
even demand a down-payment from the widows when they
first arrive. They say it is to cover the cost of their cremation,
but after a death they simply put the woman's body in a sack
and throw it in the Yamuna.'

Shukla walked with me along the *parikrama*, through the
crowded streets of the town. As we walked, we passed long
lines of widows, all shaven-headed and with begging-bowls
stretched towards us.

'My family have been priests in Vrindavan for many
generations,' said Shukla as we walked. 'The town used to be
very beautiful. But now it has expanded and become very
dirty and polluted. Before, people came here and they found
peace. Now they just find corruption and mental pollution.'

I asked the priest about the stories that appeared
occasionally in the Indian press claiming that the ashram
managers were in the habit of taking beautiful teenage widows
as concubines, or selling them at ten thousand rupees a time.

'It happens,' he said. 'Many of the ashrams are now run
by criminal elements. Even some of the sadhus are involved.
They lure young girls in, then sell them to local landowners.
When the landowners are finished with them, they can sell
them to the brothels in Delhi. They pay the police off, so they
don't intervene.'

What Shukla said was confirmed by local women's groups:
'Go to the villages around Vrindavan,' said Kamala Ghosh, 'and
you'll see that all the landowners have little widows as mistresses.
When they tire of them the widows are sold to whorehouses in
Delhi and Bombay. And we have had widows here as young as
ten.' Among those I talked to in Vrindavan, there was agreement

that nothing was being done to save the widows from such exploitation, least of all by the police.

Shukla and I were now standing outside the Shri Bhagwan Bhajan ashram, the biggest of them all, where I had met Kanaklatha that morning. A prayer shift had just finished and the street was full of tired old women in white saris. On the steps of the ashram sat a fat man in white homespun who Shukla pointed out as one of the managers. I asked him about the allegations, but the fat man simply shrugged.

'The widows come here because they love Krishna,' he said. 'After they sing we give them some rice and two rupees. That is our duty. But we are not their keepers. What they do when they go is their business.'

Inside, the ashram consisted of two vast halls. On the floor of each squatted about a thousand widows in their identical white saris. Most of them seemed to be in their fifties or sixties, but there was a thin scattering of much younger women, while around the edge of the hall, leaning against the walls, or occasionally completely prostrate on the ground, were a number of much older women. Some of them were clearly mentally disturbed, letting out high-pitched shrieks like wounded birds, while others compulsively combed their hair or brushed away imaginary flies. The windows of the two halls were shuttered, and the only light came from a pair of naked bulbs suspended from the centre of the ceiling, leaving the edges of the rooms in a deep, Dickensian darkness. The whole establishment stank of urine and dirty linen.

Then a woman stood up in the centre of each room and began clashing cymbals; from another place a bell started to ring. A new shift was beginning. A cantor started up the chant, answered by two thousand widows singing as one, on and on, faster and faster: 'Hare Ram, Hare Krishna, Hare Ram, Hare Krishna...'

This form of devotion was the invention of the great sixteenth-century Bengali sage Shri Krishna Chaitanya, an Orpheus-like figure believed by his followers to be an incarnation of Krishna. After Chaitanya's wife died from a snake bite, the sage became a wanderer, travelling to all the sites connected with the life of Krishna, building many new temples and rescuing others from decay, particularly

Vrindavan, whose shrines and temples had become overgrown and ruined.

Chaitanya's devotion to Krishna was of a deeply emotional kind, and his contemporary biography, the *Chaitanya Charit Amrita*, is filled with accounts of him falling into mystical raptures, 'breaking into song, dancing, weeping, climbing up trees, running to and fro like a madman and calling out the name of Radha and Krishna'. He encouraged his followers to come together and chant devotional songs called *kirtans* which, sung with a rising tempo and accompanied by the ringing of cymbals and bells, were supposed to lift the devotee into a mystical rapture. In Chaitanya's own time there are many accounts of thousands of devotees caught up in the mesmeric beat, falling into a state of trance, dancing and jumping as if in a frenzy, carried away in torrents of religious hysteria. So unruly and ecstatic did many of Chaitanya's prayer gatherings become that the Moghul governor of the area tried to ban his cult, and to arrest its leader for disrupting public order. According to the *Chaitanya Charit Amrita*, even the wild beasts were affected by his *kirtans*:

> When the herd of elephants saw Chaitanya coming through the woods of Vrindavan they shouted 'Krishna' and danced and ran about in love. Some rolled on the ground, others bellowed. As the master sang a *kirtan* aloud, the deer flocked thither and marched with him on two sides. Then six or seven tigers came up and joined the deer in accompanying the master, the deer and the tiger dancing together shouting 'Krishna! Krishna!', while embracing and kissing each other. Even the trees and creepers of Vrindavan were ecstatic, putting forth sprouts and tendrils, rejoicing at the sound.

Yet anything less ecstatic than the singing of today's widows in Vrindavan would be hard to imagine. At the back, the madwomen are shrieking. In the foreground, the exhausted old widows struggle to keep up with the cantor's pitch, many nodding asleep until given a poke by one of the ashram managers walking up and down the aisles with a stick. It is difficult to think of a sorrier or more pathetic sight. Vrindavan, Krishna's earthly paradise, is today a place of such profound sadness and distress that it almost defies description.

At the end of the shift, as darkness was beginning to fall outside, a pair of Brahmin priests walked into the hall and began to perform the *arti*. Taking a burning charcoal splint, they revolved the flame in front of the idol of Krishna which stood at the centre of the room. As they did so the widows let out an unearthly ululation: an eerie, high-pitched wailing noise. Bringing their hands together in the gesture of supplication, they all bowed before the idol as the priests closed the temple doors for the night. Then slowly the women began to file outside.

'This is not life,' said one old woman who came up to me out of the shadows, begging for a rupee. 'We all died the day our husbands died. How can anyone describe our pain? Our hearts are all on fire with sorrow. Now we just wait for the day when all this will end.'

# 4

# The South

# At the Court of
# the Fish-Eyed Goddess

MADURAI, 1998

Look down over the Tamil temple town of Madurai in the predawn glimmer of a summer's festival morning, and you will see an extraordinary sight.

The city sits in a broad, flat plain, as level and as green as a ripe paddy field at harvest time. Out of this flat tropical planisphere rises a series of four man-made mountain peaks, each echoed by a ripple of lesser man-made hillocks. These are the *gopuras*, or ceremonial gateways of Madurai's great temple to Meenakshi, the Fish-Eyed Goddess, a town within a town and one of the most sacred sites in India.

The *gopuras* dominate the city as completely as the cathedrals of the Middle Ages must once have dominated the landscape of Europe. They rise in great, tapering, wedge-shaped pyramids— each layer swarming with brightly coloured images of gods and demons, heroes and *yakshis*—until three-quarters of the way to their apex, they terminate in a crown of cobra heads tipped with a pair of cat's-eared demon finials. The astonishing complexity and elaboration of the *gopuras'* decoration is something you can see from far away, long before you are able to distinguish even the beginnings of its detail.

To the Tamils, this is a sacred landscape, and the origins of every feature are elaborately catalogued in the myths of Madurai. This rock was an evil elephant who attempted to trample the town's Brahmins to death before being turned to stone by Lord Shiva; the river there, the Vaigai, was created by Lord Sundareshvara, the husband of Meenakshi, to quench the thirst of one of his wedding guests, a dwarf named Pot Belly who had developed an unbearable thirst after eating three hundred pounds of rice.

At the very centre of the plain lies the temple itself, the most sacred place of all. For the temple, so the Brahmins will tell you, is a *tirtha*, a crossing-place linking the profane to the sacred. The pious pilgrim who steps within the temple enters a zone of transition, a ford between different states of perception, where the celestial can become suddenly imminent, manifest; it is a doorway to the divine, where you can cross from the world of men to the world of the gods as easily as you might cross a slow-flowing stream at the height of the dry season.

Though the sun had yet to rise, from my vantage point on the edge of town I could see the beginnings of frenzied activity around the temple. The *gopuras* were spotlit, and all around in the streets which circled the temple, flames and lights were heading towards the sacred enclosure, like a cloud of moths circling a lamp in the darkness of a summer's night.

As I walked further into the labyrinth of streets, the crowds thickened: groups of women with flowers in their hair were hurrying in the direction of the temple, all carrying offerings in their hands: packages of milk and ewers of coconut oil, pots of *ghee* and bags of *prasad*. In one place a huddle of old buses had parked in a sidestreet, and from them lines of shaven-headed pilgrims, all dressed in matching yellow *lungis*—devotees of Lord Venkateshwara, who had shaven their heads then offered their hair as gifts to the great temple at Tirupati—spilled out and set off into the slipstream of the bicycles and rickshaws. A few stalls had already opened, selling marigold garlands, glass bangles, sandalwood and incense sticks, and around these the pilgrims collected, haggling with the vendors for charms and offerings, before setting off again into the mêlée.

By the time I got to the temple it was first light, and the enclosure was already humming with life. Ranks of beggars had begun assembling under the eves of the *gopuras*, hands outstretched, and between them the pilgrims were prostrating themselves before the entrance gate. Some were lighting small camphor fires on the stone slabs under the gateway and commencing their *puja*, utterly unconcerned by the passing throng of mendicants and festival-goers, some of whom only narrowly avoided stepping on the praying figures. From inside came the sound of drums, and with it the soft beating of the wings of startled pigeons.

I passed under the Gate of Eight Goddesses and into the long, arcaded passage beyond. Inside, it was dark and magnificent. A forest of carved pillars—on closer inspection lines of heavy-breasted Hindu caryatids: *yakshis*, courtesans, goddesses and dancing-girls—flanked me on either side. Everything about the architecture was deeply, and consciously, feminine: heading towards the innermost sanctuary of the presiding goddess, one sunk deeper and deeper into the darkness, down a long, straight, womb-like passage.

There is a reason for this all-pervading femininity. The temple at Madurai is one of the few in India containing both male and female deities where the goddess is always worshipped before the gods. As far as most of the pilgrims are concerned, this is the Temple of Meenakshi; to them, her husband Lord Sundareshvara, 'the Beautiful Lord', is a thoroughly secondary deity, only to be worshipped when joined to his wife, even though he is technically a form of the most powerful of all the gods, the great Shiva himself. For it is because of Meenakshi, not her consort, that the temple is famous throughout India. She has a reputation as a uniquely generous goddess who invariably gives boons to those who honour her, particularly in the matter of children. Pray before the shrine of Meenakshi—or *Amma*, the mother, as the pilgrims call her—then tie a twine around the banyan tree in the courtyard, and in nine months' time a child will be born; or so they say.

The conscious fecundity of the temple is evident in every aspect of its decoration. Spiralling out over the cornices and the finials of the arcades are a great anarchic cavalcade of mask heads, demons, demi-gods and godlings, peeping out from the angles, coming to roost under the pendetives; a great spiralling pantheon of Hindu deities that is repeated with even greater vigour over the towering *gopuras*. It is as if Meenakshi's fertility is such that every inch of the stonework is organically sprouting with supernatural forms, just as the bare desert sprouts with camel-thorn after the rains.

Then, quite suddenly, a carved wooden temple *rath* appeared in the centre of the principal ceremonial avenue from a side passage, pushed by a swarm of half-naked figures. Their progress was lit by a succession of temple priests holding brightly burning yellow splints dipped in camphor oil. In a silken tabernacle at the top of the *rath* lay the golden image of the goddess herself, garlanded and draped in cloth-of-gold, her nose-jewel flashing in the flames of the priests' burning splints. This was followed by another temple cart, containing an image of both Meenakshi and Lord Sundareshvara, with their son, the six-headed war god Murugan, standing between them. Then came a pair of brahminy cows led by two priests and hung with drapes and drums and anointed with dots of saffron and turmeric.

As the cavalcade began lining up in the main axis, with a ringing of gongs and bells, a caparisoned temple elephant and a third *rath* carrying a huge golden horse joined the procession. From another passage emerged a temple band, banging cymbals and drums and blowing a succession of fanfares on the *nagashwaram*, the giant Tamil oboe whose rasping, raucous notes filled the air with a noise like the screech of peacocks. Then, with a last great fanfare from the *nagashwaram*, they were off, the whole procession moving slowly up the ramps, out of the temple and into the streets, cheered on by the crowds of waiting pilgrims.

'Where are they going?' I asked a passer-by, a dark-skinned Keralite in a green *lungi*.

'To the tank,' he replied. 'Once a year the gods are taken from here for a boat ride on the holy waters.' He added: 'Every year my friends and I walk here from our village in Kerala just to see this sight.'

'You must have sore feet,' I said. 'It's a long way.'

'We feel happy to come,' he replied. 'The goddess gives us strength. Sometimes it takes us only nine days to walk here.'

'To see the *Teppam* festival brings many boons,' said the man's friend, another wiry Keralite. 'Every year we feel the benefit.'

'And is that why all these people come?'

'Of course,' said the first pilgrim. 'This temple is one of the most holy places in India, and this is one of the most auspicious days. On this day, if you ask anything of the goddess you are sure to get success.'

'Is there anything in particular that you will be asking for?'

'We all want children,' said the first pilgrim. 'And for

this we look to Meenakshi. She has much energy, much power.'

'You have no children?' I asked.

'I have three sons. But I want six.'

'How many does your wife want?'

'She wants only three. So she has stayed in Kerala.'

'Meenakshi Devi looks after her devotees,' said the second pilgrim. 'She is like a mother to us. She gives us energy and strength. She clears obstacles from our path. Just to see her, to have *darshan*, is enough.'

We had left the temple behind us and were now heading through the middle of Madurai. The sun had risen and the shopkeepers were beginning to open their stalls: Durga's Veg and Tiffin; Anand Vests and Briefs; the Bell Brand Umbrella Shop; the Raj Lucky Metal Store. As the streets filled with people, so the procession began to make slower and slower progress. An escort of four fat policemen now led the way, lazily waving their lathis at cyclists who were trying to head against the flow. Every hundred yards or so the *raths* would pull to a halt and the priests would accept the offerings given to them by the devotees who lined the way, anointing the pilgrims' heads with *vibhuti* and *kumkum* (the red powder symbolising the sexuality of the goddess), and lighting the lamps on the pilgrims' outstretched trays of offerings. Those who gave money were blessed by the temple elephant, who first took the rupee notes in its trunk, gave the money to its priestly *mahout*, then momentarily cupped the tip of its trunk over the devotee's head.

In some places little temporary wayside temples had been erected along the route—often little more than trestle tables covered in lamps and framed and garlanded lithographs of gods, goddesses and saints. These were easily confused with the roadside booths set up by the various political parties for the forthcoming election, as both were covered with almost identical sets of images of heroes, political bosses and gods. After all, in India the division between religion and politics is notoriously porous, and with so many gods being played by film stars, and so many film stars entering politics (particularly in the south), there is an easy drift of iconography between temple, silver screen and election rally.

Moreover, Meenakshi and Sundareshvara are both believed by the people of Madurai to have jointly ruled their town as king and queen in ancient times, so they are themselves in a sense politicians as well as gods. Certainly, at both sets of stalls the procession would halt, garlands would be draped over the Brahmins and the political candidates, and coconuts would be cracked over the rath.

It was nearly ten o'clock before the procession reached the sacred tank at the edge of town, an open expanse of water with an island temple standing in its middle. Here the golden idols were decanted on to the temple rafts for ferrying around the lake.

'The goddess is having her bath now,' explained one of the elderly Brahmins as I watched the boat set off around the tank. 'We should leave her to her privacy. Come back at ten o'clock tonight if you wish to see the climax of the festival.'

'This is our custom,' said his son, also a temple priest. He was a handsome boy, and but for the sacred thread hanging over his shoulder, was naked from his white *lungi* upwards. 'You see, this is a very ancient ceremony,' he continued. 'Over two thousand years old.'

'I am the sixty-third generation of temple priests in my family,' said the father, 'and my son is the sixty-fourth. These traditions about our goddess have been handed down to us from the most ancient times. The same festivals, the same holidays, are celebrated just as they were at that time.

'Nothing, not one detail,' he said, 'has been changed.'

What the Brahmin said was quite true. The temple at Madurai is contemporary with those of ancient Greece and Egypt, yet while the gods of Thebes and the Parthenon have been dead and forgotten for millennia, the gods and temples of Hindu India are now more revered than ever.

Hindu civilisation is the only great classical culture to survive intact from the ancient world, and at temples such as

Madurai one can still catch glimpses of festivals and practices that were seen by Greek visitors to India long before the rise of ancient Rome. Indeed, it is only when you grasp the astonishing antiquity, and continuity, of Hinduism that you realise quite how miraculous its survival has been.

Madurai is one of the most ancient holy towns in India, a Benares of the south, and long before its existence was first noted in the West in the fourth century B.C., it was already an important centre. For from the very earliest period, Madurai was a major terminus of the Spice Route, linking the pepper groves of India with the groaning tables of the Mediterranean. Megasthenes, the Greek ambassador who visited India in 302 B.C., recorded the town's legendary riches, and it is given pride of place in the earliest document detailing the spice trade, the *Periplus Maris Erythraei*, written by an anonymous Alexandrian Greek in the first century A.D.

The *Periplus* gives a wonderful picture of the courtly lifestyle of the time when it records that the area around Madurai imported Mediterranean eye-shadow, perfume, silverware, fine Italian wine and beautiful slave-girl musicians for concubinage; in turn the town exported silk, ivory, pearls and, crucially, pepper. Both Strabo and Ptolemy mention Madurai, the former in the same breath as complaining about the drain of silver from the imperial Roman treasury that the trade with India was causing. This picture is graphically confirmed by the recent find of several huge Roman coin hoards around Madurai, as well as the discovery of a Roman coastal trading post near Pondicherry, where the goods destined for the town were unloaded. At the peak of the trade, during the reign of Nero, an embassy from Madurai was received in Rome, and there is even a reference to a Temple of Augustus being erected on the Indian coast, presumably for the use of Roman traders permanently settled in the Carnatic. Even today the English 'pepper' and 'ginger' are loan words from Tamil—from *'pippali'* and *'singabera'* respectively—having entered our language in the Middle Ages via Byzantine Greek.

This picture of Madurai's cosmopolitan connections is confirmed by Tamil sources which record that the kings of the Pandyan dynasty used to keep *Yavana* (Greek or Roman) mercenaries, alongside a regiment of Tamil Amazons, as their personal bodyguards. We know this because around the temple at Madurai there grew up a flourishing literary culture based, according to tradition, at the Sangam or academy of Tamil poets.

The surviving work of the Sangam is wonderfully graphic and accessible and gives a picture of a heroic society that would not have been altogether strange to Homer, Virgil or the author of *Beowulf*: a world of chariots and warriors where the refusal of one king to give his daughter in marriage to another was a cause for war, and where soldiers, and even their mothers, welcomed death in battle, for such an end led the hero straight to nirvana.

The wiles of dancing-girls and courtesans is another popular theme. The *Shilappadikaram*, one of the most famous Sangam works, tells the tragedy of a Prince Kovalan, who neglects his wife and loses his fortune because of his love for the celebrated courtesan Madhavi of Puhar; in the end, penniless, Kovalan is accused of theft and cut down in the streets of Madurai, while his faithful wife wreaks revenge by consigning the city to flames.

Arguably the most beautiful of the poems to emerge from the Sangam is *The Garland of Madurai*, a celebration of the city's festivals probably written in the second century A.D. One section almost exactly describes the scene I saw seventeen hundred years later: '[Madurai is] a city gay with flags, waving over homes and shops selling food and drink; the streets are broad rivers of people, folk of every race, buying and selling in the bazaars, or singing to the music of wandering bands and musicians...[Around the temple], amid the perfume of *ghee* and incense, [are stalls] selling sweet cakes, garlands of flowers, scented powder and betel *paan*...[while nearby are] men making bangles of conch shells, goldsmiths, cloth dealers, tailors making up clothes, coppersmiths, flower sellers, vendors of sandalwood, painters and weavers.'

Both the city and the temple you walk through today retain the configuration described in *The Garland*, with the streets forming a series of concentric circles around the temple. Although both town and temple have been burned down and rebuilt many times over, and little of the city's present-day fabric predates the seventeenth century, the plan of Madurai's centre still corresponds fairly closely to its original classical Hindu design of the *mandala,* a geometric diagram oriented to the four cardinal directions and symbolising the ideal cosmos, a street plan that in Madurai's case probably dates from no later than the first century A.D.

Yet perhaps the most extraordinary example of Madurai's astonishing continuity is the fact that the Sangam poem *The Sacred Games of Shiva,* which tells the legend of Sundareshvara's marriage to Meenakshi, is still very much current in the city; so much so that its myths are known to every shopkeeper and rickshaw-driver. Moreover, the events described in the stories of *The Sacred Games* remain the basis of the city's calendar, inspiring both the cycle of festivals around which Madurai's civic life still revolves, and the details of the daily worship inside the temple precincts.

Meenakshi, then as now, is the city's great fertility goddess, and the focus of her cult lies in her union with Sundareshvara. Every night in the temple the images of Meenakshi and Sundareshvara are brought together in the latter's bedchamber. The last act of the priests before they close the doors is to remove Meenakshi's nose-jewel, lest the rubbing of it irritate her husband when they make love—an act, so the priests will tell you, that ensures the preservation and regeneration of the universe.

So spectacular and addictive is the love play between the two deities that Sundareshvara—uniquely for a form of that most adulterous god Shiva—remains strictly faithful to his goddess. Once a year, an image of the lovely Tamil goddess Cellattamma is brought to the god 'to have her powers renewed by Sundareshvara'. But Sundareshvara refuses her, and the spurned goddess returns to her temple in such a fury that she can only be propitiated by a buffalo sacrifice. The *Teppam* festival which I attended is also related to the goddess's irresistible sexuality. For Meenakshi's boat trip with Sundareshvara is understood by the faithful to be part of her seduction of her Lord, a seduction which she finally achieves later that night.

All this, of course, makes the festival one of the most fecund and auspicious times in the year to get married. On its eve, as I was wandering through the temple precincts, I found myself in a long file of competing marriage parties as village after village queued up to marry off its young. The parties waited, excited and expectant, in the principal ceremonial passage leading to the shrine of Meenakshi. After the rites had been celebrated they retired to the southern range of the cloister surrounding the temple tank, to relax and to remove the more encumbering of their marriage clothes.

As I watched, a pretty Tamil bride of no more than seventeen entered the cloister surrounded by a gaggle of ten of her girlfriends. They surrounded her on all sides and, holding up an unwound sari, allowed her to remove her garlands and change in privacy out of her heavy red silk marriage sari and into a less formal cotton one. Other guests appeared carrying the accumulated wedding presents, while to one side, on his own, stood the groom, if anything even younger than his bride, and looking profoundly dazed and uncertain about the day's events. After some of the older villagers had blessed the couple, the girls led the bride purposefully off. Intrigued, I followed at a discreet distance to see where they were taking her.

They led her through the temple's labyrinth of halls and passages, eventually coming to a halt before a carved pillar. The girls bowed before the image, then anointed it with powder from a small pot carried by one of the bride's friends. After they had gone, I went up to see which god or goddess they had dedicated themselves to. In fact the image was not of a deity, but of some sort of fertility *yakshi*, a naked, heavy-breasted and heavily pregnant sprite shown bent-legged in the act of giving birth. The entire image glistened with oil where devotees wishing for a child, or an easy delivery, had covered it with *ghee*, while around the breasts and navel it was heavily stained with vermilion and *kumkum*.

Nearby, among the caryatids carved on each of the temple's ten thousand pillars, I found many other images of fecundity. One, for example, showed a Tamil village woman with a coir shopping basket and a baby strapped to her breast. Her head was turned so she could see a second baby she was carrying in a backpack, while beside her walked a third child, a little boy eating an apple; the woman's hand rested gently on her son's head. It is an image of startling humanity—the same sight can be seen today in any bazaar in Tamil Nadu—yet the statue predates the beginning of the Italian Renaissance by over a century.

'Just to enter the goddess' temple brings great good fortune,' explained K.R. Bhaskar, a tall, dhoti-clad devotee who had come up and introduced himself as I wandered around. 'Meenakshi *amma* certainly blessed my family: we now have two children after coming to pray here.'

'And the villagers believe this? That you only have to come here and children miraculously appear?'

'Not just the villagers,' replied Mr Bhaskar, 'the educated class too. I myself am a financial consultant in Bangalore. I have a post-graduate M.Sc. in Biochem from Mysore University. But I believe in Meenakshi. This is my sincere feeling. I know she exists. I myself have seen her, in the mist, in shadows. She comes in my dreams, my subconscious. What is going on here is hundred per cent truth.'

'When you say you can see the gods, do you actually believe that they look the way they do in temples, with three faces and six arms and so on.'

'No, no,' said Mr Bhaskar patiently. 'These things are symbols only. Not all devotees have the same level of spiritual achievement. Some people can see God in a flame when they meditate, but most others need something more concrete, something on which they can focus their devotion. These images here are just indications of the different moods of the gods, mere reflections. They are paths to reach the infinite, not an end in themselves.'

'And do many educated people feel like you?' I asked.

'Many,' said Mr Bhaskar. 'At one time maybe the educated stayed away from the temples, thinking they were backward, but these days educated people are coming back in ever-increasing numbers. You see, this is not superstition. This is our culture. It is in our blood, in our veins. It is not so much a religion as a way of life. It is not something that will stop when our people are educated. Hinduism will never die. Already it is beginning to make a comeback in our India.'

'Why do you think that is?' I asked.

'When you come to the temple you feel total peace of mind,' said Mr Bhaskar. 'You feel total involvement in the spiritual powers of God. In Bangalore many people have made much money, but they found that this did not satisfy them. It was not enough.

'Only with faith in God,' said Mr Bhaskar, 'can they have full satisfaction.'

The next evening at ten o'clock I again made my way along the dusty, pilgrim-clogged streets of Madurai, and through the labyrinth of horn-hooting, rickshaw-squealing lanes leading up to the great sacred tank.

Everything had been transformed since the morning procession. Temple bells rang out over a hot, thick blanket of darkness, lit here and there by the naked electric lights of the tea-stalls and the flickering camphor flames of the pilgrims' lamps. Around the side of the tank the crowds were massing, all dressed up in their neatly-pressed new *lungis* and their best silk saris. Some sat up on the parapet, nibbling from cones of chickpeas and roasted *dal*, while all around them balloon-sellers and ice-cream *wallahs*, peanut-roasters and sweetmeat vendors sold their wares. Here and there, among the sea of milling pilgrims and townsfolk, stood crowded bullock carts full of families who had driven in from their villages to see the festival: burly, moustachioed farmers and their womenfolk and children. From their eminence they peered eagerly over the heads of the crowd towards the illuminated spire of the island temple rising into the sky, its image perfectly reflected in the still waters of the tank.

'We come for every festival,' said Pandyan, a farmer sitting in the front of one especially-heavily laden cart, bearing no fewer than fifteen women and children from his extended family. 'Our village is only twenty kilometres away, so if all goes well we can get back home before dawn.'

'In our village we have a small temple to Meenakshi,' said Pandyan's wife, Kasi Ama. 'But it is better to come and give our offerings to her here.'

'On a festival day,' said Pandyan, '*Amma* cannot refuse anything, if you ask her with a clean mind.'

It was now well after eleven, an hour after the ceremony should have begun, and the Brahmins were still waiting for the exact moment, determined by the astrologers, for Meenakshi and Sundareshvara to begin their journey around the lake. As we spoke, a ripple of expectation passed through the crowd. From the small Maryamman temple by the lakeside the Brahmins were now emerging in a file, their oiled bodies glistening in the light of their flickering camphor torches. As they processed out, the crowd parted before them, and they made their way slowly to the *ghat* steps leading down to the waters of the tank, where the raft was waiting. In the morning it had looked a rather flimsy and makeshift object, with its crude woodwork and *naïvely* painted papier mâché; but now, ablaze with lamps in the burnished darkness, it was transformed into something gilded and magnificent: a huge floating temple, suspended on the dark waters of the tank. In the centre of the raft, reclining in their silken *palkis* amid their robes and garlands, were the golden images of Meenakshi and Sundareshvara.

With a beating of drums, forty or fifty well-built villagers filed out of the temple and took up their stations along the side of the tank parapet.

'These are villagers from Antonedi,' said Mohan Pundit, a temple priest I had met earlier that morning. He had just helped me manoeuvre through the police cordon to a spot on the edge of the *ghat* from where I was now watching proceedings. 'It has been the privilege of these people to pull rope since the time of our King Tirumala Nayyak, four hundred years ago.'

At a signal from the head priest, the men picked up a great thick rope several hundred feet long that was attached to the raft, and with a fanfare from the temple band—all wailing *nagashwarams* and dancing drums—they shouldered the burden and began to pull.

Slowly the raft began to move around the tank, followed by a small flotilla of Brahmins in overloaded dinghies, some of which contained as many as twenty people and were listing dangerously. As the villagers pulled, and the boat slowly circled the tank, the overexcited crowd surged around the tank, cheering and clapping and singing *bhajans*.

For an hour the raft circled and the crowd sang and cheered. Children giggled on the shoulders of their fathers, licking ice creams and begging their parents to buy them more chickpeas, or perhaps some milky *ladoos* from the *mithai-wallah*. The band played and the crowd clapped. This, I thought, not for the first time that day, is what one of the great medieval festivals must have been like.

Finally it was time to prepare the goddess for her final seduction of Lord Sundareshvara. The raft pulled into the *ghat* and the idols, still on their palanquin, were raised on to the shoulders of the priests and carried ashore. It was a heavy burden, and as the priests staggered to the top of the steps, bowed under the weight, the crowd let out one last great cheer.

'I've never seen a crowd enjoying themselves so much,' I said to Mohan Pundit.

'The people come here,' he replied, 'and for one day they forget that they are hungry and poor. The goddess takes them away from themselves. *Amma* does this for them, and for this reason they love her and are happy.'

# Under the Char Minar

'Fibs,' said Mir Moazam Husain. 'That's what everyone of your generation thinks I'm telling, at least when I talk about Hyderabad in the old days. You all think I'm telling the *most* outrageous pack of fibs.'

The old man settled back in his rocking chair and shook his head, half amused, half frustrated. 'My grandchildren, for instance. I can see the wonder in their eyes as I talk. For them the old world of Hyderabad is almost inconceivable: they can hardly imagine that such a world could exist.'

'But what exactly can't they imagine?' I asked.

'Well, the whole bang-shoot, really: the Nizam and his nobles and their palaces and their *zenanas* and the entire what-have-you that went with old Hyderabad State. But it's all true. Every world.'

Mir Moazam was a sprightly and intelligent eighty-four-year-old with a broad forehead and sparkling brown eyes. Though he talked elegiacally about the past, there was no bitterness in his voice. 'The palace I grew up in', he continued, 'had a staff of 927 people including three doctors. There was even a small regiment of women eight or ten of whom were of African extraction, who were there just to guard the main gate. But tell that to my grandchildren. They've seen how we live today, and they just think that I'm making it up. Especially when I start telling them about my grandfather.'

'Your grandfather?'

'My grandfather, Fakrool Mulk. The name means "Pride of the Realm". He was a remarkable man, a great servant of the state, but he was also – how shall I put it – a larger-than-life character.'

'Tell me about him.'

'You probably wouldn't believe it.'

'Try me,' I said.

'Well, where shall I start?' said Mir Moazam. He paused while he cast around for a suitable place to begin his tale.

'You see, although my grandfather was Deputy Prime Minister in the Nizam's government, his real passion was building.'

'Building?'

'Building. It was like an addiction for him. He just had to build. Over the course of his life he built a great series of vast, rambling palaces, one after the other. But he was never satisfied. As soon as he had finished one, he immediately began to build another. Sometimes he would just give an entire palace away. Once he heard that the Nizam had privately said that he envied him owning a palace looking on to the Fateh Maidan, where all the tent pegging and polo matches took place on the ruler's birthday. At the first opportunity he just gave the Asad Bagh to the Nizam, even though it was his principal residence and all nine of his children had been born there. But that was absolutely typical of him and his buildings. He never lived in half of them, yet even when he was seventy-five he was still at it. Of course, he built up enormous debts in the process.'

'Was he a trained architect?'

'Well, that was precisely the problem. No, he wasn't. But every evening he would go out for a walk, and with him he would take his walking stick and this great entourage of his staff, which always included his secretary, his master mason, his builders, a couple of his household poets and the paymaster general of his estates—some thirty or forty people in all.

'Anyway, on these walks, when the inspiration came, he would begin to draw in the sand with his walking stick: maybe a new cottage, or a new stable block, or possibly a new palace, or whatever it was, according to how the fancy took him. The draughtsmen he had brought with him would jot it down on paper and then draw it up when they got back. The next day he would be shown the pictures after breakfast. He would say, "No enlarge that tower, and let's put two cupolas on top." Or maybe: "That's good, but it has to be triple the size." His buildings were always something of a hotchpotch, as he would change the style according to his mood. Some have a classical ground floor, a tropical Gothic first storey, and then change to art deco or even Scotch Baronial halfway up.

'Finally the plan would be approved, the masons would get to work, and—hey presto!—the Hyderabad skyline had a new palace. Except that then he would go and visit it and say, "This door is not wide enough. I can't possibly fit through this with the Resident's wife on my arm." So the whole thing would be torn down and work would restart. Even as an old man he was still adding new wings and towers and porticoes to his palaces, and despite his debts, none of his sons even had the guts to argue with him.'

'Did he have a favourite palace?'

'I don't know about a favourite, but the one he lived in for longest was Iram Manzil, just around the corner from here. It wasn't the largest of his palaces, but one of the reasons he loved it was the stuffed tiger.'

'The stuffed tiger?'

'You see, after building, my grandfather's other great love was tiger shooting, and the season for tiger shooting was only a few months each year, so on the hill outside Iram Manzil he built this miniature railway track, and on the track he placed a stuffed tiger on wheels. It would be let loose from the top of the hill and we would all line up and fire away with our double barrels: *bang! bang! bang!* all of us aiming at this wretched tiger as it careered down the hill, shooting in and out of the rocks, down the gradient, getting faster and faster as it went down. By the time it reached the end of the track it was completely peppered: blown to bits, poor thing. So the men who were employed to look after the tiger would patch it up and pull it back, and off we'd go again.'

'I can see why your grandchildren might find all this a little...fantastic.'

'But I think what they find *most* difficult to believe is not this sort of thing, but the simple business of my grandfather's eating habits.'

'Eating habits?'

'Well, Fakrool Mulk was a most fastidious man, but he did like his food.'

'He ate a lot?'

'He would always work it off with long walks, horseback rides and by swinging Indian clubs, but yes, he did get through a bit of *khanna*.'

'So,' I ventured, 'on any given day what might be on your grandfather's table?'

'I'll never forget Fakrool Mulk's dinners,' said Mir Moazam. His face lit up at the memory: 'He would sit in the middle of this huge table, with the doctor, the butler and the assistant butler looking on, while his secretary read to him from the *Hyderabad Bulletin*. First they would bring a tankard of wonderfully thick, creamy chicken broth, then came the pomfret from Bombay – two pieces. He would finish that, then followed the whole chicken, so tender it would fall apart at the touch. Only when he had single-handedly demolished this fowl would the next course be brought in: a selection of spectacular Mughlai dishes, eight curries or so in silver bowls, and a great plate of the finest ground Hyderabadi kebabs. They would just melt in the mouth: I've never tasted anything like them anywhere else. Of course there was always a mountain of soft white pilaf rice, and everything was served on the most beautiful monogrammed porcelain. When he had finished he would pass the plate to me, and I would transfer what was left to my plate: in our tradition that was considered a great privilege, and I would *salaam* profoundly as I did so. There was very strict protocol: we wouldn't sit until asked to, and wouldn't dream of talking until talked to. He did the talking, we responded.'

'And that was the end of dinner?'

'No, no. There was still pudding. After the curries had been carried away, then in came the sweets: two different kinds of English pudding – hot and cold – followed by a silver platter of Mughlai sweets, all of which were served with a great big bowl of clotted cream. Then he'd get up and go next door to drink soda water and receive the gift that the Nizam would send him every day: it might be a box of mangoes or something. So he would call in the secretary he employed solely to write letters to the Nizam, and dictate a letter of thanks, at least half of which would simply be the usual list of highly exaggerated Persian titles. When that was finished he would take his hubble bubble and puff away at that, until he was ready to go downstairs and play billiards, after which it was off to bed. A story-teller would be brought into an alcove covered with a curtain, and from there he would tell stories from the *Shahnama* about Sohrab and Rustam, or perhaps tales from the *Mahabharat*, or Deccani tales about the deeds of the Qutb Shahi kings. Those old story-tellers could talk for days without stopping. Only when they heard snoring from the other side of the curtain would they stop.'

Mir Moazam looked up, and again slowly shook his head: 'Now, of course, almost everything has gone,' he said, 'and I suppose I'm one of the last who can remember that way of life. We're going pretty fast, and after us there will just be the same monotonous uniformity. All that will be left of that would be what is recorded in books and memoirs.

'But like my grandchildren,' he added, looking me in the eyes, 'you probably find it difficult to even conceive the life I'm describing. And why shouldn't you? This entire world was almost completely destroyed and uprooted years before you were born.'

But I did believe Mir Moazam, for I had long heard equally fantastical stories about the State of Hyderabad. Years ago, Iris Portal, an old friend of my grandmother, had told me a story I had never forgotten: How one day in the late 1930s she had been taken to see some of the Nizam's treasure which was kept in open-fronted sheds in the grounds of one of the palaces. This was at a time when Iris' husband ran the staff of the Nizam's younger son, and Iris had befriended his wife, Princess Niloufer.

Niloufer had led Iris past the Bedouin Arab guards all lolling about in a state of dishabille, and there at the back of the sheds were lines of trucks and haulage lorries. The trucks were dusty and neglected, their tyres rotting and flat and sinking into the ground, but when the two ladies pulled back a tarpaulin, they found that the trucks were laden with gems and precious stones and pearls and gold coins. The Nizam apparently lived in fear of either a revolution or an Indian takeover of his state, and had equipped the lorries so that he could get some of his wealth out of the country at short notice if the need came. But then he lost interest in his plan, and left the lorries to rot, quite incapable of going anywhere, but still full of their consignment of jewels. The guards did little to protect the riches in the lorries: what really protected them, thought Iris, was the aura of the ruler.

Other stories of Iris confirmed this picture of Hyderabad as a sort of fantastical Indian Ruritania, where an unreconstructed feudal aristocracy preserved extravagantly rococo rules of etiquette, and where life revolved around fabulously intricate and elaborate orders or precedence.

The Nizam, said to be the richest man in the world, had no fewer than eleven thousand servants: thirty-eight dusted the chandeliers, others were employed only to prepare betel nut. In addition, he had three official wives, forty-two concubines and nearly twenty children.

'He was as mad as a coot, and his [chief] wife was raving,' Iris told me. 'It was like living in France on the eve of the Revolution. All the power was in the hands of the Muslim nobility. They spent money like water and were terrible, irresponsible landlords, but they could be very charming and sophisticated as well. Many had English nannies, and had been to English schools or universities. They would take us shooting – snipe and partridges – talking all the while about their trips to England or to Cannes and Paris, although in many ways Hyderabad was still living in the Mughal Middle Ages and the villages we would pass through were often desperately poor. You couldn't help feeling that the whole great baroque structure could come crashing down at any minute.'

For all the fairy-tale quality of Iris's tales, they were confirmed in every detail by the most sober history books. The Nizam, Major-General Sir Osman Ali Khan, did indeed possess the largest fortune in the world: according to one contemporary estimate it amounted to at least £100 million in gold and silver bullion and £400 million in jewels, many of which came from his own Golconda mines, source of the Koh-i-Noor and the legendary (though now lost) Great Mughal Diamond which, at 787 carats, is thought to have been the largest ever discovered.

The Nizam was also the most senior Prince in India, the only one to merit the title 'His *Exalted* Highness', and for most of the first half of the twentieth century he ruled a state the size of Italy—82,700 square miles of the Deccan plateau —as absolute monarch, answerable (in internal matters at least) to no one but himself. Within this vast area he could claim the allegiance of fifteen million subjects. The grandest members of the Hyderabad aristocracy—known as the Paigah nobles—were richer than most Maharajahs, and each maintained his own court, his own extraordinary palace—or palaces—and his own three or four thousand strong private army. Nor despite all the dreadful inequalities of wealth, was Hyderabad a poor country: in its final year of existence, 1947-48, the state's income and expenditure rivalled that of Belgium and exceeded those of twenty member states of the United Nations.

Moreover, from what I could gather from my reading, the Nizam appeared to be every bit as eccentric as Iris had indicated. While most Indian Maharajahs dressed in magnificent costumes and bedecked themselves with jewels the size of ostrich eggs, according to one British resident the Nizam resembled 'a snuffly clerk too old to be sacked'. All his life he wore the same dirty old fez, a grubby pair of pyjamas, and an ancient sherwani; towards the end he even took to knitting his own socks. In 1946, when the Divan of Hyderabad brought a distinguished Persian visitor to see the Nizam at the Azakhan Zehra, and said in Persian *'Een Shah-i-Dekhan ast,'* (This is the King of the Deccan), the startled visitor could only comment *'Panah-ba-khuda!'* (God save us!) When he died in 1967 *The Times* described the Nizam as a 'shabby old man shuffling through his dream world', and described his hobbies as 'taking opium, writing Persian poetry and'—a wonderful detail—'watching surgical operations'.

Yet for all this, under the Nizam Hyderabad grew to be an important centre of learning and the arts. After the fall of Lucknow to the British in 1856, Hyderabad remained the last redoubt of Indo-Islamic culture and the flagship of Deccani civilisation with its long heritage of composite Qutb Shahi, Vijayanagaran, Mughal, Kakatiyan, Central Asian and Iranian influences. Its Osmania university was the first in India to teach in an indigenous Indian language, and it was far ahead of most regions of India in the spread of education. In the early twentieth century it was the most important area for

the production of Urdu literature in the subcontinent, and
the people of Hyderabad had evolved their own distinctive—
and often very sophisticated—manners, habits, language,
music, literature, food and dress. Moreover their capital was
famous as a city of palaces, rivalling in grandeur and
magnificence anything in South Asia.

It is often hard to believe this as you drive through
Hyderabad today. For while the city is still fairly prosperous
—certainly a far cry from the urban death rattle that is
modern Lucknow – fifty years on it is a pretty unprepossessing
place, ugly, polluted and undistinguished, all Seventies office
blocks and bustling new shopping centres: 'Darshan
Automobiles' and 'Dervish Home Needs', the 'Jai Hind Cycle
Store' and 'Posh Tailors: Ladies and Gents a Speciality'. The
trees have all been cut down and attempts at urban planning
utterly abandoned. New buildings are mushrooming
everywhere, often built over the old Indo-Islamic bazaars and
colonial townhouses, so that only piles of discarded pillars
remain to hint at what once occupied the site of the new
concrete jeans emporium or pizza restaurant.

In the older bazaars, the great cusped gateways of the
old Hyderabadi *havelis* still stand, but now they lead nowhere,
except perhaps to a half-built matrix of foundations and
concrete piles. The palaces of the Paigah nobility have mostly
been knocked down or else taken over by the government,
and have been so badly kept-up, or so unsympathetically
converted into offices, that they are virtually unrecognisable.
At first sight there is nothing remotely charming or magical
about Hyderabad today.

But look a little further, and you discover that small
pools of the old world do still survive, often out of bounds
to the casual visitor. The Falaknuma Palace is one such place.
A huge and magnificent complex of white classical villas and
mansions raised above the town on its own acropolis, the
Falaknuma was the principal residence of the sixth Nizam,
the father of Osman Ali Khan. But today it is the subject of
bitter legal dispute between the Taj group, who wish to turn
it into a hotel, and the last Nizam's grandson, now mainly
resident on a sheep farm in Australia, who claims never to
have sold it. While the buildings await the decision of the

courts, they lie empty and semi-ruinous, locked by court order, with every window and doorway sealed with red wax.

Wipe the dust from the windows and peer inside, and you see cobwebs, the size of bedsheets, hanging in the corners of the rooms. The skeletons of outsized Victorian sofas and armchairs lie dotted around the parquet floors, their chintz entirely eaten away by white ants, so that all that remain are the wooden frames, the springs and a little of the stuffing. Vast imperial desks, big enough to play billiards on, stand on rotting red carpets peppered with huge holes, as if they have been savaged by some terrible outsized supermoth. On one wall hangs a giant portrait of Queen Mary, on another a strange, faded Victorian fantasy of Richard the Lionheart on the battlements at Acre. Beyond are long, gloomy corridors, leading to unseen inner courtyards and *zenana* wings: mile upon mile of empty classical arcades and melancholy bow fronts, now quite empty but for a pair of lonely *chowkidars* shuffling around with their lathis and whistles. Outside stretch acres of scrub flats, once presumably soft green lawns, dotted here and there with kitsch statues of naked cupids, waterless fountains, giant silver oil lamps and paint-flaking flagpoles leaning at crazy angles.

That this fairy-tale extravagance has always been part of the culture of Hyderabad is demonstrated by the mediaeval Qutb Shahi tombs, a short distance to the east of the Falaknuma. They are wonderfully ebullient and foppish monuments dating from the fifteenth and sixteenth centuries, with domes swelling out of all proportion to the bases, like a watermelon attempting to balance on a fig. Above the domes rises the craggy citadel of Golconda, source of the ceaseless stream of diamonds which ensured that Hyderabad's rulers would never be poor. Inside the walls you pass a succession of harems and bathing pools, pavilions and pleasure gardens – a world that seems to have jumped straight out of the pages of *The Arabian Nights*. When the French jeweller Jean Baptiste Tavernier visited Golconda in 1642 he found a society every bit as decadent as this architecture might suggest. He wrote that the town possessed more than twenty thousand registered courtesans, who took it in turns to dance for the King every Friday.

The romantic and courtly atmosphere infected even the sober British when they arrived in Hyderabad at the end of the eighteenth century, and the city is the location of one of the most affecting Anglo-Indian love stories to emerge from the three-hundred-year interaction of the two peoples. The old British Residency, now the University College for Women, is an imposing Palladian villa which shelters in a massive fortified garden in the south of the town. A pair of stone lions lie, paws extended, below a huge pedimented and colonnaded front, looking out over a wide expanse of eucalyptus, breadfruit and casuarina trees, every inch the East India Company at its grandest and most formal. Yet surprises lurk in the undergrowth at the rear of the compound.

The complex was built by Lieutenant-Colonel James Achilles Kirkpatrick, Resident between 1797 and 1805. He was an unusually imaginative and sympathetic figure, whose love and respect for the people of Hyderabad was symbolised by his adoption of Hyderabadi clothes and ways of living. Shortly after his arrival he fell in love with Khair-un-Nissa ('Excellent among Women'), a great-niece of the Divan of Hyderabad, whom he married in 1800 according to Muslim law. This caused great alarm in London, as it was thought—probably correctly—that Kirkpatrick had become a Muslim, an impression that was reinforced by the report of Mountstuart Elphinstone, who wrote that Kirkpatrick had become perhaps dangerously assimilated with his surroundings:

> Major Kirkpatrick is a good-looking man...but he wears [Indian] moustachois; his hair is cropped short, and his fingers are dyed with henna, although in most other respects he is like an Englishman...[At the durbar of the Nizam] he goes in great state. He has several elephants, and a state palankeen, led horses, flags, long poles and tassels, etc., and is attended by two companies of infantry and a troop of cavalry...Major Kirkpatrick behaves like a native, but with great propriety.

I found a battered token of Kirkpatrick's love for his wife in the garden at the back of the Residency. As Khair-un-Nissa remained all her life in strict purdah, living in a separate *bibi ghar* at the end of Kirkpatrick's garden, she was unable to walk around her husband's great creation to admire its wonderful portico. The Resident hit upon the solution of building her a scaled-down plaster model of his new palace, so that she could examine in detail what she would never allow herself to see with her own eyes. The model survived intact until the 1980s, when a tree fell on it, smashing its right wing. The remains of the left wing and central block now lie under a piece of corrugated iron, near the ruins of the Mughal *bibi ghar*, buried deep beneath a jungle of vines and creepers, in an area still known as the Begum's Garden.

As in Delhi and Lucknow, the extravagantly aristocratic culture of Hyderabad filtered down to the streets. 'The people of other cities say we are a little lazy,' said a shopkeeper in the bazaar, 'that we all behave as if we are little Nizams. That we work slowly, eat slowly, wake up slowly, do everything slowly. Many shopkeepers in Hyderabad don't open their shutters until 11 a.m. We like to take life gently, to take lots of holidays and only to work when we have no money in our pockets.'

Another legacy of the nobility to filter down to the streets is a fondness for witchcraft and sorcery. In the Lad Bazaar, a short distance from the Char Minar, the ceremonial centrepiece of the city, I found a shop which sold nothing but charms and talismans.

'In the Nizam's time the Hyderabad princes were always hiring a *murshad* to make spells on their enemies,' said Ali Mohammed, who ran the shop. 'Now Hyderabad is famous for its magic. Everyone is making too many spells. So they must come here to get protection.'

Ali showed me his stock: silver *ta'wiz* blessed by famous Sufis, special kinds of attar that deflected the Evil Eye, nails worried into the shape of a cobra to protect from snake bites. On one side of the shop were piled huge bundles of thorns: 'Its name is *babool*. Put it at your gate along with a lime and a green chilli and it will take on any bad magic that someone may cast on you.'

'Do you really believe such curses work?' I asked.

'Definitely,' said Ali. 'I have seen it for myself. We are four brothers in my family, but my father had an argument with my oldest brother and threw him out. After that my brother paid a *murshad* to put a curse on our house. The *murshad* wrote a curse and put it in a bottle which he hid in the tree in our courtyard. Soon after that everything fell apart. We became ill, the business became dull, we could not sleep. My father grew near to death. Finally we realised what was happening and hired a good *murshad*. He came to our house and after making many prayers he discovered the bottle and took it away. Immediately my father recovered.

'The *murshad* of Hyderabad are very powerful,' said Ali. 'They can kill a man with just a look, if they want to.'

'Magic? Oh yes, there was no shortage of magic,' said Mir Moazam's wife, the Begum Meherunissa, when I told her about my conversation in the bazaar later that afternoon. 'What that shopkeeper said is quite true. In the time of the Nizam the head of police kept an entire department to deal with *bhaha mati* and exorcism. Oh yes, there were many such stories.'

'Can you remember any stories?' I asked.

'Of course,' she said. 'I remember very well the most powerful *murshad* in Hyderabad. I came to know him quite well. But of course he had a very tragic end.'

'How did you meet him?'

'On summer evenings the womenfolk of my family would go out for a stroll in one of the Mughal gardens. One day after they had returned from a walk my aunt began to shiver and to behave very oddly. Moreover, there was this strange smell of roses wherever she went. Luckily my grandfather realised what had happened, and knew exactly what to do. He called a *murshad* who questioned my aunt closely. Quite suddenly she started speaking with a man's voice, saying, "I am the djinn of the rose garden and I am in love with this woman." The *murshad* performed an exorcism, and the djinn was sent off. After that the *murshad* became a regular visitor at the house.'

'What did he look like?' I asked.

'Oh, he was a strange, dark-complexioned man, with a black waistcoat and white *kurta-pyjamas*. He never walked straight, but rocked from side to side. People said he was a *qalander*, a holy fool, and very close to God. Certainly he could work small miracles, some of which I saw myself.'

'You saw him work miracles?'

'Many times. Or rather, not him, so much as his djinn.'

'He had his own djinn?'

'That's right. To master a djinn and make him your servant, you must first fast for forty days. Very few succeed. But this man succeeded, and the djinn gave him the strong powers. The children all knew him as *Misri Wallah Pir* and they would run after him and shout, "Pir Sahib, give us sugar." So he would bend down and pick up a handful of mud and throw it, and before it reached us, midway in the air it would turn to sugar! It did; I tasted it myself. It was delicious – clean and white, with no sand or impurity or anything. My mother was very angry when I told her I had eaten some of Misri Wallah Pir's sugar, and said that it would become mud or a stone again in my stomach. But as far as I was aware it never did, or if it did it never did me any harm.'

'So you saw him turn mud into sugar more than once?'

'It was his favourite spell. We children would follow him around and spy on him. He was like a child, talking and laughing to himself. Sometimes he would appear to be talking directly to a wall, but if you got close enough you could hear what sounded like the wall talking to him. I would sit beside him to see if the *pir* was making the noise himself, but it wasn't him. It was his djinn, Mowakhal, replying to him. Sometimes he would read the Koran, and the djinn would correct him when he made a mistake. At other times the *pir* would reach out his hand and from nowhere sweetmeats would come, which he would feed to cows.

'Once we were on the verandah watching a lady in the street walking past with a great basket of fruit on her head. Pir Sahib was walking down the road in the opposite direction, so I shouted to him, as a joke, "Pir Sahib, get me some of that fruit." And there and then that huge basket of fruit flew from the woman's head and came to rest at my feet! The fruit carrier was used to Pir Sahib's tricks, and smiled and said, "Pir Sahib, give it back," so after I had taken a banana, Pir Sahib did send the basket back to her. The banana tasted sweeter than any other I have ever tasted.

'Once my friend asked Misri Wallah Pir for some biryani. Pir Sahib said, "I am a poor man. How can I afford biryani?" But she pleaded with him, and eventually he called his djinn: "*Idder ao Mowakhal!*" And within seconds a delicious biryani appeared before her out of the thin air. Another time a sick man begged him for grapes. It was not the season, and there were no grapes in Hyderabad, but the djinn brought them all the same.'

There was a pause, and the begum looked up, I think to see if I was secretly laughing at her memories. 'It's up to you whether you want to believe all this,' she said simply. 'But I witnessed it.'

'You mentioned that the *pir* had a very tragic end,' I said.

'His djinn left him and he lost all his powers,' she replied. 'He died in great poverty.'

'What happened?'

'After Mowakhal left him I never saw the pir again. But the story I heard—much later, in about 1979—was that one day a poor man had come to him and said that he had never seen a diamond. So Misri Wallah Pir called Mowakhal and sent him off to fetch the diamond necklace of the Queen of Mysore. The necklace arrived, and the *pir* gave it to the beggar to examine. But the man had blood on his hands, and it got on the necklace, so Mowakhal refused to take it back again. No djinn will carry anything that has been touched by blood. The pir was furious, because he didn't want to be accused of stealing the necklace, so he began to curse the djinn, who simply disappeared, and never came back.

'After that the *pir* took the necklace to a police station and told the constable what had happened. But of course he didn't believe a word the *pir* said, and when he asked the *pir* to prove that he had a djinn, he couldn't, because Mowakhal had gone. So the police beat him up and asked him how he had stolen the necklace, and what else he had taken. After he was released the *pir* became very sick, and his condition just got worse and worse. Eventually he died alone and penniless and was buried in an unmarked grave.'

As we were talking, Mir Moazam had appeared from his study where he had been busily writing a lecture to deliver the following day.

'You see what I mean?' He said to me when his wife had finished her story. 'The world we grew up in was a different age.'

'Were you aware at the time that it was all about to be swept away?' I asked.

'Up to a point,' said Mir Moazam. 'Looking back now, Hyderabad during my childhood seems like it was going through a period of glorious sunset. But at the time, of course, I thought it would all go on for ever. It was only as I grew older that I realised that it couldn't last, that the sunset must be pretty close. You could feel it coming.'

Mir Moazam sat down in the rocking chair beside his wife and rested his chin on his palm before continuing: 'You see, I was from the Mughal nobility. And so of course I felt a certain loyalty to that world. But I was not blind to the defects of the Nizam. As a graduate of Madras University I had been exposed to fiery speeches by Gandhi, Nehru and other Congress leaders, and I realised then that the old order could not last. What had been possible in the Nizam's father's time was no longer feasible. After that I was in a real dilemma, I could see both sides of the picture.

'As the British prepared to leave, I think the Nizam should have negotiated realistically with Nehru. He might have got a viable deal, a treaty that would have allowed him to keep some form of real autonomy. That way a lot of bloodshed might have been avoided. In 1947 the place was already in chaos, with the [overwhelmingly Muslim] Razakar movement attacking Congress supporters, and *agents provocateurs* burning down the railway station and looting the district treasuries. But despite all this, the Nizam still couldn't see that he had been sustained in power by the British, and that now they were going he had reached the end of the line. Half-hearted negotiations dragged on, until eventually the Nizam decided to declare outright independence from India. It was utter madness. Legally and constitutionally he may have had the right to do so, but it was still quite unrealistic.'

Mir Moazam shook his head. 'He was living in a make-believe world,' he said. 'I knew that, of course. But when the crunch came I realised that my loyalty had to be to the Nizam. After all, my ancestors had given everything for the

throne for two hundred years. I couldn't just abandon ship.
I had to do my duty.'

So far I had avoided the subject of the Indian Army's
1948 invasion of Hyderabad State, then known as 'Operation
Polo', and referred to today in nationalist historiography as
'the Police Action', as if all that had been involved was a few
parking tickets and the odd restraining order. I had steered
clear of the topic because I had been warned by mutual
friends that the invasion had been an extremely difficult and
painful period for Mir Moazam, who in the aftermath had
been unjustly arrested and had spent several years in prison
before being acquitted. But it was Mir Moazam himself who
brought the matter up.

'After university I had joined the Hyderabad Civil Service,
and as fate would have it, on 13 September 1948, when the
Indian Army finally crossed the frontier into Hyderabad, I
was the Collector in charge of the area facing the main
Indian attack from the south. We had no tanks, no planes
and virtually no artillery. Nothing: just a pile of old .303
rifles. And with those we had been ordered to take on the
might of the Indian Army.

'The morning of the attack I was still shaving when I
heard the first shells falling near my house. We had a few
platoons of civil guards, so we lined them up along the
banks of the River Musi. They were facing a fully mechanised
Indian Army unit, with tanks, armoured cars and field guns,
and before long the Indians began picking off our men like
rabbits. Our first plan was to blow up the bridge, but it
turned out the soldiers didn't have the correct equipment. As
head of the district, I was sitting with the Brigadier in the
staff car, trying to decide what to do, when the Indian Air
Force started strafing us from the air. Our car windows
exploded. I lay flat on my belly with bullets shooting over
my head. In the end the Brigadier and I took refuge under an
arch of the bridge we had been supposed to blow up. The
rest of our troops tried to find cover behind clumps of trees
along the river.

'The Brigadier and I managed to escape under intense
firing and strafing, and after that we just retreated and
retreated. The whole resistance was completely unrealistic.

There was heavy aerial bombardment on all fronts: bombs falling everywhere. Yet in all Hyderabad there wasn't a single anti-aircraft gun. The next day I was in a jeep retreating with the army towards Hyderabad when a bus we were overtaking was blown up by a plane. I had to hide in the paddy. We managed to delay them a little by opening the sluices and flooding the roads, but that was only for a few hours. When the Emperor Aurangzeb invaded Golconda [in 1687], the Hyderabad troops managed to keep the Mughals at bay for seven or eight months. In our case we only held them up for four days. It was a total collapse.'

What Mir Moazam said was confirmed by the casualty figures: on the Indian side seven killed and nine wounded, of which one died later; on the Hyderabadi side, an estimated 632 were killed.

'How did the Indian Army behave when it got to Hyderabad?' I asked.

'When an army invades any country – whether it's Alexander the Great, Timur, Hitler or Mussolini – when it gets into a town, you know what the soldiery does. It's very difficult for the officers to control them. I can't tell you how many were raped or killed, but I saw the bodies of many. Old scores were paid off across the state.'

I discovered later that it is in fact possible to make an informed estimate of the numbers killed in the aftermath of the 'Police Action'. When reports of atrocities began to reach Delhi, Nehru, 'in his private capacity', commissioned an unofficial report from a group of veteran Congressmen made up of two Hyderabadi Muslims who had prominently opposed the Nizam's rule and chaired by a Hindu, Pandit Sunderlal. The team made an extensive tour of the state and submitted their report to Nehru and Sardar Patel in January 1949. Its findings were never made public, presumably because of its damning criticism of the conduct of the Indian Army. It remained unpublished until recently, when a portion of it, smuggled out of India, appeared in America in an obscure volume of scholarly essays entitled *Hyderabad: After the Fall*.

The report, entitled 'On the Post-operation Polo Massacres, Rape and Destruction or Seizure of Property in Hyderabad State', makes grim reading. In village after village across the state, it meticulously and unemotionally catalogues incidents of murder and mass rape, sometimes committed by troops, in other cases by local Hindu hooligans after the troops had disarmed the Muslim population. A short extract, chosen at random, gives the general flavour:

> Ganjoti Paygah, District Osmanabad
>
> There are 500 homes belonging to Muslims here. Two hundred Muslims were murdered by the *goondas*. The army had seized weapons from the Muslims. As the Muslims became defenceless, the *goondas* began the massacre. Muslim women were raped by the troops. Statement of Pasha Bi, resident of Ganjoti: 'The trouble in Ganjoti began after the army's arrival. All the young Muslim women here were raped. Five daughters of Osman Sahib were raped and six daughters of the Qazi were raped. Ismail Sahib Sawdagar's daughter was raped in Saiba Chamar's home for a week. Soldiers from Umarga came every week and after all-night rape, young Muslim women were sent back to their homes in the morning ...

And so on, for page after page, in all, the report estimates that as many as two hundred thousand Hyderabadi Muslims were slaughtered, which, if true, would make the 'Police Action' a bloodbath comparable to parts of the Punjab during Partition.

Even if one chooses to regard the figure of two hundred thousand dead as an impossible exaggeration, it is still clear that the scale of the killing was horrific. Although publicly Nehru played down the disorder in Hyderabad, telling the Indian representative at the United Nations that following the Nizam's officials deserting their posts there had been 'some disorder in which Hindus had retaliated for their suffering under the [overwhelmingly Muslim] Razakar militia,' privately he was much more alarmed. This is indicated by a note he sent to Sardar Patel's Ministry of States on 26 November 1948, in which he wrote that he had received reports of killing of Muslims so large in number 'as to stagger the imagination', and looting of Muslim property 'on a tremendous scale'—which would seem to confirm the general tone of Pandit Sunderlal's report.

I asked Mir Moazam what happened to him while all this murderous anarchy was taking place around him.

'Several of the officers who were under suspicion by the new regime went to Pakistan,' he replied. 'Arrangements were made for me, as it was clear I was going to be arrested. But my father said, "Face the firing squad. I will disinherit and disown you if you run away from your post." So I stayed, and after a farcical trial full of paid witnesses, I was sentenced to death. I could see the noose from my cell.'

Mir Moazam described his ordeal bravely and straight-forwardly, with barely a flicker of self-pity or bitterness: 'Later that year the sentence was reduced to life imprisonment,' he said quietly. 'After three years in solitary cells, following an appeal in the High Court, I was honourably acquitted. Other officers were less lucky. Many were framed with trumped-up charges. Others were forced to flee to Pakistan, though they dearly wished to stay in Hyderabad. Very few retained jobs of any importance: they were weeded out. Some were removed, some were reduced in rank, others were put in jail. Seeing this, after I was released, I decided to go to London. There English friends of mine and old Civil Service colleagues eventually helped me get a job in UNESCO, and I spent much of the next thirty or forty years either in Paris or as Chief Liaison Officer in Libya and Afghanistan.'

'You must have seen quite a few changes on your return,' I said.

'I hardly recognised the place,' said Mir Moazam. 'I arrived back with a friend who was head of a French bank. All the way I had been telling him about the wonders of Hyderabad, and particularly about the City Palace complex. I told him about the Blue Palace, the Green Palace and, most lovely of all, the Pearl Palace. So as soon as we arrived we went over there. I found the chowkidar and got him to open the gates. Inside it was completely flat: they had totally levelled it. Nothing was there except a few goats. I'll never forget the humiliation as I turned to my friend to try and explain what had happened.

'But of course I soon discovered that it wasn't just the City Palace: almost all the great houses had gone. Even King Kothi [the Nizam's palace] had been bulldozed, or at least most of it. There was one wing left, converted into some sort of hospital.'

'Were the palaces confiscated by the government?' I asked.

'No, not as such,' said Mir Moazam. 'But the aristocracy lost all their status and their income after the Police Action, so they just sold everything: land, houses, even the doors and windows. They knew almost nothing about business. Selling their heritage was the only way they could make ends meet.'

The old man shook his head in disbelief. 'No one thought to protect anything,' he said. 'They sold their history just to survive. Now there's virtually nothing left: just dusty high-rise buildings everywhere. Outside Salar Jung's palace, for instance, was a garden easily comparable to the Tuileries. I'll never forget its shady walks and ancient trees, its soft green lawns and parterres bursting with flowers. There was an octagonal fountain so large you could row about it in a skiff. Now it's a filthy lorry park. So much was lost, unnecessarily, through sheer ignorance.'

I asked Mir Moazam what had happened to his own family.

'After the Police Action, the family simply disintegrated,' he replied. 'Some went to the Gulf. Now we are scattered to the winds, and Iram Manzil [Fakrool Mulk's last palace] is a government office. It's just around the corner from here, but it's almost unrecognisable. For me it stands as a symbol of all that has happened to this town.'

'Could you show me?' I ventured.

'Why not?' said Mir Moazam.

The old man got to his feet, and collected his stick. Two minutes later we were heading through the new housing estates that seemed to be springing up everywhere in Hyderabad.

'When I was a boy all this was part of my grandfather's estate,' said Mir Moazam. 'In those days Iram Manzil lay miles outside the town, five hundred acres of land, all beautifully maintained. Where those houses are, that was my grandfather's nine-hole golf course. See those shacks? That was a polo field. And that mess over there? That was the palace's orange groves. It's impossible to visualise now.'

We turned down a gradient, and drew up outside a large office complex. On the gate was posted the stencilled notice:

GOVERNMENT OF INDIA
OFFICE OF THE ENGINEER-IN-CHIEF

'This was it,' said Mir Moazam. 'Unrecognisable.'

I looked where he was pointing. From among a cluster of shacks and lean-tos and concrete outhouses, clinging to the central building like barnacles on an oyster, I could see the outlines of what had once been a magnificent palace. But garages had been built in front of the central portico, obscuring the symmetry of the façade. The paint was peeling, and air-conditioning units hung out of every arched window. A feeling of neglect hung over the whole complex, almost completely masking the grandeur of the original plan.

'You used to arrive through a gatehouse with two double-storeyed towers,' said Mir Moazam. 'A bugler would blow as you passed. The bugler's name was Joseph, and he used to play the reveille first thing in the morning and sound the retreat each night at sunset. But they bulldozed the tower long ago. Over there, where that ugly garage is now, used to be the tennis courts, and beyond were the French Gardens, with their fountains playing. On the other side, at the bottom, there was a big lake. As you drew up in front of the palace, at a sign from the major domo our band would play 'God Save the Nizam' and 'God Save the King Emperor'. Later, after a game of tennis, you used to have tea on that terrace, over where that temple is now.'

We walked together around the complex, Mir Moazam pointing out where the *zenana* gate stood, before it was bulldozed, and where the African guards used to drill. Here was the pool they used to fill with coloured liquid to play *holi*, there the hall where Mohurram was celebrated and where the Christmas tree stood. Over there, where the arches were now blocked up, used to be the *baradari* hall. At the end of Ramadan, on the night of Eid, the room would be full to bursting, with everyone sitting on the floor, eating a great Mughlai dinner.

'I remember the Nizam coming here, and the Viceroy, and a whole succession of British Residents. Outside there would be gorgeously caparisoned elephants and over a hundred polo ponies. There were, palanquins and teams of palanquin bearers, four-in-hand coaches, and in 1934 nearly fifty cars, mainly Rolls-Royces and Daimlers. I remember the polo matches and the times we used to stand over there and try to shoot coins thrown in the air, or to pepper that old stuffed tiger on wheels. Then there were the tennis matches and the trips to the Malakpet races and the shikar trips into the jungle. It all seems very long ago now.'

'So what of the future?' I asked. 'What do you think will survive of the old culture of Hyderabad?'

Mir Moazam shrugged his shoulders. 'Very little,' he said. 'You can't keep out change. In fifty years an entire world has been levelled, much has been destroyed. The process is nearly finished now. I think that everything that is special about Hyderabad is going. Day by day the old ways are disappearing and being replaced by a monotonous standardisation. What we had in Hyderabad was a distinct Deccani culture, the product of a very particular mixture of peoples and influences. It was based on religious tolerance, courtesy, hospitality, love of the arts and a first-rate civil service which made no distinction between creeds or caste or class. But much of the old élite went to Pakistan, and a flood of new people have come, bringing their own ways with them. What is left are the vestiges and fragments—is still vital and has a life and an extraordinary stamina. But who knows how long it can last?'

The old man took my hand and led me sadly back towards the road. 'My children tell me you mustn't live in your memories. One must try to move with the times, and face the future rather than always dreaming about what has gone.'

Mir Moazam turned to face me: 'And they are right, of course,' he said. 'That is why I do not like to come back here. At every step there are fragments of my past. And frankly it breaks my old heart to see it like this.'

# *Parashakti*

Something was clearly wrong with the woman.

As I walked past, she jumped up, rocked unsteadily one way and the other, then lunged towards my face with her long, dirt-stained fingernails. I sidestepped, and she lurched after me, one foot dragging slightly behind the other. Then, as abruptly as she got up, she sat down again on the floor, and curled herself up into a little ball. Nearby, three other women rolled around beside her, cackling to themselves in deep, broken voices.

Mr Venugopal put a calming hand on my shoulder: 'You must not worry about these ladies,' he said, smiling at my alarm. 'Each of them has a devil in her. But soon all these evil spirits will be exorcised.'

He patted me reassuringly on the back: 'By tonight our goddess Parashakti will have all these devils tamed. By eleven o'clock, I promise you, sir, all these ladies will be right as rain.'

Mr Venugopal was a kind and devout old man. We had met a little earlier that morning in a roadside tea-stall; as we shook hands, Mr Venugopal had handed me his card. It read:

Venugopal—
Chief Engineer to All-Kerala Electricity Board
(Retired)

Mr Venugopal, it was true, looked a slightly unlikely Chief Engineer. As he sat at his breakfast, gobbling down great plates of *idli sambhar*, he was naked but for a thin white cotton loincloth, over the top of which spilled his sizeable paunch. He wore heavy black glasses, and his forehead was marked by a prominent sandalwood *tilak* mark. Over his chest, attached to a thin black thread, hung a Hindu charm.

'I am a retired person interested in spiritual affairs only,' he explained. 'Now my career is over I visit temples and pray to God. But of all the temples I have visited, the goddess of this place is by far the most powerful. I tell you: if you surrender to her you will get total peace of mind.'

Perhaps I had looked a little sceptical, for Mr Venugopal had immediately offered to take me around the great temple of Chottanikkara himself. Although all the major temples in Kerala are officially closed to non-Hindus, Mr Venugopal insisted that he was a personal friend of one of the temple officials, and that his friend would be happy, as he put it, 'to expedite everything'. Sure enough, twenty minutes later I was through the great wooden gatehouse with its upturned Chinese flying eves, past the burly temple guards, and inside the temple's first compound.

'Listen,' said Mr Venugopal. 'Before I take you into the presence of the goddess, let us sit down in the shade and take our rest. Then I can tell you about the Mother.'

We found a stone wall-bench under an arcade of the cloister garth, and Mr Venugopal started to explain.

'We Hindus believe that some of the symptoms of epilepsy—delirious convulsions and mad utterances—are due to the effect of *yakshis*, or evil spirits. These spirits have astral bodies only, and are invisible. Their identity can only be guessed at by the symptoms of the possessed person, and also by the astrological calculations of our Brahmins. Our feeling is that every evil spirit would like to unite with the Almighty. But thanks to his bad deeds he cannot. For this reason there are too many evil spirits roaming around in the atmosphere.

'Now, the aim of these *yakshis* is to get inside the bodies of weak-minded peoples. Then they think they will be brought to a temple where some compensatory *puja* will be done for them, and in this way they will get salvation.'

We walked past the first shrine and through a courtyard lined by a succession of small cells, each with a simple wooden door. Walking in the same direction as ourselves there flowed a continuous stream of pilgrims. Many were plump Brahmins over whose oiled and glistening torsos hung thin sacred threads. I remarked to Mr Venugopal on the number of visitors.

'Each year this shrine is more and more popular,' he replied. 'Twenty years ago people did not have belief. They were materialistic and said that all temples were just humbug and nonsense. Now many have learned the error of their ways. They think materialistic things are not everything. They realise you cannot get happiness even with all the material benefits in the world. So, like all people who are in trouble, they call for their Mother and she is answering them.'

We had arrived at the bottom of a great stairway. Here a second gatehouse led past a tank into a second compound.

'Mr William. At this stage you must please take off your shirt. If you wish to go into the inner temple, you must be wearing only a pant or a *lungi*. This is our custom.'

'Why here?' I asked. 'Why not at the entrance?'

'Our goddess Parashakti reveals herself in different forms in different parts of the temple,' explained Mr Venugopal. 'At the top she is in her most gentle and wise and motherly form: there she shows herself as the goddess Saraswati and the goddess Lakshmi. But here in this lower compound she appears in her most terrible form. Here she is Kali. We must be most respectful. To anger her...'

He broke off, and ran his fingers melodramatically across his throat.

'Finish,' he said, arching his eyebrows for emphasis.

The inner compound was much smaller than those we had already passed. A wall pressed in around the small, dark shrine where the believers were bowing in front of the idol. To one side stood a tree. Its trunk was punctured by hundreds of long steel nails.

'This is the Devil's Tree,' said Venugopal. 'By hammering nails into the bark with the heads of the patients we clamp the spirits to the goddess Kali so they will not disturb any other person.'

'Did you say with their *heads*?'

'Oh yes. But first the possessed person must be in a state of trance. She must be seized by the goddess, then she will feel nothing.'

'And how do you persuade Kali to seize the person?' I asked.

'Oh, that is easy matter,' said Mr Venugopal. 'We feed her twelve basins full of blood.'

Who is Parashakti?

Her names are as many as her devotees, though sometimes she is called simply Mahadevi—the Great Goddess—for the world was created when she opened her eyes, and it is destroyed whenever she blinks.

Some call her Jagatikanda, the Root of the World. Others know her as Supreme Ruler, She who Supports the Galaxy, She who is Ruler of All the Worlds, Mother of All. Her most sacred title is the Root of the Tree of the Universe.

Yet if Parashakti is Life itself, she is also Death. She can destroy all she creates, and for this reason many of her devotees choose to worship her as Pancapretasanasina, She who is Seated on a Throne of Five Corpses. She is also known by the names She who is Wrathful, She who has Flaming Tusks, She who Causes Madness, She whose Eyes Roll about from Drinking Wine, the Terrible One, Night of Death.

To summon her, the Brahmins chant a Sanskrit invocation:

> Come, come in haste, oh goddess, with thy locks
> bedraggled, thou who hast three eyes, whose skin
> is dark, whose clothes are stained with blood, who
> hast rings in thy ears, who hast a thousand hands,
> and ridest upon a monster and wieldest in thy
> hands tridents, clubs, lances and shields.

Though she is fierce, terrifying and destructive, the goddess is said to be quick to come to the aid of her devotees. In times of drought she appears in a form having many eyes. When she sees the condition of her creatures she begins to weep, and her woe has the force of a hundred monsoons. Soon the rivers begin to flow, the ponds and the lakes fill to overflowing, and verdure covers the earth. Through Parashakti the world is reborn.

At no place on this earth is the Great Goddess so accessible as in her principal shrine of Chottanikkara. For there, so it is said, her idol sometimes comes to life and in physical form takes action to protect her devotees against devils and demons.

Once, Mr Venugopal told me, a demonic *yakshi* desired a handsome young Brahmin. The Brahmin was crossing the jungle in order to perform a *puja* at the temple at Chottanikkara when the *yakshi* first saw him. She joined him on his journey and began to talk sweetly to him. It was late in the evening and the *yakshi's* outer form was that of a tall and lovely Tamil girl. She knew that if she were able to persuade the Brahmin to spend the night with her she would be able to devour him alive.

But on his way through the forest the Brahmin happened to stop at the hut of a holy man. He invited his beautiful companion to come inside and take some refreshment, but she refused and hovered among the trees outside. The holy man, through his spiritual powers, realised then the true nature of the *yakshi*. He gave the Brahmin a red cloth and told him to leave the woman and to go on as fast as he could to the shrine of Parashakti. When he got there he should throw the cloth over the idol; only then would he be saved.

The Brahmin ran from the holy man's hut, and the *yakshi*, realising that she had been discovered, abandoned her disguise and changed into her real form. She became as tall as a mountain, with a mouth like a cave, and her hair was a mass of hissing cobras. The *yakshi* chased after the boy, and by the time he had neared the temple gatehouse she was virtually upon him. She grabbed at his leg and he just managed to throw the red cloth over the idol before the *yakshi* pulled him from the gateway.

At that moment the Kali idol came to life. Seeing that her devotee was in trouble, the goddess brandished her sword and chased the *yakshi* into the forest. Beside a jungle pond the goddess caught up with the demon and cut off her head. Then she drank the *yakshi's* blood. So much gore flowed from the corpse that to this day the pond beneath the temple still has a reddish tinge.

But the drinking of the *yakshi's* blood also had its effect on the goddess. As Mr Venugopal put it when he first told me the story, 'finally the drinking of blood became her habit. Now she cannot live without it. Every day we must feed her twelve full basins. In return she still rids us of our demons.'

In 1830 a Bengali Maharajah slaked the thirst of the Mother Goddess with the blood of no fewer than twenty-five of his youthful retainers; as recently as 1835 a boy was beheaded every single Friday at the altar of the Kali temple at Calcutta. Many temples in Kerala still quietly sacrifice cocks, goats and sheep to the goddess, but at Chottanikkara, where Parashakti requires her full twelve basins of blood every day, the goddess has been gradually weaned (or perhaps detoxed) on to a blood-coloured solution of lime juice and turmeric.

Parashakti is fed her supper at nine o'clock every evening. After she has drunk her fill, music is played for her entertainment. It is then, Mr Venugopal told me, that the goddess makes the devils dance.

By night the temple precincts were more eerie than by day.

The postcard-sellers had gone and the tea-shacks were shuttered and closed. In the dark, unseen palm trees rustled in the wind.

A figure stepped out of the shadows.

'Mr William?'

It was Venugopal. He looked agitated.

'Come quick,' he said. 'We are late.'

Together, we passed through the empty gatehouse. On the far side, lit by flickering reed torches, we were confronted by a large and completely silent crowd. All the pilgrims and devotees were facing the shrine, bowed double before the image of the goddess. Some of the men had prostrated themselves flat on their faces, arms outstretched towards the idol.

Then quite suddenly the silence was broken. One of the priests clashed a pair of brass cymbals; simultaneously four of his colleagues began to blow conch shells and large curved trumpets of a design familiar from Cecil B. de Mille Biblical epics. From around one corner of the shrine another priest appeared, sitting astride a huge tusker elephant. The *mahout* bowed to the goddess, hands arched in the gesture of *namaskar*, then began circumambulating the shrine, followed by the cymbal-clashers and the trumpet-blowers. As the priests circled round and round, the other devotees joined in, until the shrine was ringed by a great collar of moving pilgrims.

The elephant was eventually driven away by its priestly *mahout*. By the light of the full moon, the cymbal-clashers led the way down the great flight of steps to the inner enclosure.

The Kali temple was brightly lit by a nimbus of smoky, acrid-smelling torches. As the devotees streamed in, two half-naked priests lit the last wicks of a great rack of flickering candles in front of the shrine. The priests opened the doors, and the pilgrims bowed down before the many-armed image of Parashakti-Kali.

I drew closer to try and catch a glimpse of the image in the flickering torchlight. The goddess was shown as a hideous black-faced hag, smeared with blood, with bared teeth and a protruding tongue. She was naked but for a garland of skulls and a girdle of severed heads; a thug's strangling noose dangled from her belt.

Soon more half-naked Brahmins appeared. Their sweat-wet flesh glistened in the light of the lamps; they began to intone Sanskrit *mantras* to the goddess. As they chanted, the chief priest squatted cross-legged on the ground, and I noticed for the first time the deep copper basins lying in ranks amid the shadows at the priests' feet.

Then the possessed women were led in: twelve or thirteen young girls, mostly adolescent, and a single boy, in his late twenties. They were arranged in an arc around the shrine, and for a few minutes they stood quite still while the Brahmins continued to chant their mantras. Then the chief priest nodded to the cymbal-clashers, and the music began.

At first the cymbals merely kept time with the metre of the *mantras*, but then the conch-blowers and the trumpeters struck up too, and the band was joined by four priestly drummers, each holding a tall wooden *tabla*. Soon the *mantras* were completely drowned out by the primeval rhythm of the temple musicians.

In the shadows, I could see that the chief priest was now splashing the blood-solution around the shrine, literally throwing it out of the basins with cupped hands so that as it landed it splattered red over the other priests, then ran down towards a conduit that passed it in turn towards the roots of the Devil's Tree.

The pulse of the drums rose to a new peak, the conch shells blew; then suddenly something very strange happened. One of the possessed girls started to shake, as if in the grip of a violent fever. Her eyes were open, but there was a lost look on her face. Beside her, the other girls were beginning to sway as well; the trance passed from one to the other, like a contagion.

'Look!' whispered Mr Venugopal. 'See how powerful our goddess is! She is making the spirits dance. Soon maybe they will surrender to her.'

One girl in a blue sari was shaking her long mane of hair backwards and forwards as she was seized by a series of impossible convulsions. Behind her, a woman—presumably her mother—was trying to make sure her sari did not unwrap itself beyond the limits of Indian modesty. Every so often the girl's hands would fly up in the air, her robes would fall out of place and her mother would rush forward and pull the material back into its proper position.

Three of the other girls were by now writhing on the floor as if in pain; a fourth was spinning like a top, screaming and shrieking as she did so. It was an extraordinary sight. I felt as if I had stumbled back several millennia into some distant druidical ritual. Yet no one except myself seemed in the least bit surprised by the spectacle, and of the several children who were present, a couple looked positively bored. One was playing with two glass marbles, rolling them from hand to hand, completely ignoring the unearthly commotion going on around him.

After about five minutes—though it seemed much longer—the music reached its throbbing climax. In front of the shrine the chief priest tired of ladling out his solution and began simply upending the bowls of blood so that the red liquid began to lap around the prostrate bodies of the women. The drums pulsed faster and faster; the cymbals clashed; more and more of the possessed fell twitching to the floor.

When the last one went down, a conch blew a deep note and two priests stepped forward and closed the doors of the shrine. The drums stopped dead. It was over.

As the limp, almost lifeless bodies of the possessed were carried away by relays of the younger priests, I asked Mr Venugopal whether the women were now cured.

'Sometimes they are, sometimes not,' he replied, inclining his head. 'For a particularly troublesome devil it may take a month before the demon will surrender.'

We wound our way slowly back up the grand staircase.

'Has anyone you know been cured?' I asked him as we neared the top.

'Oh, many people,' he replied.

'Tell me an instance.'

'Well—last month a cousin of mine brought a boy from Bombay. The boy was from a good family, but he was deranged in some way: he wouldn't eat, he quarrelled with everyone, and he refused to go out to work. Anyway, the boy was brought here, and he stayed inside the temple for five days.

'Every night the goddess entered him and asked the demon to leave. Then in the morning the priests fed the boy a little *ghee* that had been kept in the goddess' shrine overnight. At first he refused more than a drop, but by the third day he was eating again—great plates of rice and vegetables. It was the first time he had touched real food for several weeks.

'On the final day the chief priest did some special *puja*, and that night the devil finally left the boy. Now he is quite normal and has resumed work in his father's insurance company as if nothing had ever happened. This I have seen for myself only one month ago.'

'It sounds like a classic case of faith healing,' I said— then, seeing Venugopal's expression, immediately wished I hadn't.

The old man shrugged his shoulders: 'If after what you have seen this evening you want to call it faith healing, that is your affair only.'

He looked upset by my rudeness, and I began to struggle to explain myself. But Venugopal held up his hand for me to be silent: 'Every day I see people coming and getting relief. For me that is enough.'

'You think the goddess can exorcise any demon?' I asked.

'For me this is the most powerful temple in India,' said Venugopal. 'There is no doubt about it: this is the most powerful temple for destroying the evils of the world.'

We were at the outer gate of the temple now. The old man turned to go back inside. He said: 'In India, if you wish to get something done it is best to go first to the Prime Minister. So it is with spiritual affairs. Parashakti is the Supreme Goddess. But to see her work...'

Here Venugopal turned and smiled at me.

'To see her work, maybe you must first be god-fearing and god-loving,' he said. 'Only then can you really understand her power...'

# 5

## On the Indian Ocean

# Bombay Glitz: Shobha Dé

BOMBAY, 1992

Question: How do you outrage nine hundred million Indians without leaving your desk?

Answer: Write two filthy-dirty semi-autobiographical airport-slush novelettes, and set the action in Bombay.

This is the story of Shobha Dé, a clever Indian lady who looks good, lives well and writes dirty. For these unforgivable crimes her books have been panned by the reviewers and her lifestyle vilified in a couple of hundred different Indian papers. The headline writers (who are fond of alliteration) have described her as the Maharani of Malice, the Empress of Erotica and the Princess of Pulp. She gets sackfuls of hate mail; she has even received death threats.

Sticks and stones may break her bones, but bad publicity has left her laughing all the way to the bank. Shobha Dé has garnered some of the most spectacularly bad reviews ever written in India—'the language smacks of the gutter in its putrid contents'; 'Amoral...she betrays her own sex'; 'distasteful'; 'downright muck'—but at the end of it she has become by many leagues the country's best-selling writer, moving more books than any Indian writer since Independence (she's also a top seller in Romania, to the delighted bafflement of her Delhi publishers). And her books are avidly read. On the plane to Bombay, both my neighbours had devoured her complete *oeuvre*.

'This is very dirty lady,' said Mr Sanjay Aggarwal, the nice fertiliser executive sitting on my left. 'Her books are full of wicked and filthy thoughts.'

'I am reading everything she is writing,' said Mr Satish Lal, who makes carbuncle grinders in Bangalore. 'In one book I am counting seventy-three copulations. I am shocked only. Really—her head is full of perversions.'

Shobha takes her vocation seriously. Turning herself into the Jackie Collins of India has not been easy: her notoriety is the product of hard work. Born Anuradha Rajadhyaksha, daughter of a Brahmin district judge from small-town middle class India, she has spent forty-three years becoming Shobha Dé, the rich and fashionably unfashionable pulp novelist from metropolitan Bombay.

She kicked off as an exceptionally beautiful model, at a time when joining a modelling agency in India was considered about as respectable as joining a brothel. Then, at the height of her modelling success, she suddenly threw the whole thing in and became a glamour journalist. When Nari Hira launched *Stardust*, India's first film-gossip magazine, in the early 1970s, he made Shobha the editor. She was just twenty-three. Under her direction, the venture was an incredible success. In a matter of months *Stardust* had six million readers and was India's third-biggest magazine. Within a year it was the largest-selling film magazine in the world.

The reason for the success of *Stardust* was simple: it had a gossip column that became essential reading for India's numberless film-goers. 'Nita's Natter'—as the column was called—was written by Shobha, and it did what no one had ever dared to do before: gave uncensored accounts of the affairs and debauches of Bollywood, the Bombay film world. Its style was almost a parody of Glenda Slagg in *Private Eye*, full of three-word sentences punctuated by an equal number of exclamation marks: 'Rekha left Pran's party in a hurry!! Was she missing someone???' 'Ajit Singh was seen playing in the surf at Juhu with an ultramod model in the wee hours of the morning! Afterwards rumour has it that they went back to a wayside inn for kebabs and…some red hot pickle!!!'

For all its sledgehammer subtlety, 'Nita's Natter' made Shobha the hottest journalistic property in Bombay. 'It was the bitchiest column I've ever read,' remembers Nari Hira. 'It was wonderful. She ran down everyone she met, literally *everyone*: she made fun of socialites, mocked film stars, broke up marriages. That sort of thing had never been done here before. It is still not done.'

The column may have made Shobha's name, but it won her few friends. The success of her novelettes did not improve things. The books were full of easily identifiable Bombay society characters, and those portrayed in them were furious; those left out even more so. Yet her enemies could only sit and watch while Shobha's Glenda Slag prose was moulded into a series of massive bestsellers.

At the same time, in a country where divorce and extra-marital relations are frowned upon, in quick succession Shobha ditched her first husband, publicly took a French lover, then left him and married another man—who just happened to be a shipping magnate. To go with her millionaire husband she has diligently collected all the other trappings of the super-rich pulp-novelist: the white Mercedes and the vintage Jaguar; the penthouse suite and the hideaway retreat; the private launch and the attentive, liveried servants. You name it, if Jackie Collins has it, Shoba Dé has two.

Part fantasy lifted from a second-rate American soap opera, part marketing exercise by a clever publisher, part the deliberate creation of a very ambitious woman, Shobha Dé is a calculated construct living on the very boundary of plausibility. Spend a week with her, meet her friends, ride in her cars and go to her parties—at the end of it you are still left with a lurking suspicion that you have stumbled on to some sort of film set peopled with actors speaking lines from a Jilly Cooper script. Back in your hotel room you look through your notes and ask yourself yet again: *Is this woman for real?*

'Put it this way,' she says knowingly: 'I seem to be stuck with an image, and the smart thing to do is to *flog* it...'

The voice on the phone is difficult to place, a silky-smooth mid-Atlantic drawl with only the faintest hint of Indian intonation.

'Anyway, I'll send the boat to pick you up,' she continues nonchalantly. 'Just walk out of the Taj Mahal hotel and down the steps to the jetty.'

Shobha Dé is not only difficult to place, she requires a leap of the imagination to believe. To be ferried across the waters of a tropical bay to interview the glamorous lady-writer in her country estate: *Haven't I read this somewhere before?*, you wonder.

Millions of Indians certainly think so, and they don't like it. For India, once the land of the Kama Sutra, is now one of the world's most buttoned-up and prudish places. Despite a dazzling variety of Sanskrit terms for every shade of sexual arousal, no modern Indian language has a word for orgasm. Although the possibilities of sex have never been so exhaustively catalogued as in the Hindu *shastras* (where every conceivable type and variety of conjunction is described and analysed—upside down, as a team sport, conjoined with every animal in the bestiary), India has for thirty years resisted the onslaught of the sexual revolution which swept much of the rest of the world in the Sixties.

In the 1990s the subcontinent is the last bastion of the chaperoned virgin, the double-locked bedroom and the arranged marriage. A sex scene in a traditional Indian film consists of the camera panning away from a converging couple and coming to rest on a bee pollinating a flower, or a violently shaking bush. The result is sexual repression on a massive scale, with hundreds of millions of Indians having no outlet for their erotic tensions. As the writer Khushwant Singh has noted, 'Nine-tenths of the violence and unhappiness in this country derives from sexual repression.'

While all this may be very frustrating for hundreds of millions of young Indians, it provides Ms Dé with considerable opportunities. She has built her fortune on the stress lines of the frustrated Indian libido. It's not just that her books are cheaper than imported romances, and easier to find than banned foreign pornography. Dé realised early on that it did not take much effort to outrage an Indian audience; even the vague hint of a falling sari can register a high reading on the Richter scale of subcontinental titillation. Before her first book, *Socialite Evenings*, had even hit the streets in 1989 it had caused a major scandal; advance orders poured in.

But it is her second book, *Starry Nights* (1991), that is by far her most successful bash at the sex and shopping novel.

There are endless sequences in which the characters buy, wear or talk about Gucci shoes, Dior sunglasses or Lanvin watches, but most of the book is focused single-mindedly on sex.

The story follows the mango-breasted heroine, Aasha Rani, as she sleeps her way to stardom—and then makes her fatal mistake: she falls in love with India's number-one hunk, a steely-eyed, smooth-skinned, cast-iron lump of machismo called Akshay Arora. There is no hanging about in Shobha's novels: Aasha Rani's clothes have been removed by page 3, and by page 5 we have encountered the f-word for the first time (but not the last). On page 6 we have a deflowering, on page 9 a wet sari scene (Indian cinema's traditional alternative to nudity), and on page 17 an innovatory passage involving an elderly Bombay film star, a nubile starlet and some ceremonial oil from a Hindu temple. There are six more major copulations (on pages 28, 54, 60, 79, 122 and 181) and a galaxy of minor conjunctions, including one notable encounter in the lavatory of an Air India Boeing—which the author admits lifting from *Emmanuelle*.

One of the (apparently unintentional) pleasures of the book is the background of high kitsch against which the action takes place. Aasha Rani has a fetish for furry toys—'pink kittens, blue rabbits, silky black leopards with yellow eyes, polka-dotted pandas, even a four-foot giraffe...'—which she piles high in her magnificent pink boudoir: 'all gauzy pink drapes, quilted bedcovers and pink heart-shaped cushions trimmed with lace'. It is a truly wonderful bedroom—full, as another description has it, of 'velvet bedspreads, Rexine love seats, pink telephones, gilt-edged mirrors and a fountain'. The reader can only agree with Aasha Rani, who 'thought it was the most gorgeous room she'd ever seen'.

It is here, in this sequinned pink lovenest, that the temple oil gets rubbed, the heroine debauched and the most memorable bits of dialogue spoken: 'All through my bad days one thought has kept me going,' says Akshay Arora in a rare moment of eloquence: 'I knew I had to see you. I couldn't leave this world without saying goodbye...' It is also in this room that one producer 'hammers away...grunting like a wild pig', and that another lays his masculinity out on the tabletop, where Aasha Rani mistakes it for a Havana cigar.

Only when the heroine moves to London and becomes a call girl does the interest begin to flag. 'There are some wonderful seventeenth-century estates going,' suggests another character at one point. 'Why don't you retire to the country?'

After trudging through 250 pages of this sort of thing, the reader feels that that would not be a bad idea.

Before she rang off, Shobha told me that she had invited a couple of her friends over for lunch in the country. They would be coming on the same launch as me, she said.

She did not indicate that 'a couple' meant seventy-two gushing Bombay socialites—fat-cat industrialists and their glitzy wives, actors and starlets, glamour journalists, society painters and producers. As I stepped out of my hotel I found myself ambushed by a set of characters straight out of one of Shobha's novels.

'Hi!'

'Hi!'

'Hi-ee!'

'I *love* your Dior sunglasses.'

'Thanks. Oh *golly*—I'm *so* hung over!'

'I didn't get to bed until five a.m.'

'Are you going to Laxman's tonight?'

'Of course. But have you heard? Vinod hasn't been invited!'

'Why?'

'Don't you know about Vinod and Dimple?'

'No?'

'Bunty saw them on the beach at Juhu, and do you know what Dimple was wearing?...'

I listened fascinated. So, I thought, people really do speak like this. As the crowds of Sunday trippers gathered to gawp at the socialites, someone spotted a minor film star ('*Ae woh dekh*! Moon Moon Sen!') and everyone crowded around to get a picture of themselves standing beside the screen goddess. The chatterers pointedly ignored the *hoi polloi*.

'Moon Moon! Sweety, it's so good to see you! Baby, are these kids *really* yours?'

'Hey, don't you start. I'm sick of people telling me how beautiful I look. Do I look so bad in my films, huh?'

'What a *lovely* Lanvin watch.'

Eventually the launch turned up, and with a clatter of stilettos the cocktail party moved aboard. We dropped our moorings and set off across the bay.

The incongruous half-timbered Swiss gables of the Bombay Yacht Club, the flashing white domes of the Prince of Wales Museum, the palm trees of Marine Drive all slipped away into the distance. The shoreline widened, unveiling the mini-Manhattan of the business centre and the spider-like cranes of the dockyards. Then, slowly, the whole vision sank into the consumptive pollution-fog that hung thinly over the bay. The boat rocked from side to side. The sun shone through the haze. The socialites swapped addresses.

Forty minutes later, the morning mist parted to reveal a white beach, a windbreak of bottle palms, and the bobbing wooden outrigger canoes of village fishermen moored to a rickety jetty. Beyond stretched an avenue of eucalyptus and casuarina, flanked on either side by banana plantations. Shobha was there to meet us.

She is tall and clear-skinned, with a mane of fabulous dark hair, and is far more attractive in person than she appears in photographs. Her movements are graceful and languid, but she has alert alley-cat eyes which are constantly darting backwards and forwards, ready to pick up anything interesting, controversial or scandalous.

As her guests moved towards her, Shobha swooped down on them, embraced them, showered them with kisses and compliments, then ushered them through her house and out into the garden, where the servants hovered with Bloody Marys. Soon brunch was served.

The house was decorated in very much the same spirit as Aasha Rani's bedroom in *Starry Nights*. There were fake escutcheons on the gates, and mock-crystal chandeliers hung from the ceilings. There were soft-focus photographs of Shobha and her shipping magnate on the piano, and twirly-wirly fake-ironwork gaslights in the garden. More portraits of our host and hostess, in thick chocolate-box acrylic, hung from the walls. There may have been no pink telephones, but I still felt sure that Aasha Rani would have approved of this house.

I finally managed to corner Shobha in the lull which followed brunch. The chatterers were falling silent: they lay with their legs raised on wickerwork Bombay fornicators or stretched out on the hissing lawns.

'You want to talk?' she said. 'Sure.'

Shobha flicked her hair to one side and clicked into interview mode.

'Maybe I'm into bondage' she volunteered. It was by any standards an unusual *entrée*. 'Without the leather and whips,' she added.

'I don't understand,' I said.

'Writing,' she explained. 'I'm a typewriter-junky. I need that fix. Writing is for me a kind of bondage.'

'But without the leather and whips.'

'Right.'

We looked at each other. I must have seemed puzzled, as she tried another tack.

'Do you know what the women in this town are really after?' asked Shobha. 'I'll tell you. They want jewels in their bank vault, Chanel clothes in their wardrobe, a Porsche in their garage, a tiger in their bed—and an ass of a husband who pays for it all.'

Perfectly formed designer-quotes slipped out as if by magic. The whole monologue appeared to have been meticulously rehearsed. But at least no one can say that Shobha Dé has any pretensions about her *oeuvre*.

'What do you think of your books so far?' I asked after a while.

She smiled: 'You want the honest answer?'

'Yes.'

'I write readable trash—commercial novels,' said Shobha. 'But I don't think "commercial" is a dirty word. The bottom line for any product is whether it's going to sell. There is a market out there, and I'm filling a slot. The anguished little novels my critics churn out about suffering women at the kitchen hearth, they all lie unsold and eventually get pulped. I've had it up to here with moaning, groaning, oppressed females.'

She shrugged her shoulders.

'I am cold-bloodedly catering for *mofussil* fantasies,' she said. 'I want to provide a tantalising peep into the lifestyle of the rich and famous. I want to entertain, and most of all I want to sell. I'm not going for any literary awards.'

'But if you want to provide fantasies, why are your characters all so unhappy?' I asked. 'Are you saying that all that debauchery makes everyone miserable?'

'I don't think the wrath of God descends on bad girls. No—I think bad girls have a ball and die having a ball.'

'So you aren't trying to make a moral point?'

'No—and I hate those sort of judgements. The life my characters lead—having affairs, living from one party to the next...'

'...and going shopping...'

'...and going shopping—this is their idea of a ball. It's not up to me to say, "Girls: this isn't the sort of ball you should be having." '

She paused.

'But to come back to your question—I don't want to make it too perfect. No. I'm aware that if I make it all too desirable, well...'

Shobha arched her eyebrows and sipped her Bloody Mary.

'Well...there might be a revolution...'

Two days later, the white Mercedes drove up to the Taj Mahal Hotel promptly at ten p.m. The chauffeur held the door open. Inside was Shobha—wearing a pearl choker, a gold tikka mark and a sari of expensive-looking gilt silk—and beside her sat Dilip, her shipping magnate. Dilip grunted a greeting. I got in. The car glided away.

It was Christmas Eve in Bombay, the poor man's Rio, and outside, on the sidewalks of the ten-lane highway, the beggars were massing at the lights.

'Our hostess will have been busy all day,' said Shobha, ignoring a leper clawing at her window. 'She always shampoos her gravel on the afternoon before her parties.'

We glided out of crumbling central Bombay. We passed the airport and headed on towards Juhu, towards Bollywood, where the beggars sleep on discarded film magazines. Along the Lido is India's Beverly Hills.

'Just wait until you see this house,' said Shobha. 'It's like something out of James Bond.'

It was: a marble palace surrounded by giant bottle palms and facing out on to the rolling breakers of the Arabian Sea. Oceans of Veuve Clicquot bubbled into fluted champagne glasses. Liveried servants carried lighted kebab-skewers among the guests. Courtyard after courtyard was filled with millionaires, film stars, politicians, editors, sex symbols: everyone who was anyone in Bombay.

'No one is here yet,' said Shobha, looking around dismissively. 'The real heavy-duty Bombay society won't turn up until one or two o'clock. Otherwise it will look as if they haven't been invited to three other parties.'

Loudspeakers hidden in the palm trees were playing the Lambada. Shobha took to the floor with her shipping magnate. You could see the rocks on her fingers glinting in the lights. Nearby, the former Chief Minister of Kashmir, Farooq Abdullah—dressed in a long, thick Kashmiri coat despite the heat—was bobbing around with a woman in a voluminous sari. Both were trying to avoid stepping on her flowing silks.

I stooped down and picked up some gravel. Shobha had not been joking. It really had been shampooed.

In the first courtyard the marble was white, and glistened like a mirror. In the second, water bubbled down a rock-face, wove its way through a hanging garden and came to rest in a huge swimming pool. A suite of rooms filled with Kashmiri rugs led on to a third courtyard facing out on to the breakers. On a line of linen-covered trestles whole turkeys lay stuffed and ready for consumption; beside them were ranks of lobsters, great cauldrons full of hot curry sauces, caviar and blinis, mountains of pineapples, dates and guavas.

Fragments of different conversations wafted over the music:

'Anyway, when Imran said he was bored in Sharjah I told him to come over...'

'She thought she was getting a millionaire. What she *did* get was five children and two poodles...'

'He'd love to be royalty. But he claims his grandmother turned the title down...'

'She's just a common *bania's* daughter...'

'Of course, when Imran comes here he has this queue of adoring women stretching as far as Marine Drive...'

'He has over *one hundred* vintage cars. He drives whichever happens to match his cufflinks...'

'Do you know what semen is in Gujarati?'

Through it all you could hear the voice of Dilip, Shobha's tame shipping magnate: 'Do you know who is here tonight?' he said. 'The edible-oils king of India. He controls the export of thirty-seven different kinds of edible oils.' Over the next hour Dilip pointed out the prawn king of India, the soap king of India and the washing-machine king of India: 'Big men,' said Dilip approvingly.

Meanwhile I was watching Shobha and the reception she was getting from the guests. Our hostess, whom Shobha had very obviously parodied as a society slut in *Socialite Evenings*, gave her a peck on both cheeks, seemingly unbothered by Shobha's indiscretions. One of India's leading sex symbols, Pooja Bedi—whom Shobha, with her usual subtlety, had christened 'Boobs Bedi'—came up and welcomed her; they sat and discussed Pooja's recent photo-shoot for an advertising campaign by India's new Kama Sutra condoms.

Sometime after midnight I was sitting with Shobha, our plates overloaded with turkey, when she remarked on how few people ever came and struck up conversations with her. Why did she think she attracted such hostility, I asked her.

She answered very simply: 'A four-letter word—envy.'

'Your columns and books can hardly have helped.'

'None of my critics have read the books. They were just a take-off point to vent their spleen. The general reaction to the reviews was "It served the bitch right." '

'But why? Why should you attract all this?'

She called for champagne: 'Waiter! *Sahib ko champagne chahiye!*' While it was being poured, she considered. 'As I see it, ballsy women have a hard time here,' she said. 'That's just the way it is.'

There was no self-pity in the way she spoke, just resignation. She had left herself wide open to all the flak, of course, had courted it even, but still you couldn't help feeling a certain sympathy. In a culture which has elevated sycophancy into an art form, Shobha Dé doesn't play the game. In what is still a rigidly conventional and conformist society, she has stood out of line, and has always been prepared to pay the price. Certainly her writing is no great shakes, but that's not the issue. The real problem is that Shobha has guts.

'I detest subterfuge and hypocrisy,' she said. 'I live my life openly, and in my writing I describe what really happens in this town—I tell it how it is. My attitude exacts a price.'

'Is it just Bombay that's the problem?' I asked.

'No. I love this town. At least here I can live on my own terms. I wouldn't be able to function anywhere else.'

She shrugged her shoulders: 'I don't think Shobha Dé would be allowed to exist anywhere else in India. Another city,' she said, 'would have crushed me.'

# At Donna Georgina's

The history of Goa is written most succinctly in the portraits of the Portuguese Viceroys that still line the corridors of the abandoned convent of St Francis of Assisi in Old Goa.

The early Portuguese Viceroys were giants among men: chain-mailed warlords like Pedro da Alem Castro, a vast bull of a man with great muttonchop whiskers and knee-high leather boots. The boots terminate in a pair of sparkling golden spurs; his plate-metal doublet is bursting to contain his massive physique. All around Castro are others of his ilk: big men with hanging-judge eyes and thick bird's-nest beards. Each is pictured holding a long steel rapier.

Then, some time in the late eighteenth century, an air of ambiguity suddenly sets in. Fernando Martins Mascarenhas was the Governor of Goa only a few decades after Castro had returned to Portugal, but he could have been from another millennium. Mascarenhas is a powdered dandy in silk stockings; a fluffy lace ruff brushes his chin. He is pictured leaning on a stick, his lips pursed and his tunic half-unbuttoned; he looks as if he is on his way out of a brothel. In north India, a couple of generations in the withering heat of the Gangetic plains turned the Great Mughals from hardy Turkic warlords into pale princes in petticoats. In the same way, by the end of the eighteenth century the fanatical Portuguese *conquistadors* had somehow been transformed into effeminate fops in bows and laces.

The Portuguese first visited Goa in the last days of the Middle Ages. In 1498 Vasco da Gama discovered the sea route from Europe to the Indies, and immediately began planning ways of wresting control of the Indian Ocean from the Muslims, so diverting the spice trade to Portugal. By August 1507 Afonso de Albuquerque, 'the Caesar of the

East', had built a fortress on the island of Socotra to block the mouth of the Red Sea and cut off Arab traders from India. In March 1510 Albuquerque arrived off the coast of Goa. With him came a fleet of twenty-three caravels, galleons and war barques. Albuquerque massacred the Muslim defenders of the local fort, then carved out for himself a small, crescent-shaped enclave clinging on to the western seaboard of the Deccan. From there the Portuguese controlled the maritime routes of the East.

The *conquistador* chose his kingdom well. Goa is an area of great natural abundance, and the state is envied throughout India for its rich red soils and fertile paddy fields, its bittersweet mangoes and cool sea breezes. From its harbours, Albuquerque's fleet brutally enforced the Portuguese monopoly of the spice trade.

In its earliest incarnation Old Goa was a grim fortress city, the headquarters of a string of fifty heavily armed artillery bastions stretching the length of the Indian littoral. But by 1600, the process that would transform the *conquistadors* into dandies had turned Old Goa from a fortified barracks into a thriving metropolis of seventy-five thousand people, the swaggering capital of the Portuguese Empire in the East. It was larger than contemporary Madrid, and virtually as populous as Lisbon, whose civic privileges it shared. The mangrove swamps were cleared, and in their place rose the walls and towers of Viceregal palaces, elegant townhouses, austere monasteries and elaborate baroque cathedrals.

With easy wealth came a softening of the hard edges. The fops and dandies had no interest in war, and concentrated instead on their *seraglios*. Old Goa became more famous for its whores than for its cannons or cathedrals. According to the records of the Goan Royal Hospital, by the first quarter of the seventeenth century at least five hundred Portuguese a year were dying from syphilis and 'the effects of profligacy'. Although the ecclesiastical authorities issued edicts condemning the sexual 'laxity' of the married women who 'drugged their husbands the better to enjoy their lovers', this did not stop the clerics themselves keeping whole harems of black slave-girls for their pleasure. In the 1590s the first Dutch galleons had begun defying the Portuguese monopoly;

by 1638 Goa was being blockaded by Dutch warships. Sixty years later, in 1700, according to a Scottish sea captain, the city was a 'place of small Trade and most of its riches lay in the Hands of indolent Country Gentlemen, who loiter away their days in Ease, Luxury and Pride'.

So it was to remain. The jungle crept back, leaving only a litter of superb baroque churches—none of which would look out of place on the streets of Lisbon, Madrid or Rome— half strangled by the mangrove swamps.

The most magnificent of the surviving buildings is Bom Jesus, the church which now acts as the enormous vaulted mausoleum of Goa's great saint, the sixteenth-century Jesuit missionary Francis Xavier. To modern tastes, Xavier seems to have been a brute—when he visited Goa he was so shocked by the lingering pagan practices performed by the colony's converted Hindus that he successfully petitioned for the importing of the Inquisition—but this does not stop Goans of all faiths revering his memory four hundred years later. Indeed, a decade ago, when the miraculously undecayed body of St Francis was last put on public display on the altar of Bom Jesus, one Hindu lady was so overcome with devotional fervour that she bit off the little toe of the saint's left foot and smuggled the relic out of the church in her mouth. She was only apprehended when she removed it from her mouth in the queue for the ferry.

Ironically, the healing powers of St Francis are today particularly sought after by those same 'pagan' Hindus Xavier sought either to convert or to persecute. Outside Bom Jesus stand the usual lines of postcard- and trinket-sellers. But among the Catholics selling effigies of the Virgin and pictures of the Pope are a group of Hindus who squat on the pavement and sell wax models of legs, arms, heads and ribs. I asked them what the models were for.

'To put on the tomb of St Francis,' replied one. 'If you have a broken leg, you put one of these wax legs on Mr Xavier's tomb. If you have headache, then you put one wax head, and so on.'

'How does that help?' I asked.

'This model will remind the saint to cure your problem,' replied the fetish salesman. 'Then pain will be finished double- quick, no problem.'

Today the best view of the old metropolis can be had from the Chapel of Our Lady of the Mount. To get there you must climb a long flight of steps, once a *passeggiata* for the Goan gentry, now a deserted forest path frequented only by babbler birds, peacocks and monkeys.

Scarlet flamboya trees corkscrew out of the cobbles. Bushes block the magnificent gateways into now collapsed convents and overgrown aristocratic palaces. The architrave of a perfect Renaissance arch has rotted to the texture of an old peach-stone. Roots spiral over corniches; tubers grip the armorial shields of long-forgotten Goan dynasties. As you near the chapel, its façade now half-submerged under a web of vines and creepers, there is no sound but for the creak of old timber and the eerie rustle of palms.

The panorama from the chapel's front steps is astonishing. The odd spire, a vault, a cupola, a broken pediment can be seen poking out of the forest canopy. You look down past the domes and spires of the churches and monasteries, and see the evening light pick out the wandering course of the Mandovi river beyond.

The river is empty now: the docks are deserted; the galleons long sunk. Of one of the greatest cities of the Renaissance world, almost nothing now remains.

'But of course, despite everything they hung on,' said Donna Georgina, leaning back on her wickerwork divan. 'Despite the loss of the trading empire, they ruled us for another three hundred years. They were in Goa for a full two and a half centuries before you British conquered a single inch of Indian soil; and they were still here in 1960, more than a decade after you all went home again.'

'Until Nehru threw them out at the liberation of Goa in 1961.'

'Liberation?' said Donna Georgina, her face clouding over as quickly as a Goan sky at the height of the monsoon.

'Did you say *liberation*? Botheration more like!'

I had clearly said the wrong thing, and Donna Georgina Figueiredo was now sitting bolt-upright on her divan, rigid with indignation. We were talking in her eighteenth-century ancestral mansion, not by any means the largest of the Indo-Portuguese colonial *estancias* that still dot Goa, but certainly one of the most perfectly preserved. I had driven to Donna Georgina's village, Lutolim, along a lagoon edged by coconut groves, breadfruit trees and flowering hibiscus. At the centre of the village was the large white baroque church. In front of it stood a small *piazza*; to one side was the school, on the other side the taverna, the Good Shepherd Bar. In it, appropriately enough, the village priest was sitting at a table in a white cassock, reading the daily paper. Scattered around the vicinity were the grand houses of the village, and the grandest of them all was the Estancia Donna Georgina.

Inside, a servant had ushered me into the formal drawing room. On one side, next to an eighteenth-century Indo-Portuguese tallboy, stood a superb tall Satsuma vase. On the walls hung dark ancestral portraits. Other treasures—Macau porcelain, superb statuary, Mannerist devotional images— were dotted around the wooden galleries.

As she entered the room, Donna Georgina clapped her hands. Within seconds another barefoot servant came running down the passage from the kitchen.

'Francis, bring Mr Dalrymple a glass of chilled mango juice. I will have a cup of tea.'

The servant padded off down the bare wooden floorboards. It was not long afterwards that I made my gaffe about the liberation of Goa.

Donna Georgina clasped her hands and raised her eyes to heaven.

'Now, understand *thees*, young man,' she said in an accent heavy with Southern European vowels. 'When the Indians came to Goa in 1961 it was hundred per cent an invasion. From what were they supposed to be liberating us? Not the Portuguese, because the Portuguese never oppressed us. Let me tell you exactly what it was the Indians were freeing us from. They were kindly liberating us from peace and from security.'

Donna Georgina had fearsome beady black eyes and her hair was arranged in a tight quiff. She wore a flowery Portuguese blouse bought in Lisbon, offset by a severe black skirt. She nodded her head vigorously.

'We were ruled from Portugal for exactly 451 years and twenty-three days!' she said. 'The result of this is that we are completely different from Indians—*completely* different! We Goans have a different mentality, a different language, a different culture. Although we are now under Indian occupation, I feel awkward when I cross the border into India—everything changes: the food, the landscape, the buildings, the people, the way of life...'

Donna Georgina stared over my shoulder towards the open window: 'In the Portuguese days we never had to lock our houses at night. Now we can never be sure we are safe even during the day. And you know who we fear most? The Indian politicians. Absolutely unscrupulous people. They have razed our forests, ransacked our properties. They have made life impossible for everyone—particularly all us landowners. They offer our land to the people in their election promises: never give anything that belongs to them—oh no, not a pin— but they never think twice about offering people what belongs to others. Oh yes. That's very easy for them.'

What Donna Georgina said reflected stories I had heard repeated all over Goa. The sheer length of time that the Portuguese had hung on in their little Indian colony—some four and a half centuries of intermingling and intermarriage— had forged uniquely close bonds between the colonisers and the colonised. As a result most Goans still consider their state a place apart: a cultured Mediterranean island, quite distinct from the rest of India. As they quickly let you know, they eat bread, not *chapattis*; drink in tavernas, not tea-shops; many of them are Roman Catholic, not Hindu; and their musicians play guitars and sing *fados*. None of them, they assure you, can stand the sound of sitars or *shehnai*.

Moreover, like Donna Georgina, many educated Goans still talk about 'those Indians' and 'crossing the border to India', while happily describing their last visit 'home' to their cousins in the Algarve or their brothers in Cintra. Absorption into a wider India, they would admit, had certainly brought prosperity to the previously stagnant colony—but at a price. Public life had become corrupted, and the distinct identity of Goa was being forcibly and deliberately eroded.

Portuguese, for example, was no longer taught in the Goan schools; Portuguese place-names were everywhere being Sanskritised; the superb colonial buildings in Panjim were being systematically pulled down to make way for anonymous Indian concrete: the mansion of the Count of Menem, the last of the great Panjim aristocratic townhouses, was destroyed only in 1986 to make way for a six-storey block of flats.

There were, it was true, still some last remaining corners left: the haphazard, narrow cobbled lanes of Fontainhas, for example, the oldest quarter of Panjim. Fontainhas looks like a small chunk of Portugal washed up on the shores of the Indian Ocean. Old spinsters in flowery dresses sit on their verandahs reading the evening papers, chatting to each other in Portuguese. Wandering through the quarter in the evening you come across scenes impossible to imagine anywhere else in India: violinists practise Villa-Lobos at open windows; caged birds sit chirping on ornate *art nouveau* balconies looking out over small red-tiled *piazzas*. As you watch, old men in pressed linen trousers and Homburg hats spill out of the tavernas, walking-sticks in hand, and make their way unsteadily across the cobbles, past the lines of battered 1950s Volkswagen Beetles slowly rusting into oblivion. A Mediterranean *douceur* hangs palpably, almost visibly, over the streets.

But such corners, insisted Donna Georgina, were becoming harder and harder to find. For twenty minutes my hostess listed the now familiar litany of complaints.

'We could not fight the Indians in 1961,' she said. 'They were too many. Goa was a small place and could not defend itself. Even today we are only one million people. What can we do against nine hundred million Indians? But their seizure of Goa was an act of force. The majority here were opposed to the Indian invasion. That was why they had to come with their army, their air force and their navy. That day we all cried bitterly. It was the end of the good old days.'

Donna Georgina brought out a small handkerchief and dabbed her eyes.

'In fact, since 1961 we've had two invasions. First it was the Indians. They plundered Goa: cut down our forests and took away our woods. Their politicians created havoc. Then after that it was the turn of the hippies. Disgusting. That's what those people were. *Dees-gusting*. All that nudism. *And* sexual acts: on the beach, on the roads—even in Panjim. *Panjim*! Imagine: kissing *in public* and I don't know what else. Disgusting.'

The previous afternoon I had seen what remained of Goa's once-vibrant hippy community. At Anjuna Beach, instead of the rusting Volkswagens of Fontainhas, a line of Enfield Bullet motorbikes were parked beneath the palm trees. The weekly flea market was packing up as I arrived: a German holy man was returning his stock of Hindu charms to his bag, while under the next palm tree a Mexican bootlegger was putting his remaining cans of imported lager back into his knapsack. On the dunes by the shore, a bonfire was roaring, and what appeared to be a topless six-a-side female football team—an odd sight anywhere in the world, but an astonishing one in India—was kicking a ball around. A group of bangled backpackers was cheering them on while passing a ten-inch joint from hand to hand.

'Shoot!'

'Intergalactic!'

'Cos-mic!'

In the Sixties, Anjuna had been the goal of every self-respecting hippy in Asia. From Hampstead and Berlin, from the barricades of Paris to the opium dens of San Francisco, streams of tie-dyed teenagers crossed Asia to reach this shore and make love by the breakers. Whole nomad communities formed around the beaches: Anjuna, Chapora, Colva and Calangute, previously backwaters barely known even to the sophisticates of Panjim, became mantras on the lips of fashion-conscious acid-heads across Europe and the United States.

But in time, as the Sixties turned into the long hangover of the Seventies, the hippies either died of overdoses or went home. The young who come today are mostly students, generally a pretty affluent middle-class bunch who in due course will no doubt cut off their ponytails and become merchant bankers or commodity brokers.

Very few of the genuine diehard flower children of '67 still remain. Some have become very rich—it doesn't take much imagination to work out what trade their fortunes have come from—but most of the stayers-on are good-natured old freaks who grow their own, flap around in flared denim, hold forth on dragon lines, the Gaia theory and world harmony, and make ends meet by selling chocolate hash-brownies, aromatherapy oils and Indian waistcoats to the backpackers. This fossilised relic of Haight-Ashbury is actually pretty tame stuff, but you would never guess that from talking to Donna Georgina.

'Of course, it's because of *drugs* that their behaviour is like it is,' hissed my hostess. 'Disgusting people. Drugs and sexual acts and I don't know what else. I don't know which is worse: those hippies or our modern Indian politicians. The Portuguese wouldn't have allowed either.'

Donna Georgina sipped her tea defiantly. 'Mr Salazar would have known what to do with those hippies. He wouldn't have let them behave the way they did.'

The old lady took me around the house. She showed me the great ballroom, where they held the last ball in 1936, and the sunken cloister where she grew all the essential ingredients for her kitchen—chillies and asparagus, coconut and lemongrass, tea rose, papaya and balsam.

'Despite the hippies and the politicians, you seem at least to have maintained your house,' I said, looking around at the succession of perfectly preserved colonial Portuguese rooms that surrounded us.

'Thanks to hard work,' said Donna Georgina. 'Hard *labour*, I might call it. I'm currently fighting *twenty-five* lawsuits in an effort to keep the family property intact. That's right: *twenty-five* of them. Then there are the monkeys: big monkeys who jump on the roof and try to tear it apart. And as for preparing for the monsoon rains, it's worse than a wedding. The amount of work: checking the drains, making sure nothing leaks...But let me tell you this: it is my duty so to do. It is my duty to my ancestors, to myself *and* to society.'

We ended up in front of the ancient *oratoria*: a cupboard-like object which opened up like a tabernacle to reveal ranks of devotional images, crucifixes, sacred hearts and flickering candles. Twice every day, the household met there to say a decade of the rosary. On the wall beside it, Donna Georgina had hung a pen-and-ink drawing of the Holy Family.

'I drew it myself,' she explained, seeing where I was looking. 'The baby is Jesus and the lamb that he is feeding symbolises humanity. The old lady is St Anne, Jesus's grandmama. All the ancient families of Goa have St Anne as their patron saint.'

Donna Georgina paused, leaving the last phrase hanging in the air.

'It's entirely through St Anne's intercession and God's protection that this house is standing and that I am still alive. People always ask me: "Living alone, you must have someone to look after you. Who is it?" To which I reply: "God Almighty, Jesus Christ and St Anne."

'And, young man, let me tell you this. Between them they are doing a very good job.'

# The Sorcerer's Grave

On 5 April 1721, two pirate ships appeared off the coast of the Île de Bourbon, a mountainous Indian Ocean island known today as Réunion. Commanding them was a French corsair, Captain Olivier Levasseur. The captain was more commonly known as 'La Buse', the Buzzard, and with good reason: prior to his appearance off Réunion, he had been busy plundering the shipping off the Malabar Coast of India; only when the British East India Company sent out the entire Bombay Fleet to hunt him down did he beat a retreat towards his base on Madagascar.

As they sailed homewards, the pirates found they were running low on water, and La Buse decided to call in at Bourbon to replenish his tanks. Approaching the harbour of Saint-Paul, he saw moored there a massive seventy-gun Portuguese man-of-war, the *Nostra Senhora de Cabo*. Without hesitation La Buse sailed straight in, fired a broadside at the galleon, then boarded it, almost without resistance. It turned out to contain what was probably the richest prize that ever fell to pirates: over £1 million-worth of Indian gems being shipped by the Viceroy of Goa back to his masters in Lisbon.

It was nine years before La Buse returned to Réunion, and then in rather different circumstances. In 1730 he was captured by a slave-trading bounty hunter, brought back to Réunion in fetters and sentenced to death. But on the scaffold, La Buse made a speech which would assure him a measure of immortality. As the noose was placed around his neck, he scattered a bundle of parchment charts among the crowd. The maps, he said, indicated exactly where on Réunion his treasure lay buried. But first the finder would have to crack his code. To this day the treasure has never been found, despite adventurers coming to Réunion to search for it for over 250 years.

The grave of La Buse is, however, somewhat easier to locate than his treasure. It lies in the old Marin Cemetery, overlooking the deep fragmented blue of the ocean, on a flat apron of land lying between the tall black basalt cliffs and the rustling palms on the shore. On my first evening in Réunion, intrigued by what I had read of the exploits of La Buse, I walked barefoot along the coral beach from my hotel to pay my respects to the old pirate.

Today much of the coast around Saint-Paul is like a miniature St-Tropez: a little down the coast, at Boucan Canot, lines of topless Parisians can be seen splayed out under the palms, frying in Ambre Solaire. But inside the footfall-soft silence of the cemetery the atmosphere is very different. Within the high walls, hidden by a long screen of ilexes, you are suddenly back in the eighteenth century, surrounded by the obelisks and mausolea of sea-captains and corsairs, exiled aristocrats and shipwrecked plantation-owners.

These low basalt tombs are classical in inspiration, but naïve in execution: pillars rise through Ionic capitals to oddly misshapen pediments; below, rough inscriptions record the often brutal deaths of the early colonists: '*Ici repose Capt. de Bellegarde tué par les corsaires*'; '*Ici repose la famille Chandemerle morte dans une naufrage...*' As the night draws in and the ocean wind gusts through the graves, you suddenly realise how remote this island on the Tropic of Capricorn must once have been: seven months' voyage from Marseilles, visited by only one supply ship every six months.

It did not take long to find the grave of Levasseur, although there was no grandiloquent mausoleum marking it, like those erected by the colonial gentry who now keep him company. Instead there was just a headstone of black basalt. On it was inscribed a skull and crossbones, and the brief epitaph:

> *Olivier Levasseur dit la Buse—pirate,*
> *cumeur des Mers du Sud,*
> *Executé à Saint-Paul 1730.*

Yet while the other graves in the cemetery were forgotten and overgrown, that of La Buse was clearly much-visited. Piles of flowers and the wax of innumerable candles covered the graveslab, while to one side stood several newly opened rum bottles, apparently left as offerings. Stranger still, alongside the bottles there had been placed three or four packets of Gauloises and Gitanes. The packs had been torn open at their base and the cigarettes left to burn out, so all that remained were the charred filter-tips. On some of the packets had been scribbled incantations and petitions to La Buse.

Outside the cemetery I approached a large Créole woman. In the gathering darkness she had set up a brazier on an old oildrum, and was now roasting corncobs on the embers. I bought one, and asked her in the course of conversation why she thought offerings had been left on the grave of an eighteenth-century pirate.

'I don't believe in it,' she replied, her tone suddenly becoming sharp.

'Don't believe in what?'

'In...all that business.'

'But some people clearly do.'

'I don't know them.'

'But what exactly is going on?' I persevered. 'Why do people...'

'It's their business!' snapped the old woman, turning away. 'Why don't you ask them? They come here every night *pour gratter le bois*.' ('To scratch the wood', i.e. sorcery.) 'But I tell you this,' she continued: 'whatever they say in Saint-Paul, it's no secret that half the wickedness in Réunion comes from that grave...'

The first thing that strikes you when you arrive in Réunion is the sheer—almost ridiculous—*Frenchness* of the place.

The island may lie at the heart of the Indian Ocean, halfway between Madagascar and Sri Lanka, but it was uninhabited until the French began colonising it in 1646, initially by dumping convicts on its beach, later turning it into an important naval base and refuelling point for French East Indiamen on their way to and from the *Compagnie des Indes'* headquarters at Pondicherry in Tamil Nadu. Legally, it is as if the French East India Company still ruled the waves. For Réunion is still part of France; indeed, at first sight it appears to be every bit as Gallic, as developed and as prosperous as its distant mother country. The people all have French passports, and male school-leavers are obliged to go to France to perform their national service. The language is French, the television is French, the cars are French, the croissants and baguettes at breakfast are French, and the wines in the restaurants are defiantly and exclusively French. Nine-tenths of the island's trade is with France. It is as if Réunion lay just off the coast from Cannes, not ten thousand miles to the south.

It is only later, after you have been on the island for several days, that you notice the degree to which this Frenchness is modulated by Réunion's tropical geography and what the Réunionnais call the *métissage*: the racial intermixture that has made the island a model of melting-pot multi-culturalism. 'If anyone born on this island tries to tell you he has "pure" French blood,' I was told by one Réunionnais friend, 'don't believe him. It's simply not true. In the *métissage* lies the very essence of this island.'

By the mid-nineteenth century, Réunion had a population of several thousand French exiles: a mixture of down-at-heel aristocrats turned plantation-owners and a leavening of *pauvres blancs*—usually impoverished, landless Breton farmers who had emigrated in the hope of opening hill farms in the island's mountains. These colonials were outnumbered roughly two to one by ex-slaves, most of whom were of Madagascan origin. The mixture was spiced up in the years that followed by an infusion of Tamils, north Indian Muslims, Canton Chinese and Yemeni Arabs, all of whom were brought into work the plantations as indentured labourers after slavery was abolished in the 1840s.

Today, these very different communities are intermixed in the most astonishing manner: there can be few places on earth—and few moments in history—where so many radically different peoples, religions, cultures, languages and cuisines have become so spectacularly intermingled.

This *métissage*, combined with the island's extreme isolation, affects every aspect of life on Réunion. The process of intermingling and cross-fertilisation has, for example, moulded much of the island's folklore and religious practice— as the bizarre offerings at the grave of La Buse so intriguingly indicated. Grandmère Kale, who is said to live in the island's volcano, emerging to eat up Réunionnais children who don't finish their greens or who refuse to do their homework, is a cross between the witches of European and African folklore, and Kali, the Hindu goddess of destruction. The mixture of different faiths, often within a single family, has had a profound influence on the Réunionnais' attitude to the world. It has made them unusually tolerant and open-minded, but also deeply heterodox.

'Beliefs and ways of living are forever mingling on this island,' I was told by Father Samy Anarche, a Tamil Catholic priest who ministers to a parish in Réunion's capital, Saint-Denis. 'In the same family you can find a Chinese Taoist, an Indian Muslim, a Metropolitan Catholic, an African witch-doctor and a Tamil Hindu. Inevitably ideas percolate from one religion to another. I have many Chinese Catholics in my parish who are involved in ancestor-worship, as well as Indian ones who believe in reincarnation. It all makes a lot of work for the priesthood: we are continually having to explain to our parishioners what is and is not Christianity. *Bien sûr*, it is the same with other religions: the Hindus here all eat meat and perform blood sacrifices. That's something you'll rarely see in India these days, and it probably derives from the influence of African *gris gris* (voodoo).'

The *métissage* has also formed the islanders' language: they speak both conventional modern French and an impenetrable Créole patois which mixes Malagasy, Tamil and Arabic on a base of eighteenth-century nautical French.

More enjoyably for the traveller, the island's brand of Créole cooking is also wonderfully multi-cultural, and quite unique. It mixes French and Indian culinary enthusiasms with a dash of Arab, Chinese and Malagasy influence. The result is a fusion startlingly unlike any of its parent traditions. A typical Réunion meal might consist, for example, of *cari z'ourite et cari poulpe* (a creamy sea urchin and octopus curry) with a scattering of side dishes of lentils, *choux choux* (crystophene), *rougaille* (a spicy tomato chutney) and *bredes* (a spinach-like digestive); pudding might be *gâteau patate* (a sweet, heavy potato-cake). To add to the complexity of the island's cuisine, in some areas of Réunion Arab influence results in the use of cloves and nutmeg, Chinese influence in a taste for ginger, and Malagasy influence in a variety of delicious dishes with a coconut-cream base and several memorably disgusting ones involving roasted wasp grubs.

With an island of Réunion's racial complexity and degree of isolation, none of this should be a surprise. But it is, if only because of the strong initial impression of French modernity that greets you on your arrival at the island's western coastal strip—the glossy Renault garages, the wide motorways, the suburban villas and the neon-flashing nightclubs. All this lulls you into thinking that you are somewhere settled and unsurprising, when in reality Réunion is a crucible positively fizzing with bizarre practices, strange ideas and unexpected juxtapositions.

As I soon discovered, the offerings at the grave of La Buse were barely the tip of the iceberg.

Although the *métissage* is everywhere on Réunion, it is not evenly distributed throughout the island. You only have to look at a map to see that while the coastline is full of straightforwardly French place-names—Saint-Denis, Saint-Paul, Saint-Pierre—the hinterland contains names of more complicated derivation: thus Cilaos, Salazie and Mafate, the three volcanic craters that dominate the mountainous interior, all have names derived from the languages of Madagascar.

The reason for this lies in the island's history. While the coast has always been dominated by French colonists, the mountains were traditionally the hideaways of escaped Malagasy slaves: Cilaos, for example, is a corruption of the Malagache *tsy laosana*—the place from which you never return.

It is easy to see how Cilaos came by its name. For although parts of the coast are to this day dominated by Parisian immigrants, who buy up the beachfronts, opening hotels and surfing clubs, the mountainous interior has escaped this fate, and remains firmly in the hands of the native Réunionnais.

Here, up beyond the high passes can be found the real essence of the island's Créole identity. In the *cirques* (volcanic craters), cut off from the rest of the island by mountains of terrifying verticality, live isolated communities of mountain shepherds whose way of life has not changed for a hundred years. One crater, the Cirque de Mafate, still cannot be reached by road. Here, just ten miles as the crow flies from the bars and nightclubs of Saint-Denis, is a deeply inward-looking society, some of whose members have never left the crater or seen a car.

Anyone who wishes to see the heart of Réunion must brave the treacherous roads and head up into the mountains. At the fine old colonial town of Saint-Louis—all eighteenth-century churches, ruined sugar mills and grand *Compagnie des Indes* townhouses—you turn inland, leaving the hot white glare of the palmed and coraled coastline behind. Less than a mile from the coast, the scenery changes beyond recognition.

Nothing you have seen on the island prepares you for what lies ahead. For from the coast, the first range of the hills looks green and rolling, like the gentle contours on other Indian Ocean islands. But cross these foothills and you see for the first time the massive volcanic peaks that lie further inland: successive ranges of mountains and craters rising and receding into inky cloudbanks of thunderous cumulus. You expect geological acrobatics like these on great landmasses where continents collide, not on an island the size of Réunion, little more than forty miles across and represented on most maps by the smallest of dots. Yet the scenery is of Andean, or even Himalayan, grandeur. These are jagged, angular, peremptory ranges with ridges that jut out like fractured bones—as sharp and angular as fragments of broken glass, but on such a scale that they rise to form whole ranges of pyramid peaks—great lines of aspiring Matterhorns and Sugarloaf Mountains, with names like 'the Rhino's Horn' and 'the Priest's Bonnet'.

There is something profoundly violent, even frightening, about the geological processes at work, made more terrible still by the impenetrable blackness of the basalt: it neither refracts nor reflects light, but seems rather to absorb it, to draw it in. Not even a glint of mica breaks the rocks' terrible black monotony, and only on the gentler slopes can ferns or moss find purchase on the hard, brittle, volcanic geomorphology.

The road through this landscape moves with serpentine indecision: it rises, curves and doubles back, hesitates, sinks, then curves back on itself once more. On either side cliffs tower upwards, with dark cloudbanks masking their peaks; small waterfalls cascade down the abyss and on to the windscreen. The effects of the towering peaks, mist and cloud combine to give the landscape an oddly primeval feel: it is as if you are rising up to some lost world—so much so that you feel you might not be surprised if a pterodactyl were suddenly to appear and glide gently down the mountain thermals.

Cilaos, the bleak, mist-shrouded spa-town that dominates the topmost *cirque*, is an isolated, end-of-the-world sort of place.

It grew to fame in the mid-nineteenth century as a hill station and sanatorium for European soldiers and colonial officials whose health had been damaged by too long in the jungles of Bengal or the swamps of Vietnam. Its climate was deemed 'European'—the ultimate accolade in the eyes of homesick colonials—its mildly radioactive mineral waters were credited with healing powers, while its baths were said to instantly cure rheumatism and a whole anthology of muscular complaints.

For a century Cilaos filled every summer with bedridden brigadiers and crippled colonels—until a landslide soon after the Second World War suddenly blocked the source and killed the town dead. The unexpected return of the waters in 1971 has done little to renew the town's prosperity, and it remains oddly time-warped. Its clapboard, candy-floss houses with their corrugated-iron roofs and nasturtium-filled gardens still seem to be locked in the past, as if all the town's clocks had stopped the moment the source was blocked.

Every day, as late afternoon gives way to evening, the clouds descend on Cilaos, shrouding it in a thick, misty gloaming. Yet overnight the clouds pull back, so that each morning the town awakes, miraculously refreshed, to crisp, chilly sunrises that briefly turn the great basalt amphitheatre of rock surrounding it as pink as smoked salmon. Finding at breakfast that the bleak vision I had seen on arrival had given way to a scene of Alpine freshness, I pulled on my walking boots and headed straight off into the hills.

Three hours later I was passing up a wooded mountain path, with wild strawberries and meadow campion underfoot; in the valley below I could hear the bells of the convents of Cilaos. In contrast to the geological pyrotechnics of the passes on the way up to Cilaos, the mountainsides above the town were surprisingly gentle: conifer forests gave way on the steeper slopes to bamboo and flowering bromeliads. Unseen birds were singing in the forest canopy, the ground was soft and springy, and the sun shone brightly overhead.

Then, turning a corner, I found myself in a meadow, at the top of which was a thatched hut. A tall Créole farmer was standing beside it, feeding his two donkeys. He was lean and wiry, and on his head he wore a Homburg hat; but he had no shoes, and his feet were large and dusty. He introduced himself as Loulou, and invited me inside his shack. There he offered me a glass of orange juice, squeezed before my eyes from his own oranges. I was hot and thirsty after the walk, and as we sat and savoured the cold liquid I asked Loulou about himself.

He had been brought up in this meadow, the Îlet des Trois Salazes, he said, and since finishing his national service he had rarely left it: it was over thirty years since his last visit to Saint-Denis, even though the bus from Cilaos could get him there in a morning.

'Why should I go?' he said. 'I have everything I need here. And the people down on the coast...'

'What about them?' I asked.

'They're all z'oreilles.'

I had not heard the island's French immigrants called this before. I later learned that z'oreilles—literally 'ears'—was supposedly a reference to the immigrants' habit of cupping their ears to catch the islanders' Créole patois, though one Réunionnais friend I talked to believed it actually derived from a more sinister source: the old French predilection for cutting off the ears of slaves, leaving the plantation-owners as the only people with their *oreilles* intact.

'To us it seems the *z'oreilles* have a totally different mentality,' continued Loulou. 'They're always rushing about here and there. They've got no manners. Down bottom, if you ask directions they'll not answer—or they'll send you the wrong way. And they call anyone with a Cilaos accent a *choux choux*-eater. So why go and risk trouble? Better stay here with my family. Us *yabs* (highlanders) shouldn't mix with the *z'oreilles*...It never does any good.'

As Loulou talked, I looked around the hut. It was a classic mountaineers' den, low and cosy, with a fire licking at the logs on the hearth. A *coffee-pot*, a kettle and a couple of pans containing rice and cari poule rested on a steel grill suspended over the embers. From the roofbeams hung Loulou's worldly goods: an axe, two rainproof capes, a box of candles, a torch and a guitar.

Loulou's father, so he told me, had been a palanquin bearer. His job had been to carry invalids up the mountains from Saint-Louis to Cilaos; until the building of the road in 1935 it had been impossible for carriages or cars to make it up, so impassable were the mountain tracks. In his childhood, said Loulou, there were seven families living in the Œlet; now it was just him and his sons.

'The young are all leaving this area, said Loulou. 'Things are changing so fast. In the old days we would say that Réunion was like a book: every now and again the page would turn. Now it's like a wind is blowing and all the pages are changing at once. Even up here, things are changing like you can't imagine. They say that we'll soon have electricity. And after that, who knows? Maybe even the telephone.'

When Loulou came back from his national service, he found the Îlet virtually deserted. Only his widower father was left; everyone else had given up and gone to seek work on the coast. Moreover, in his absence the French forestry agency had removed the Îlet's right of pasture over the mountain; they had planted trees on the grazing land and fenced the area off. There was no compensation.

'We lived off our sheep,' said Loulou. 'But after our pasture was taken away we had no option but to shoot them. After that everyone moved away. I came home to find that everything had broken up. I had to start again from scratch.'

Since then he had devoted his waking hours to trying to coax a living from the Îlet, to turning the thin soil of the mountainside into productive land. As he took me around, he proudly showed me where he had built terraces, planted fruit trees and established herb and vegetable gardens. He now had two patches of grain and maize, and apricots, cherries, plums and quince hung heavily from boughs covered in thick grey lichen. There was watercress in the stream and sweet-smelling passionflowers hanging from a trellis in front of his hut. In addition he had two milk-cows, a bull and his donkeys. In summer his sons joined him in the Îlet. Life was hard, he said, but he managed to make ends meet.

As we said goodbye he showed me the ruined hut where the village sorcerer had lived when he was a child. It was then that Loulou told me one of the most extraordinary stories I heard on Réunion.

Some time in 1931, a box of sacred relics arrived in Réunion from the Vatican.

It seems that somewhere in transit the label detailing the saint's name had been removed from the box, and the only indication as to its contents was a stamp on the side reading, in Italian, 'SPEDITO' (expedited). So began the cult of St Expedit, whose popularity grew year by year, until what had started as a clerical error ended with St Expedit becoming Réunion's unofficial patron saint, a saint whose unwritten biography has come to crystallise the most profound hopes and fears of the island's multiple ethnicities. There are now around 350 shrines on Réunion dedicated to St Expedit. They sit beside every road junction, crown every hilltop, lie deep in the bottom of the island's wildest ravines. They act both as oratories for the faithful and as sacred sentry-boxes, guarding against the terrors of the night.

For it is not just Réunion's Catholics who look to St Expedit for help: all the communities of the island pray to him, and each has brought something to his cult.

Probably due to a confusion with the popular French cult of St Elpiduce, the local Catholic Church has given the saint the trappings of an early Christian martyr, and his image has stabilised as that of a young Roman legionary, with a silver breastplate and a red tunic. In one hand he holds a spear, in the other the martyr's palm; under his right foot he crushes a raven, a symbol of his victory over the demons of temptation. But to this conventional image of Catholic piety have been added a number of more exotic trappings. Hindus have adopted into their pantheon this image clothed in the Hindus' sacred colour, and now treat St Expedit as an unofficial incarnation of Vishnu; those wanting children come to his shrine and tie saffron cloths to the grilles. In the same way, Indian-Réunionnais Muslims tie short cotton threads to his shrine, just as they would at Sufi shrines in the subcontinent.

The cult has also proved popular with the descendants of those slaves who clung to the old spirit-worshipping beliefs of their Malagasy ancestors. In Madagascar the palm is associated with death, while St Expedit's spear and raven are taken to be symbols of sacrifice, as if he were a white witch-doctor. More exotic still, some of the island's sorcerers have given the cult a slightly sinister aspect by decapitating the saint's image, either to neutralise his power or to use the head in their own incantations. According to Loulou, the sorcerer at Îlet Trois Salazes had a small oratory in which he kept several heads of St Expedit.

'He used them to cast spells,' said Loulou. 'He thought that by cutting the saint's head off he was taking his power and stealing it for himself.'

'Did you believe he had power?'

'We were all terrified of him: everyone believed he had very strong powers. But in the end the people kicked him out. He was too dangerous—he began to demand bribes not to cast spells on us all. In the end we had enough.'

'Weren't you frightened that he would take revenge on you for throwing him out of the Îlet?'

'We took precautions,' replied Loulou.

'What sort of precautions?'

'We used stronger magic. We sent someone to the grave of La Sitarane in Saint-Pierre. It is the most powerful grave on the island. With La Sitarane on your side, no one can harm you at all.'

On my last evening on Réunion, I drove into Saint-Pierre to look for the grave of La Sitarane.

Beyond the mosque, just before the Hindu temple of Kali, a group of old Créole men were playing *boules* on a square of carefully clipped grass; through the palm trees I could see the surf exploding on the coral reef out to sea. After the clear but chilly air of the mountains, the coast seemed gloriously hot and humid.

Graves seemed to form a grim symmetry to my journey through Réunion. I had visited the tomb of La Buse the night I arrived; now here I was, on the eve of my departure, making for another cemetery, intent on seeing the grave of an even more reprehensible character than the piratical Buzzard. For La Sitarane, it emerged, was not just a sorcerer, but also a murderer who had been executed after committing a number of bloody killings at the turn of the century.

'He only killed three people,' said a Réunionnais historian I quizzed on the subject, 'but according to legend he first drugged his victims with *datura*, then afterwards drank their blood. Just before he was guillotined, he made a speech vowing that he would return from the dead to punish his captors. It caused such a shock in Réunion that La Sitarane has never been forgotten. But I'll tell you an odd thing.'

The historian leant a little closer to me: 'When I first visited his grave, twenty years ago, there were no visitors, no offerings and no burning candles. But now the grave is more visited than even that of La Buse. All these offerings, this sorcery: far from dying away with development and education, it actually seems to be on the increase.'

This idea fascinated me, for it touched on something that had become clearer to me the longer I stayed on Réunion: that the island's ever-increasing *métissage* was leading to a fundamental metamorphosis in its character. Réunion had been born and shaped by the accidents of French colonial history, and three hundred years after the French flag was first raised at Saint-Paul, the island was still supported by an umbilical cord from Paris. Yet with Réunion's customs and traditions continually evolving through the intermixture of its different communities, it seemed that the island was visibly becoming less and less French every day. Certainly the façade was still there—the croissants, the baguettes and the burgundy—but at its heart the island seemed to be fast evolving its own quite separate identity, spinning off into its own orbit, as the *métissage* led to a constantly shifting fusion of faiths, ideas and superstitions.

Inside the cemetery, the cross head of La Sitarane's gravestone had been broken off, and the remaining shaft was painted bright red. On the graveslab, just as the historian had said, was piled a mountain of bizarre offerings: rice, potatoes, oranges, radishes, wine gums, milk, coconuts and incense sticks, as well as the inevitable bottles of rum and packets of Gitanes.

'You see, people here think La Sitarane is alive,' explained Jean-Claude, the gravedigger, who was busy preparing a plot nearby. 'That is why they bring these presents: cigarettes for him to smoke, rum for him to drink, and so on. They think that if they honour him in this way La Sitarane will help them in their work—or help them punish their enemies.'

Jean-Claude hauled himself out of his grave and wiped his hands on his trousers.

'So who is it who comes here?' I asked

'We get all sorts,' replied Jean-Claude. 'An hour ago there was a woman dancing on the grave. First she cut the head off a chicken, then she started dancing. She was Créole, I think, but lately it's been mostly Tamils who've been coming. They stand by the grave in groups and their priests read from their bad books. All the Tamils believe in La Sitarane's power. They are great sorcerers.'

I walked over to La Sitarane's grave and reached down to pick up a coconut that someone had left on it, but Jean-Claude restrained my hand.

'It's better not to touch,' he said. 'There was a gravedigger here when I was a boy. One day he drank some wine from the grave. The next day his mind was finished. Now he's in the asylum in Saint-Denis. Or so they say.'

'So you actually believe in La Sitarane's power?' I asked.

'*Bien sûr*,' said Jean-Claude. 'Of course. Everyone does.'

He smiled at the question, as if it were something only a *z'oreille* could possibly ask.

'This is Réunion, not Paris,' he explained. 'Here things are—how do you say?—a little different from *La Métropole*.'

# Up the Tiger Path

JAFFNA, SRI LANKA 1990

The band had been playing *Auld Lang Syne* before the helicopter gunship appeared over the crest of the hill. The noise of the rotor blades drowned out the pipes and drums, and throbbed down over the last commandos as they boarded the troopships. The hot dust rose in whirling eddies and the Generals' medals chinked against one another as they brought their handkerchiefs up to cover their faces. After hovering for a few seconds over the departing army, the gunship passed on. It flew out across the bay, over the aircraft carrier and the destroyers, joining the four other helicopters which were criss-crossing the harbour—a formation of giant dragonflies hovering over the waters.

The ceremony had been going on for two hours. It was an indulgent display of speeches and march-pasts and brass bands, designed to show that the occupying troops were going to take their time leaving, that they were not—heaven forbid—being thrown out, that the third-biggest army in the world was not withdrawing with its tail between its legs.

The speeches droned on, medals were awarded—but there was no disguising the tension which hung over the jetty. Somewhere around the bay, hidden under the jungle canopy, the Tamil Tigers were taking up their positions. Everyone was expecting a parting shot, a farewell mortar attack or the explosion of a last artfully disguised landmine, and all the way through the ceremony the Indian helicopters scoured the surrounding hills and clearings for the first burst of machine-gun fire, or the telltale flash of a rocket-launcher glinting in the sun.

It was the end of March 1990, and I had been sent south from Delhi to cover the withdrawal of the Indian Army from Sri Lanka. Although the event was getting little coverage in the Western press, it was, in its way, as extraordinary an event as the Russian retreat from Kabul, or, before that, the fall of Saigon. Once again, as in Afghanistan and Vietnam, a superpower army—India has 1.3 million men under arms—had suffered a humiliating defeat at the hands of a small but dedicated guerrilla group. It was a remarkable achievement—at times the Tigers had been outnumbered seventy to one—but while half the journalists in London seemed to have been into Afghanistan with the Mujahedin, and there were enough films about Vietnam to stock a fair-sized video library, the Tamil Tigers remained faceless, unsung, unknown. One reason for this was that the Tigers strongly discouraged journalists. As a result there was little in the cuttings libraries to fill me in. There were only hints, and they made me want to know more.

Firstly, it was clear that the Tigers were almost fanatically disciplined. Smoking and drinking were banned on pain of expulsion; adultery was punishable by death. It sounded an unlikely collision between the Maoist guerrilla principles of Che Guevara and the monastic ideals of the Desert Fathers; but it was clearly an effective mixture: there were few internal disputes within the Tigers, and certainly none of the petty power squabbles which fatally divided the Afghan Mujahedin. Instead the Tigers were a centralised, autocratic, almost fascistic organisation, with the senior Tiger commander, Prabhakaran, receiving a near-religious obedience from his fighters.

Secondly, the Tigers were suicidally brave. In more than a decade of continuous fighting, remarkably few of them had been taken alive. Every guerrilla carried around his or her neck a tiny phial of cyanide crystals: trapped by government troops, whole camps of Tigers had been known to swallow their phials and end their lives in two minutes of inconceivable agony.

Finally, and no less intriguingly, the Tigers were clearly completely ruthless. In the course of their campaigns they had been responsible for some of the worst atrocities against civilians in recent Asian history. Their massacres had been compared to the most revolting excesses of the Viet Cong, even of the Khmer Rouge. Car-bombs had been left outside nursery schools; whole villages had been systematically liquidated; political rivals had been hunted down and exterminated with a terrible, single-minded savagery. It was as if the Tigers actually enjoyed killing, as if to them it was a hobby, or even an art form. Yet this unpleasant cocktail of qualities has turned the Tigers into arguably the most efficient and successful guerrilla group operating anywhere in the world today.

As I watched the last Indian troopship pull out of China Bay, I made up my mind to extend my stay in Sri Lanka, and to try to discover a little more about the Tigers. With the Indians out of the country, their war was temporarily over. They now controlled the north and east of the island, the Tamil heartland, and were beginning to make noises about talks with the Sri Lankan government and democratic elections: maybe they would look on journalists more kindly than before. I returned to Colombo and extended my visa for another month.

The next day I rang a Tamil-speaking driver, George, and together we set off for Anuradhapura.

Anuradhapura is where the story begins—doubly so.

The Tamils and the Singhalese have been neighbours in Sri Lanka for nearly three thousand years, and throughout much of that time they have been fighting each other. The north and east of the island is the preserve of the dark-skinned Tamils: small and sharp and hard-working and Hindu. Elsewhere the island is dominated by the Singhalese, a languid and strikingly beautiful race of fair-skinned Buddhists. Anuradhapura is their city, and in its centre lies the sacred bo tree, grown from a clipping of the tree in Bodh Gaya under which the Buddha achieved enlightenment. It was brought to Sri Lanka in about 250 B.C. by the first Buddhist missionaries, and has always been one of the most sacred relics of Buddhism.

In 237 B.C. the city was seized and sacked by Tamil Hindus from south India. They enslaved the Buddhists, and established Hinduism as the official religion of the island. It was Dutugümunu (101–70 B.C.), the Singhalese answer to King Arthur, who liberated his people at the battle of Anuradhapura. The city became the capital of a united Sri Lanka, and has remained ever since the symbol of Singhala dominance (even though, between the fourteenth century and the beginning of the colonial period, most Tamils were governed by their own independent Kings of Jaffna).

In 1948, when Sri Lanka (then known as Ceylon) gained its independence from Britain, the old wounds reopened. With eleven million Singhalese and only three million Tamils, the advent of democracy led to the subjection of the minority: in 1956 Singhala was made the country's official language, and Tamil was banned from government offices and road signs; to gain access to senior government jobs, Tamils had to pass a Singhala proficiency test. At the same time, prime land in the north was gradually parcelled out and colonised by Buddhists, at the expense of its Hindu owners. Early Tamil attempts at nonviolent protest were brutally put down by the Special Task Force, a kind of Buddhist Gestapo.

It became clear to many young Tamils that if they and their culture were to survive, they would have to take up arms and create their own state—'Eelam', or Precious Land— in the north of Sri Lanka. In 1975 Vellupillai Prabhakaran, a teenage Tamil smuggler, brought together a small group of his friends and founded the Liberation Tigers of Tamil Eelam (LTTE). Trained partly in southern India by RAW, the Indian intelligence service, and, allegedly, partly in Israel by Mossad, they set out to fight for an independent Tamil state.

Initially only one of a number of competing Tamil guerrilla groups, the LTTE soon established itself as among the most fanatical and ruthless terrorist forces operating anywhere in the world. For ten years the Tigers bombed schools, garrotted Buddhist monks and wiped out whole Singhalese villages. They also waged a bloody—and ultimately successful—war against their Tamil rivals. Finally, a series of violent, often suicidal strikes and bombings led to a major anti-Tamil pogrom in Colombo in July 1983, which in turn plunged the country into a full-scale civil war of almost Lebanese complexity. Following the riots, one of the Tigers' first major targets, a symbolic strike at the heart of Singhala myth and national pride, was Anuradhapura.

Today the ancient city bears deceptively few scars from Prabhakaran's attack. The great white *stupas* still rise from the green of the paddy fields, as bulky as the Giza pyramids but more refined, the domes tapering to perfect fir-cone steeples. Beyond, the jungle chokes and grips at the fallen pillars of temples and palaces half-submerged by vegetation. Those buildings which were burned or shattered in the attack have been tidied up and repainted. Only if you look very carefully can you see the bulletholes or scorch-marks, the last shreds of evidence of the massacre which violated arguably the most sacred Buddhist sanctuary in Sri Lanka.

It was seven-thirty in the morning of 14 May 1985 when the Tigers arrived at the modern town on the outskirts of the Sacred Enclosure. They parked their hijacked vehicle in the middle of the bus station, calmly climbed out of the back, cocked their Kalashnikovs and began firing indiscriminately into the crowd. Two grenades were thrown into a waiting school bus; a shoulder-launched rocket hit another full of elderly pilgrims.

Mohammed Razik runs Paris Corner, a small tea-stall opposite the bus station. That morning he had just opened his shutters and was sitting down to read the newspaper when he heard the explosions. Thinking they were crackers, he went outside to have a look.

'People were running everywhere. Many had fallen on the ground, either wounded or huddled screaming over the body of a relative. Smoke and flames were rising from the buses which were on fire. The rattle of automatic weapons seemed to be coming from all directions. Then I saw about twenty guerrillas advancing slowly out of the flames of the bus stand, walking forward in a straight line, firing from the hip. Three of them were wearing uniform, the rest were in T-shirts. I saw them throw a grenade at the Bank of Ceylon— the security guard there had tried to fire his shotgun at them—before I ran out the back and jumped into the lake.'

A few minutes later the Tigers reached the bo tree temple. While they paused outside to shoot the trinket-sellers, postcard-*wallahs* and a crocodile of Buddhist nuns,

Dhanapala Herath, the temple sweeper, tried to close the great temple gates. The Tigers pushed them open before he managed to secure the bar.

'They barged in and one of them raised his gun to shoot at the great Buddha image. I pushed at the gun and the shots hit the roof. Then they shot me, three times, in the legs, the arms, and shoulder.' He paused for a second and looked down at his two amputated stumps. Then he continued: 'I remember one thing before I lost consciousness. They were all laughing. They were not frightened or horrified at what they were doing—they were joking and giggling and enjoying themselves, as if they were at a festival.'

The massacre at Anuradhapura brought a terrible new religious passion and bitterness to the violence in Sri Lanka. The following day further riots led to hundreds of Tamil deaths all over the south of the island. Up to 1990, perhaps 150,000 people lost their lives in the fighting. For an island whose total population is barely fifteen million, that is a colossal slaughter.

North of Anuradhapura, you leave Singhalese territory. You move into the Tamil zone, into Eelam. No public transport passes between the two communities: that is where George comes in.

George is a charming and companionable Singhalese taxi-driver who, unusually for a southerner, speaks good Tamil. He has, however, one serious flaw: George is heavily into home engineering. His car works fine until George begins poking around under its bonnet. Then anything can happen. On a previous trip we were spending a night in a reputedly guerrilla-infested stretch of jungle. George chose this propitious moment to fiddle with his engine. The next morning, smoke billowed out of the bonnet and the carburettor exploded. It was three days before we were on the move again.

The morning we set off from Anuradhapura was a bad day in respect both of George's car and our nerves. First there was the banner headline announcing that a Tamil militia opposed to the Tigers had apparently peppered the road we were proposing to take with landmines. Then came George's announcement that he had spent the day before washing his car: 'All-over washing,' he said, 'removing oil, flushing engine, everything coming clean. Today like new engine.'

No sooner had he turned the ignition than the effect of this washing became apparent. The car began to judder like a spin-dryer, stalled, then crawled off at the magnificent speed of nineteen miles an hour. 'Sri Lankan petrol very bad,' said George somewhat unconvincingly.

Gradually, as we headed slowly northwards, the scenery began to change. Near Anuradhapura the land had been rich and tropical: water-buffalo grazed in the drained paddy fields; Buddhist monks in orange robes strolled along holding peacock fans and yellow umbrellas; the gardens bloomed with jasmine and purple bougainvillaea. But as we moved on, the paddy gave way to arid savanna tracts broken by occasional thickets of jungle—classic guerrilla territory. Desiccated palmyra plantations replaced the tropical coconut palms. It was a no man's land—wild, guerrilla country, ideal for ambushes. It has always been so: for three thousand years northern Ceylon has been disputed, and this savanna has always been the border country, the battleground. Holes in the road—some two or three feet deep and as wide as the road itself—were identified by George as craters left by old landmines. In several places he mentioned the names of the drivers who had been killed by the blasts. We drove on in silence.

I don't know where we crossed the border, but by the time we again came to human habitation we were firmly inside Tiger country. The Tiger flag—two Kalashnikovs crossed behind a roaring man-eater—hung from every telegraph pole; Tiger graffiti and Tiger murals were painted on to every wall.

We got as far as Vavuniya before we were stopped by a roadblock. We were promptly marched out of the car by a guerrilla cradling a Kalashnikov and made to wait while a fifteen-year-old Tiger radioed for permission to let us through.

Previous experience of the Tigers had shown that it was almost impossible to enter into conversation with the cadres. Every guerrilla, it seemed, was given instructions not to speak to journalists or foreigners; even the most inoffensive questions were met with blank shrugs. But on this occasion I was luckier. The hut was full of bored guerrillas. Two guards in blue baseball hats lounged around with carbines on their knees, scratching their balls, fiddling with their safety catches. They were wearing the distinctive Tiger uniform—fatigues whose camouflage imitates the banding of a tiger-skin. I lured them into conversation—using George as translator—by asking them about their guns, a subject close to the heart of every Tiger. Gradually they opened up.

None of the Tigers in the office could have been older than twenty-five, but they all talked as if they had had years of guerrilla experience; many must have joined when they were barely out of primary school. Yet they seemed remarkably unaffected by the war. Far from it—as far as they were concerned, they'd had a good time. They talked in a strange mixture of war-comic bravado and Sixties guerrilla jargon, but just occasionally a hint of real feeling slipped through. When, after two hours, we surprisingly received permission to proceed, I asked them a final question: Had there been no bad moments?

It was one of the older boys in the room who began, a little hesitantly, to answer. He had been leading a patrol in the jungle one day in early January, he said, when they had been surprised by an Indian ambush. With him was a friend, a very poor village boy who had never had a new set of clothes in his life. Just that day he had been given his first Tiger uniform: a smart set of the new tiger-camouflage variety. The patrol leader had managed to escape, but his friend had thrown down his weapon and run for it, only to be captured. He had had no alternative but to take cyanide. 'It must have been an old phial,' said the boy. 'It didn't work properly. From where I was hiding I could see his face. It was screwed up and disfigured and there was blood and foam pouring out of his mouth. He begged the Indians to shoot him, but they didn't. He took over five minutes to die.'

As he spoke, there was silence in the room. As we left, I caught a last glimpse of him. Although he was doing his best to hide it, I could see that in his mind he was still looking at the face of his friend, alive and foaming at the mouth, writhing on the jungle floor.

We passed on, deeper into Eelam. The land grew dryer, until it could support only the palmyra trees, the bleached thickets of elephant grass and a tangle of gorse and scrub. It was uninspiring country—yet this was the setting for the Tigers' greatest battles.

In 1987 the seesaw of atrocities and counter-atrocities reached a new level of intensity when the Sri Lankan Army decided to move out from their handful of fortified camps and attempt to capture the entire Jaffna Peninsula. This first siege was followed by a ludicrous and darkly farcical interlude when the Indian Army arrived as a peacekeeping force. Fellow Hindus, they came, supposedly, as the protectors of the Tamils. Yet within a month they were at war with the very people they had come to protect, after an attempt to disarm the Tigers was violently resisted. In October 1987 the Indians besieged Jaffna, assaulting the town with tanks and heavy artillery.

The Indian troops were equipped with the very latest Soviet weaponry. They advanced north towards Jaffna on five fronts, and the Tigers were driven out—but not before they had wiped out nearly half of the Indian 'peacekeeping force', with minimal manpower and kitchen-sink technology. They discovered, for example, how easy it was to knock out a modern armoured personnel-carrier: place a lot of plastic explosive in a roadside bucket; lead some wires from it to a radio receiver in a house a hundred yards away; then activate the mine by switching on the radio. The latest Soviet battle tank, the mighty T-72, proved little more of an obstacle: a fifty-kilogram landmine could effectively take out two or three of the monsters.

It was a celebrated victory: the Tigers retreated to the jungle and the jungle villages—in classic Maoist style they mingled with the people 'like fish in water'—to build up their strength and wait for their moment. But driving north, I saw what I had never read about—the cost. As we crossed the Elephant Pass and headed into the Jaffna Peninsula, the devastation increased. Buildings were fire-blackened and shattered. Smart Imperial *façades* gave on to gaping, gutted interiors. Whole streets were shuttered up, the plaster of the shopfronts pockmarked by fragmentation bombs and phosphorus grenades. Roofs were collapsed and twisted, signboards hung loose; shards of jagged metal—the remains of reinforced concrete—jutted out of shell craters towards the sky. There had been no attempt to clear up or rebuild: the wreckage of the town had just been left to crumble.

Evening was approaching, and the late-afternoon half-light magnified the wreckage and increased our feeling of unease. In an apparent attempt to cheer us up, George began listing the treats and luxuries shortly awaiting us at the Hotel Elara in Jaffna: air conditioning and hot baths and television.

George's promises of luxury only made it worse when we arrived. The hotel—long ago it had been the best in Jaffna, and had earned three stars—did not have any televisions; nor any telephones; nor any electricity; nor indeed much of its back wall. Nor, any longer, did it have a staff—only the depressed and bankrupt manager, who welcomed us like lost sons: his first non-Tamil guests for eighteen months.

'Sir,' said George in funereal tones as we paused halfway up the stairs and looked out over the vast bomb-crater that was Jaffna. 'You must look after me. I am a married man.'

The other thing was the water. According to a notice headlined 'MESSAGE TO OUR PATRONS', it was 'highly recommended for bathing and washing, but not for drinking'. The water was brown and metallic and smelt like sewage. If you ran the bath quarter-full, you ceased to be able to see its bottom. Lowering myself into it that evening, I thought I would not recommend it even for sheepdip. Thenceforth I pioneered the expensive habit of washing with a sponge and a bottle of French Volvic water, with which, by some strange good fortune, the hotel was amply supplied.

I soon realised there was something strange about Jaffna. The town, like the hotel, was in ruins, but the prevailing atmosphere was anything but degenerate or sleazy. The guerrillas—who seemed to outnumber ordinary citizens—were upright, polite and well-disciplined. Some of the younger ones had been assigned traffic-police duties, and they stalked imperiously around the road junctions like officious school prefects. There were no beggars, touts or prostitutes hanging around the hotel. The Tiger command had banned them all and created a Morality Police to arrest and punish offenders. Moral watchdogs patrolling the ruins for evidence of illicit sex: it was something I had previously seen only in Iran.

Perhaps the most upright of all the guerrillas in Jaffna were the girls—the gloriously named Freedom Birds. After days of applying to the Tigers' Jaffna command, I was finally given permission to visit their strongly guarded barracks. The Tigers made it clear that I should be grateful for this privilege: I was the first foreign journalist who had ever been allowed to meet them. Even George was banned; the Freedom Bird on guard at the gates strutted out of her pillbox and indicated with a flick of her machine-pistol that I was to get out, and that George was to stay where he was.

It is easy to see why the Freedom Birds are kept away from the public eye, strictly segregated in their own barracks. They are the stuff of Bond movies: a regiment of beautiful Tamil amazons dressed in tight-fitting khaki fatigues, with carbines strapped across their waists. But they were very far from the Bond model in at least one respect, as I soon discovered: they had all taken a vow of chastity, and were as buttoned-up as an order of cloistered nuns.

This was something the libidinous Indian troops found out whenever they attempted to capture the Freedom Birds alive. The women carry not one, but two cyanide capsules around their neck. As my escort explained as she conducted me into the guardroom, 'A man can be tortured, but a woman has more to lose—her virtue.' She led me to a table and indicated that I should sit. 'Anyway, being captured alive is a blow to the pride of a freedom fighter. Suicide is an act of human dignity.'

It was a typical Freedom Bird aside. They look sweet and naïve, but they can be alarmingly doctrinaire and severe. None more so than their leader, the tall and lovely Lieutenant Jaya, a political science graduate with a taste for incomprehensible Maoist jargon. 'We are driven by the revolutionary optimism of our ideology,' she announced soon after we were introduced. 'We will fight state oppression and the oppression of women, male domination and caste bigotry. The people will be our vanguard.'

After five minutes of this sort of ranting I began to understand what Lieutenant Jaya was talking about: she was trying to turn her troops into a kind of paramilitary feminist death squad. In peacetime, she said, the Freedom Birds were engaged in a social struggle 'to free Tamil womanhood from male imperialism', touring the poor areas of Jaffna, talking to the women and listening to their problems. If a woman said her husband had beaten her, or insulted her, or was a notorious drunk, the Freedom Birds would take action. The Tamil men, Jaya said, were very 'counter-progressive': 'It is our duty to re-educate them.' I could just see Lieutenant Jaya indulging in a spot of re-education: visions rose before me of truckloads of manacled misogynists and recalcitrant wife-beaters being shipped off to the re-education camps, Lieutenant Jaya awaiting them, her thumbscrews and electrodes ready.

Then she invited some of the younger fighters in, and we talked of the war. It was an extraordinary sight: six beautiful and feminine fourteen-year-old girls, sitting relaxed and with their friends, giggling and joking, talking about guerrilla warfare as if it were O-level results, rock bands or boyfriends.

If I had assumed that, when it came to the military crunch, the Freedom Birds were something of a gimmick, I was very much mistaken. In the final days of the 1988 siege of Jaffna by the Indian Army, it was the Freedom Birds who held the main road, the most important of all the sectors. A soft-spoken young fighter who introduced herself as Comrade Dilani told the story.

'There was a force of three hundred crack girl guerrillas dug in at the Kopi junction. The Indian Army came forward— an endless convoy of tanks and personnel carriers. Lieutenant Maladi, our leader, stood in the middle of the road and challenged them. Without even daring to raise the man-covers of their tanks, the Indians shot her dead in cold blood. When we saw this we detonated the four landmines we had prepared, and fired off our Carl Gustav rocket-launchers. In three minutes we had destroyed six brand-new Soviet T-72 tanks and a whole string of personnel carriers. Despite the constant strafing of the Indian Air Force we held our position for three days, long after most of the other strongpoints had caved in. Of three hundred, only twenty-six of us were killed. When we fight we are ruthless,' added Dilani in her gentle, sing-song voice. 'We have no pity.'

'Don't you feel that all this killing has hardened you?' I asked. 'That you'll never be able to return to family life after this?'

'Tamils of my age have suffered oppression since our birth,' Dilani answered shortly. 'What happened at the siege is nothing new to us.'

'But didn't killing all those people upset you?' I asked. 'Didn't it give you nightmares?'

'They are our enemy,' she answered. 'They killed our people. So we killed them. Why should we be upset?'

'But you are—what? Fourteen? You can't just go around killing people at that age and remain completely unaffected.'

'They are not people,' replied Dilani simply. She was unable to understand my point. 'They are army. They are enemy.'

I frowned. She shrugged her shoulders.

'We are busy,' said Lieutenant Jaya, getting up and indicating that I should do likewise. 'We have a war to fight.'

It was clear that my interview with the Freedom Birds had come to an end.

There was one thing that I was determined to do before I left Eelam: I wanted to get into one of the Tigers' jungle camps. The camps are the nerve centres of the Tigers' operations. They are large, often holding more than a thousand guerrillas, and heavily fortified. Their locations are a closely guarded secret, and I had never heard of an outsider being allowed to see them.

On my first evening in Jaffna I went straight to the Tigers' central office and filed a request. After a week I received my answer—a polite no. They were very sorry. They would like to help, but it was strictly forbidden. No non-Tiger was ever allowed into the camps.

I did, however, still have one chance. Anton Balasingham was the Tigers' LSE-trained political chief. While Prabhakaran led the Tigers' military wing, Balasingham was the brains behind the gun. He was reputedly an intelligent man and an Anglophile; if I could talk to him, perhaps he would be willing to help me. The question was how to find him: like all the senior Tiger hierarchy his whereabouts were kept secret. I only knew that his home was in Point Pedro, a former smuggling village north of Jaffna. I decided to look there.

I found the local Tigers' office and explained what I wanted. The local commander, a small, nervous man with a deadpan civil-servant look, asked me to sit while he radioed his superior for instructions. The superior, I was told a few minutes later, was asleep. I could wait if I wanted.

Sleepy guards lounged around on wicker chairs. I took a seat beside them. All over the walls were pictures of fallen Tiger 'martyrs'. They were shown standing stiff and formal with their assault rifles, or weighed down by heavy anti-tank weapons, or posing with their friends over the bloody bodies of Indian soldiers. 'All local peoples,' said one of the guards, pointing to the pictures. 'All killed now.'

I waited in the room for five hours. I paced up and down listening to the sound of the snoring guards and the turning fan. I paced some more. The superior was still asleep. He had gone out. He was busy. Finally he awoke, and said he would call Balasingham. There was a long delay. Then he rang. Balasingham was asleep. Balasingham was out. It went on and on, like some ghastly dream, until I became certain that none of them had any intention of ever taking me to Balasingham, that they were merely stringing me along. Finally the inevitable message came through. Mr Balasingham had set off for the jungle. If I wanted to try again the next day I was welcome.

Frustrated by an entirely wasted day, I walked outside to the car and woke George. He turned the ignition key. Nothing happened. He turned it another three times, and still nothing happened. 'Battery flat,' he said with a yawn.

George went off to find some jump leads, and I hung around the car, fuming. I was still waiting when I saw two figures getting out of a jeep and walking towards the office. The first was a man with narrow, metal-rimmed glasses and, unusually for a Tamil, a slight paunch. With him was a tall blonde woman. I knew the pair instantly—I had seen their faces in posters on the walls of innumerable Tiger offices. It was Balasingham and his Australian wife, Adele.

He had, of course, received no messages. He was so sorry. Had I waited very long? Certainly he would be interviewed. He was very much the textbook revolutionary intellectual: quick-witted and intense, fond of gesticulation and dogmatic generalisation. He even spoke English with the statutory spy-film heavy accent. He talked of the founding of the Tigers and of its growth from a small group of friends into what he called a 'national freedom struggle'. We discussed his revolutionary heroes—Che Guevara, Mao Tse Tung and Ho Chi Minh, and their influence on the Tigers' tactics. He told me about the battle of Jaffna and his subsequent flight to a safe house in southern India, of his return, the reformation of the scattered units and the long months of guerrilla warfare against the Indian Army. After two hours I gently dropped the question into the conversation: did he think I could visit one of the camps?

It would be quite impossible, he said, to visit any of the Jaffna camps—Prabhakaran would never allow it. But I could try Amparai, in the east of the island, where his friend 'Castro' was the commander. If anyone would let me see a camp, it was Castro. He promised to send a message to him the next day.

That night I packed my bags and went to bed early. In the morning George and I rose at five, and were on the road before dawn.

It was a bad journey. We drove slowly along the eerie, empty roads, looking out for landmines. As we crawled, George gloomily regaled me with stories of his taxi-driver friends who had driven less carefully, and as a result had been blown up.

'My friend Dhanapala,' said George. 'Always he was having girlfriends in secret. All girls—too many girls. His wife never knew. Last October he was driving to Jaffna with girlfriend when *poof!* Car blows up. Finished. Gone. All pieces. This man Dhanapala, he gets very bad name, going with other women and all. This, and dead too.'

To make matters worse, about fifty miles outside Jaffna, George's car's air conditioner overheated. First it started leaking water on to my leg, then steam billowed from under the bonnet, then it began excreting black smoke. We turned it off, but the smell of burning plastic lingered.

We reached Amparai at six that evening. Balasingham had been true to his word. Within an hour of our arrival, a message was delivered to us at the town's one remaining hotel. It was from Castro. We were to report to his office at nine the following morning. Our transport would be waiting.

I had heard a little about Castro since I entered Tiger territory. He was regarded as the Tigers' most brilliant young commander, its finest general after Prabhakaran himself. He was the architect of one of the Tigers' most chillingly efficient operations: a seaborne attack on two military camps carried out the previous November in the middle of the night. The camps were the headquarters of a Tamil militia armed and trained by the Indians to take on the Tigers. By devastating the 'collaborators" camps and massacring those inside, Castro neutralised all the remaining pro-Indian forces. When the Indians had finally withdrawn, northern Sri Lanka fell effortlessly into the Tigers' lap.

I had expected some hardened guerrilla leader, and was not prepared for a shy, handsome figure of my own age. I asked him to tell me more about the attack, and he happily complied. He described the preparations, the spying and the intelligence work. He told me of the long, wet fifty-mile march through the monsoon jungle, the moonlit crossing of the lagoon and the silent belly-crawling as the guerrillas surrounded the camp and cut the wire. As he talked, I was aware of a growing sense of *déjà-vu*. It all sounded a bit familiar, I said. Hadn't I seen a film of this somewhere? He smiled.

'You're right. Our camps are all equipped with televisions and videos. War films are shown three times a week, and are compulsory viewing. We often consult videos like *The Predator* and *Rambo* before planning our ambushes. None of us are trained soldiers. We've learned all we know from these films.'

So, I thought: video-guerrillas. To Sri Lanka from Hanoi via Hollywood. It was an arresting idea: real-life freedom fighters earnestly studying Sylvester Stallone and Arnie Schwarzenegger to see how it was done.

Later I saw the camp's video library: complete sets of *Rambo*, *Rocky* and James Bond; all the Schwarzeneggers, including *Conan the Barbarian*, *Conan the Destroyer* and *Commando*; most of the recent Vietnam films; and, touchingly, no fewer than three copies of The *Magnificent Seven*. Moralists have often speculated that much of today's violence·is inspired by violent movies. If only they knew. Here in Sri Lanka the tactics of an entire civil war—tens of thousands killed, maimed and wounded—seem to be largely inspired by imported videos.

Overexposure to Hollywood glamour had also affected the Tigers' dress sense. As Castro led me outside to the waiting Toyota Land Cruiser, I caught another glimpse of the Tigers' taste for paramilitary chic. Not only were all his bodyguards wearing the new tiger-skin camouflage uniforms, the Land Cruiser had also been painted outside and upholstered inside with the same matching tiger-stripes.

We left Amparai and headed off, past the lagoon into flat country—paddy fields edged with coconut palms. After fifteen miles we swung off the main road and came to a checkpoint protected on either side by heavily sandbagged bunkers. Despite Castro's presence, the guards refused to let us through until they had received clearance on their radios.

We headed up a dirt track, across open country. On the way we passed three more carefully camouflaged roadblocks; at each we were stopped and checked. Then we entered the jungle, and in a minute we were there.

Again I was presented with an image very different from my expectations. This time it was the size of the camp that took me aback. It was the size of a university campus: a heavily camouflaged jungle town, built in and around a forest clearing. The buildings were surprisingly solid structures of wickerwork, bamboo and thatch: arsenals and hospitals, command huts and dormitories, restrooms and conference centres, refectories and lecture rooms. Between them, sand had been scattered thickly on the ground to prevent the mud from turning to a quagmire.

It was just as well. The place was a hive of activity, buzzing with no fewer than two thousand heavily armed guerrillas. Some were attending political lectures, sitting in rapt attention as a senior Tiger harangued them with revolutionary rhetoric; others were busy with target practice or assault courses or weapons training; some were playing volleyball; others queued up for haircuts, the barbers' chairs surreally removed from their proper place to sit between two peepul trees in the clearing.

As striking as the sheer scale of the place was the age of the guerrillas. The overwhelming majority were in their early teens—just old enough to join the Boy Scouts in England. The same had been true of many of the Tigers I had seen in

Jaffna, but then I had assumed that these were just the reserves, and that the real grown-up commandos were in the camps. Here for the first time it became clear that the Indians had been defeated by a guerrilla force whose average age cannot have been a year over eighteen.

The younger the Tiger, the more anxious he was to prove himself a full-blooded guerrilla. You did not have to talk to any of them for long before they began boasting about the operations they had been on; and they were not making it up. Did I remember the copse of palmyra trees just before I left the main road, asked two boys of about thirteen. That had been the site of a big ambush earlier in the year. They had let off two huge landmines and blown up six trucks in a convoy, then they had gunned down the survivors—killed nearly fifty Indians, they said. It was wonderful. I should have been there. Another, perhaps a year younger, began telling me of the booby-traps he had laid further into the jungle. Small anti-personnel mines hidden in tree-stumps: took off a man's legs, but rarely killed him. Good strategy, he said: wounded Indians used up more resources than dead ones. By the end the Indians were so scared they never dared leave the roads. Cowards! Chickens!

Castro had been firm that I was only to be allowed a glimpse of the camp, a taster. My last image before I was driven away was a party of ten boys carrying great lumps of raw, bloody meat into the camp. The meat was skewered through by long wooden poles which the boys carried on their shoulders, one at each end. As I saw the meat, I suddenly thought of those pictures of the Tigers standing over the dead Indian bodies, triumphant over the bullet-mauled corpses. I shuddered. There was far too much blood here. I had seen enough.

Sitting now in Delhi six months later, thinking back on that journey, I remember one incident in particular.

It was a feast day in Jaffna, and I was late for church. I hurried through the deserted streets, past the gutted houses and the bombed-out shops, to the dusty square in front of the cathedral. It was a white-hot, sticky-hot tropical afternoon, and the plaster on the front of the cathedral had been pockmarked three inches deep by the bursts of shrapnel, grenades and fragmentation bombs. Pieces of broken stained glass lay scattered under the rose window, but the grotto of the Virgin beneath it was untouched; around her neck someone had hung a garland of orange marigolds, as if she were a Hindu goddess.

Inside, Mass was just beginning. The pews were packed, and segregated: men on the left, women on the right. The Bishop of Jaffna led a convoy of white-robed clergy up the central aisle, past the bleeding image of the Sacred Heart, and up to the altar. Everyone was singing, the schoolgirls in their white veils, the seminarians in their black serge cassocks, even the odd Tamil guerrilla, gun still strapped to his waist, and as they sang the ceiling fans whirred above the pews, round and around.

Just as the opening hymn was reaching its climax, through the singing I could suddenly hear a second sound, the noise of rotor blades, first distant, then throbbing loudly down, directly above the congregation. The sound echoed around the cathedral, and everyone looked up in instant, horrified recognition: although there was now a truce, it was just a few months since the bombardment, and everybody knew the sound of the gunships only too well. Slowly the hymn tailed off, until only two or three of the children in the choir were still singing, encouraged by the frantic gestures of the choirmaster. Then even they fell quiet.

The helicopter passed on, and the Bishop began the Mass as if nothing had happened, but the tension in the cathedral remained. Jaffna was on edge; it had already been the site of two sieges, two battles, and everyone knew the third could not be far away. Everybody in the town—Christian and Hindu—was praying for peace.

In the event, of course, their prayers were not answered. The negotiations with the Sri Lankan government were a failure: the Tigers, delighted with their victory over the

Indians, became arrogant and demanded too much. There were violent clashes. Then, on 13 June 1990, the Tigers went too far. They pounded Sri Lankan Army camps with mortars and seized 650 Singhalese policemen on duty in Tiger-held northern Sri Lanka. The policemen have never reappeared, and are feared dead. On 20 June, the Sri Lankan Army moved out of its barracks and headed north. Jaffna was under siege again; its third assault in three years.

The Tigers themselves were usually fanatics: severe, doctrinaire and rigorously disciplined, they were rarely good company. But the Jaffna townfolk were friendly people, tired of war, and were always ready to gossip.

So now I think of the people I met in the town. I wonder what has happened to those I met at the cathedral: the shy seminarians, the Bishop's efficient secretary, the angry choirmaster. In the shady cloisters of the cathedral I had tea with the Bishop on Easter Saturday; he looked like Robert Morley, wore a dirty cassock and nursed a large paunch. When he talked about the last Indian attack on his cathedral town he blushed bright red: 'The Indians stopped my car fifty yards from my palace and demanded to see my papers,' he fumed. 'Imagine! Me—the Bishop!'

And what has happened to poor Anton Alfred, the civil servant appointed Jaffna GA (Government Agent) by the Sri Lankan authorities? He had no power in a town controlled by the Tigers, yet he was expected to keep the place working, to maintain the schools, to run the buses. He was a small man—dwarfed by his huge Victorian desk—but he was very brave. If the truce broke, he knew the Tigers would come for him; they had shot his predecessor, and would have no compunction about doing the same to him.

'It is not a very enviable position to hold,' he said, 'but someone has got to do this service. One must try to go on...'

And what has happened to Comrade Dilani, the prettiest guerrilla in Jaffna? Recently I read that several of the Freedom Birds had fled to India, but I doubt if Dilani was among them.

The reports from Jaffna have become ever more grim. For three months there has been neither water nor electricity in the town, and nothing works: not the telephones, not the banks, not the post offices, not even the market. There is no petrol, and food is selling for ten times its normal price. The Sri Lankan forces who are besieging the town let nothing through; even candles and matches are stopped.

But the most terrible aspect of the siege is the bombing and the strafing. The strafing, from Bell-412 helicopter gunships, is relatively state-of-the-art, with sudden swoops disrupting funeral processions, emptying streets, picking off old men at crossroads. But as the Sri Lankan Air Force has no modern bombers, the bombing is a lot less high-tech. It is, in fact, about as crude and as random as the stones flung by a medieval mangonel. The government is killing its own people with Chinese Y-12 transport planes. The slow, lumbering aircraft carry home-made three-hundred-kilogram bombs, packed into wooden barrels. These are rolled manually out of the cargo hatch—simple, but effective nonetheless: countless homes, the Tirunveli market, the central railway station and the Jaffna Memorial Hospital have all been blown to pieces in this way in the past month. One Indian correspondent reported seeing a woman scavenging in the street: it was only on closer inspection that he realised she was collecting pieces of her husband's flesh for cremation; he had been passing on a bicycle when a bomb went off nearby.

One week Jaffna was subjected to what its inhabitants called 'shit-bomb attacks'—barrels of excrement rolled out of aircraft. They caused little physical damage, but made Jaffna smell like a sewer, and the city's already frightened inhabitants suspected they were being subjected to some sort of crude experiment in biological warfare.

Actual civilian casualties in Jaffna are of course hard to estimate in mid-siege, but according to the Tigers they stand at about four thousand, a terrible toll in a town of only sixty thousand inhabitants. As a retired government official told one correspondent: 'It is a living hell—that is, for those of us who are alive.'

Meanwhile, in the centre of Jaffna, like Russian dolls stacked one within another, there was a siege within the siege.

One of the finest colonial relics in Sri Lanka was the magnificent sixteenth-century Dutch fort. Its walls had long been elegantly crumbling, but they were hastily rebuilt when the Easter truce dissolved into the June war. Like a scene from the Indian Mutiny, the defunct fort suddenly became a last place of refuge for the Singhalese trapped in Jaffna—traders, government officials, policemen and a small detachment of two hundred government troops.

The houses around the fort were quickly levelled by the Sri Lankan Air Force to provide the defenders with a clear killing-field around the walls. Undaunted, the Tigers dug a network of trenches to encircle the fort, and proceeded to pound it with mortar and heavy-artillery fire. They followed this up with a series of desperate assaults, on one occasion coming at the walls protected by the only armour they possessed: bulldozers and dumper trucks. In another attempt a fifteen-year-old boy was sent to climb the walls with explosives strapped to his body, so as to blow them at their weakest point—but at the last minute he was spotted and shot by the defenders. The explosives went off, and the blast could be heard twelve miles away, but the old Dutch walls held.

It was only after ninety-six days, with food and water running short, that the fort was finally relieved. After a preliminary bombardment, the Sri Lankan government sent a thousand crack troops across the Jaffna lagoon on dinghies. Six were sunk and an old Italian Siamarchetti fighter shot down, but the troops managed to land and fight their way through to the southern gate of the fort. The garrison was evacuated, but attempts to fan out and capture more of Jaffna failed. On 26 September the government troops abandoned the fort under cover of darkness. The Tigers raised the flag of an independent Tamil Eelam from the battlements two days later.

Jaffna remains under siege. Though the government forces will probably succeed in taking the town, as the Indians did before them, it is unlikely that they will succeed in crushing the Tigers. Like a rerun of an old movie, the Tigers will escape to their secret camps deep in the jungle, and there they will bide their time until the moment comes to counter-attack. For as long as the Singhalese continue to discriminate against Tamils, there will always be new Tiger recruits to fill the shoes of those who are killed. The Tigers are ruthless, certainly, but they survive because they are perceived by the Tamil population to be fighting genuine injustice.

In the meantime, the random bombing of Jaffna goes on, and civilian casualties continue to mount. The government claims it merely wishes to 'rid the Tigers of their lair', but rightly or wrongly, the people of Jaffna detect more sinister motives. As one of Comrade Dilani's Freedom Birds told me on my last visit: 'We must continue to fight, for if we do not, the Singhalese will not rest until they have ejected the Tamils from this island once and for all.'

*Postscript*: Seven years later, the civil war is still limping on. Jaffna fell in 1993, and at the time of writing the Tigers have indeed been driven back into the jungles. The government now controls all the towns of the Jaffna Peninsula, but it is unable to keep the roads open or to prevent the Tigers emerging from the shadows to regain effective control of the peninsula every evening after dark.

Moreover, the Tigers still retain the capacity to mount the occasional horrific 'spectacular'. On 31 January 1997 they claimed responsibility for a massive explosion in the heart of Colombo, near the Central Bank Building, where Sri Lanka's gold reserves are kept. The explosion killed two hundred people and injured fourteen hundred others. In July, four thousand Tigers, led by Castro, emerged from the jungle to launch a week-long land and seaborne operation against the government's military base at Mullaitivu, 170 miles north-east of Colombo. They eventually succeeded in storming the base, taking away large quantities of heavy weapons. Except for a handful who managed to escape, all twelve hundred military personnel in the base were killed. This was arguably the government's worst defeat in the entire civil war.

More seriously still, the government has totally failed to win the battle for the minds of the Tamils: despite offering a form of federal autonomy and other concessions, it remains deeply distrusted by the Tamil population, and the Tigers retain mass popular support. As there seems little hope of their laying down their arms in the immediate future, the prospect of any solution appears very remote.

In the fifteen years since the 1983 riots, an estimated fifty thousand lives have now been lost in the conflict.

# Index